Fragile States

UNU World Institute for Development Economics Research (UNU-WIDER) was established by the United Nations University as its first research and training centre and started work in Helsinki, Finland, in 1985. The purpose of the institute is to undertake applied research and policy analysis on structural changes affecting developing and transitional economies, to provide a forum for the advocacy of policies leading to robust, equitable, and environmentally sustainable growth, and to promote capacity strengthening and training in the field of economic and social policy-making. Its work is carried out by staff researchers and visiting scholars in Helsinki and via networks of collaborating scholars and institutions around the world.

United Nations University World Institute for Development Economics Reaserch
(UNU-WIDER)
Katajanokanlaituri 6 B, 00160 Helsinki, Finland
www.wider.unu.edu

Fragile States

Causes, Costs, and Responses

Edited by
Wim Naudé, Amelia U. Santos-Paulino, and
Mark McGillivray

A study prepared by the World Institute for Development Economics
Research of the United Nations University (UNU-WIDER)

OXFORD
UNIVERSITY PRESS

OXFORD
UNIVERSITY PRESS

Great Clarendon Street, Oxford OX2 6DP

Oxford University Press is a department of the University of Oxford.
It furthers the University's objective of excellence in research, scholarship,
and education by publishing worldwide in

Oxford New York

Auckland Cape Town Dar es Salaam Hong Kong Karachi
Kuala Lumpur Madrid Melbourne Mexico City Nairobi
New Delhi Shanghai Taipei Toronto

With offices in

Argentina Austria Brazil Chile Czech Republic France Greece
Guatemala Hungary Italy Japan Poland Portugal Singapore
South Korea Switzerland Thailand Turkey Ukraine Vietnam

Published in the United States
by Oxford University Press Inc., New York

© United Nations University—World Institute for Development Economics Research
(UNU-WIDER), 2011

British Library Cataloguing in Publication Data
Data available

Library of Congress Cataloging in Publication Data
Data available

Typeset by SPI Publisher Services, Pondicherry, India
Printed in Great Britain
on acid-free paper by
MPG Books Group, Bodmin and King's Lynn

ISBN 978–0–19–969315–3

3 5 7 9 10 8 6 4

Foreword

While no concise definition exists of which countries can be classified as 'fragile', there is no doubt that overcoming state fragility has become one of the most important international development objectives of the twenty-first century. Significant amounts of development funding are being allocated for this purpose and all indications are that this will continue in the coming years with wide-ranging implications for both development strategy and finance. Fragile states have become a hot topic in more than one sense.

This book was finalized in the midst of a global crisis—a triple crisis involving financial contraction, shocks to food prices, and the increasing threat of climate change. In a world that faces a multitude of hazards, strong states and good governance are more needed than ever. This means that fragile states— states that lack authority, legitimacy, and capacity to progressively steer their development—pose a significant threat to global security. Many fragile states have indeed turned into failed states, where hundreds of millions of people are trapped in poverty, violence, and desperation. The potential implications for peace and stability are dangerous.

The book is intended as a timely contribution to the international discourse on three dimensions of fragile states: their causes, their costs, and the responses required. These dimensions are intricately intertwined. For instance conflict, a major cause of state fragility, is often also a consequence of state fragility. Hence we cannot adequately respond to fragile states without considering the relationship between conflict and state fragility. Consequently, many of the chapters in this book focus on conflict and its relation to the state.

The costs of fragile states are not limited to their own citizens. This volume documents the far-reaching global repercussions of state fragility. Estimates are provided to suggest that the total costs of fragile and failing states may be twice the total amount of annual international aid flows. The international community faces a crucial responsibility to deal with fragile states. Hence our shared responsibility for bringing about a reduction in conflict and improving the effectiveness of aid in the context of fragility deserves the scrutiny that this book brings to bear.

The book should appeal to scholars, policy-makers, and donors who are concerned about conflict and development. The ultimate aim is to contribute to our inadequate understanding of how strong and accountable states can be fostered—states where government and civil society progressively advance human well-being, underpin households' resilience in the face of shocks, and form effective partnerships to maximize the benefits of development assistance.

Finn Tarp
Director, UNU-WIDER, Helsinki

Acknowledgements

This book would not have been possible without the encouragement and support of the community of scholars that constitute the UNU-WIDER network. This network enriched our thinking on fragile states in particular at three crucial junctions—at the conceptualization of the UNU-WIDER project on *Fragility and Development*, at the hosting of the international conference on Fragile States, Fragile Groups held in Helsinki on 15–16 June 2007, and in the conceptualization and focus of the book. We wish to extend our gratitude to this community. We hope that this book will further stimulate their research.

While we have a general debt towards our UNU-WIDER network, we have a very specific debt towards Tony Shorrocks, who as the then Director of UNU-WIDER inspired and promoted the overall project and the work contained in this book. We are also in particular grateful to the contributors of the volume for their scholarship, dedication, and also patience. Two anonymous referees provided insightful and vital comments and suggestions that we wish to acknowledge with thanks.

A special word of thanks is due to Anne Ruohonen, the project assistant, for her efficient and always enthusiastic support. We are also grateful to Neha Mehrotra and Lorraine Telfer-Taivainen from UNU-WIDER's publication team and for the professional administrative support provided by Barbara Fagerman and Paul Silfvenius. Thanks to Luc Christiaensen for his assistance in guiding the manuscript through the review process. And to our many colleagues and friends at UNU-WIDER who have all in some way indirectly contributed to this book, your loyalty, professionalism, and hard work are much appreciated—thanks for having made UNU-WIDER a warm and welcoming place to do research!

UNU-WIDER gratefully acknowledges the financial contributions to the project from the Australian Agency for International Development (AusAID) and the UK Department for International Development (DFID) towards the project on *Fragility and Development*, and to the Ministry of Foreign Affairs of Finland for supporting the conference on Fragile States. UNU-WIDER would also like to acknowledge the financial contributions to its research programme by the governments of Denmark (Royal Ministry of Foreign Affairs), Norway (Royal Ministry of Foreign Affairs), Sweden (Swedish International Development Cooperation Agency—Sida), and the United Kingdom (Department for International Development).

Wim Naudé, Amelia U. Santos-Paulino, and Mark McGillivray

Helsinki and Geelong, November 2010

Contents

Contents

List of Figures

List of Tables

List of Abbreviations

AAPs	assessment and action plans
ALC	authority, legitimacy, and capacity
ARDL	autoregressive distributed lag
BBC	British Broadcasting Corporation
BIS	Bank for International Settlements
BPAK	Banking and Payments Authority of Kosovo
CEE	Central and Eastern Europe
CFA	Central Fiscal Authority
CIDA	Canadian International Development Agency
CIFP	country indicators for foreign policy
CPA	Coalition Provisional Authority (of Iraq)
CPIA	country policy and institutional assessment
CPR	country performance ratings
CVI	Commonwealth Vulnerability Index
DAC	Development Assistance Committee of OECD
DFID	Department for International Development (UK)
DPC	difficult partnership country
ECM	error correction model
EPI	Environmental Performance Index
EVI	Environmental Vulnerability Index
FYR	Former Yugoslavian Republic
GC	governing council
GDP	gross domestic product
GMM	Generalized Method of Moments
GNI	gross national income
HDI	Human Development Index
HH	households
HIPCs	heavily indebted poor countries

HPI	Happy Planet Index
IDA	International Development Association
IMF	International Monetary Fund
ISDR	International Strategy for Disaster Reduction
LDC	least developed countries
LICs	low-income countries
LICUS	low-income country under stress
LSMS	living standards measurement study
MDGs	Millennium Development Goals
MENA	Middle East and North Africa
NATO	North Atlantic Treaty Organization
ODA	Official Development Assistance
OECD	Organisation for Economic Co-operation and Development
OLS	Ordinary Least Squares
PEFA	Public Expenditure and Financial Accountability
PFM	Public Financial Management Systems
PITF	Political Instability Task Force
PPP	purchasing power parity
PRSP	Poverty Reduction Strategy Paper
ROSC	Reports on the Observance of Standards and Codes
SIDS	small-island developing states
UK	United Kingdom
UN	United Nations
UNCTAD	United Nations Conference on Trade and Development
UN-DESA	United Nations Department for Economic and Social Affairs
UNDP	United Nations Development Programme
UNEP	United Nations Environmental Programme
UNMIK	UN Mission in Kosovo
UNU-EHS	United Nations University-Institute for Environment and Human Security
USA (US)	United States of America (United States)
WB&G	West Bank and Gaza

Notes on Contributors

Sebnem Akkaya is Senior Economist at the Middle East and Northern Africa Region, World Bank, Washington, DC, USA.

Mina Baliamoune-Lutz is Professor and Kip Fellow of Economics at the University of North Florida, USA.

Sumon Kumar Bhaumik is Reader in International Business and Economics, Aston Business School, Aston University, Birmingham, UK.

David Carment is Professor of International Affairs at the Norman Paterson School of International Affairs, Carleton University, Canada.

Lisa Chauvet is Senior Researcher at IRD (Institut de recherche pour le développement). She is based at the research centre DIAL, Paris, France.

Paul Collier is Professor of Economics and Director of the Centre for the Study of African Economies, University of Oxford, UK.

Ghassan Dibeh is Professor and Chairman of the Department of Economics at the Lebanese American University, Byblos, Lebanon.

Norbert Fiess is Senior Economist in the World Bank Latin America and Caribbean Region, World Bank, Washington, DC, USA.

Ira N. Gang is Professor of Economics at Rutgers, The State University of New Jersey, New Brunswick, NJ, USA.

Sanjeev Gupta is Deputy Director of the Fiscal Affairs Department of the International Monetary Fund (IMF), Washington, DC, USA.

Anke Hoeffler is Research Officer at the Centre for the Study of African Economies, University of Oxford, UK.

Bartlomiej Kaminski is Associate Professor of Government, University of Maryland, College Park, MD, USA, and Consultant for the World Bank, Washington, DC, USA.

Mark McGillivray is Research Professor in International Development at Alfred Deakin Research Institute, Deakin University, Melbourne, Australia.

S. Mansoob Murshed is Professor of the Economics of Conflict and Peace, Institute of Social Studies, The Hague, The Netherlands, and Professor of International Economics at the Birmingham Business School, University of Birmingham, UK.

Wim Naudé is Professor of Development Economics and Entrepreneurship at the Maastricht School of Management, a working group member of the Club de Madrid, a Senior Affiliate of the Households in Conflict Network, and associate editor of *Small Business Economics Journal*. He is based in Maastricht, the Netherlands.

Stewart Prest is a doctoral student in political science at the University of British Columbia, Canada.

Gaël Raballand is a Senior Economist in the World Bank Africa region working on governance and public sector reform, and based in Lusaka, Zambia.

Yiagadeesen Samy is Associate Professor of International Affairs at the Norman Paterson School of International Affairs, Carleton University, Ottawa, Canada.

Amelia U. Santos-Paulino is Economist in the Division for Africa, Least Developed Countries and Special Programmes, United Nations Conference on Trade and Development (UNCTAD), in Geneva, Switzerland.

Philip Verwimp is Associate Professor and holder of the Marie and Alain Philippson Chair in sustainable human development at the Solvay Brussels School of Economics and Management, Université Libre de Bruxelles where he is also affiliated with ECARES. He is based in Brussels, Belgium.

Myeong-Su Yun is Associate Professor, Department of Economics, Tulane University, New Orleans, LA, USA.

1

Fragile States: An Overview

Wim Naudé, Amelia U. Santos-Paulino, and Mark McGillivray

1.1 Introduction

As this book was approaching publication at least two news headlines dramatically illustrated that the willingness and ability of governments to promote their citizens' development and safety are crucial challenges. The first was a human-made disaster, the second a natural hazard resulting in a natural disaster. Both illustrated that people in 'fragile states' are at risk, and that their development prospects are being set back by the inability of such states to respond appropriately to crises.

The human-made disaster erupted on 15 September 2008 when the investment bank Lehman Brothers filed for bankruptcy and brought the US's sub-prime mortgage crisis to a head. Within a short space of time this financial crisis resulted in a global economic crisis as the rich countries of the world went into their worst recession in 70 years, and global growth contracted for the first time since the Second World War. For many developing countries, after enjoying a period of unprecedented growth, the contraction in global credit and collapse in their exports came as an unexpected shock, testing their resilience to the utmost (Naudé 2009, 2010). Worst affected were the world's fragile states, their problems compounded by reductions in aid receipts from their suffering donors, and by the inability and unwillingness of their governments to conduct macroeconomic policies in such a manner as to promote household resilience. An example of how fragile states can transmit external shocks back to the rest of the world is provided by the sudden rise in piracy off the coast of Somalia since November 2008, when Somali pirates began expanding their scope well outside the

Gulf of Aden.[1] Somalia, a conflict-ridden country, is by all accounts one of the world's most fragile states, seen by many as a failed state. The fact that a global economic crisis can tip it into activities with a significant cost on the rest of the world is to be expected—as Bakrania and Lucas (2009: 14) predicted:

> The financial crisis is threatening to exacerbate levels of hunger and desperation across the region caused by a combination of drought, poor seasonal rains, conflict, and the high cost of food. Given the existing state of criminality, gangs and international conflict actors across the region, but concentrated in Somalia, there is also a risk that increasing economic pressure will not only push more people into criminality and possibly radicalisation, but also that these networks will spread within the region, beyond the regional border into stable countries such as Kenya, and into international territory through activities such as piracy.

Human-made and natural disasters often go hand in hand. Indeed, natural hazards most often turn out to be disasters when human institutions fail. On 3 May 2008, Cyclone Nargis hit the poor country of Myanmar, home to more than 50 million people—a country subject, like many fragile states, to deep-seated social conflict. While estimates were coming in on fatalities ranging from between 22,000 to 100,000 the military regime in Myanmar was, according to media reports, hindering and delaying the delivery of international aid to victims of this disaster. Many other poor countries, a significant number of them small-island developing states (SIDS), are extremely vulnerable, like Myanmar, to natural hazards[2] (McGillivray et al. 2008, 2010). Indeed, in many of the poorest countries in the world, the frequency of natural disasters, particularly droughts and floods, have been on the increase. Unless their governments have the ability and willingness to address their citizens' broad development needs, natural hazards can all too easily result in terrible disasters, sparking off conflict, or exacerbating existing conflict.

We experienced the exacerbating effect of fragile states on external (human-made) and natural hazards first hand during the UNU-WIDER project on fragility and development, from which this book emanates. This was during a trip to Fiji, a SIDS consisting of more than 800 islands spread across the Pacific. We were in Fiji to organize a project meeting at the end of November 2006. Fiji, like many fragile states, has been embroiled in a long-simmering political crisis. On the second day of our meeting the crisis suddenly

---

[1] The number of pirate attacks off the cost of Somalia increased by 200 per cent in 2008 (Dingman 2009).

[2] The devasting earthquake that destroyed much of Port-au-Prince, the capital city of Haiti, on 12 January 2010 and claimed more than 200,000 lives is another recent case in point. Many deaths could have been prevented through better building standards and more efficient management of the urbanization process.

deepened. We woke up to be notified by the local press[3] that the military had given the warning: 'Prime Minister Laisenia Qarase has less than twelve hours to clean up the government or risk being removed from power'. Within days, the military made good on this threat with army Commander Commodore Voreqe Bainimarama taking over in a bloodless coup d'état. This coup d'état was the fourth in the past two decades.

Recurring conflict, such as we experienced in Fiji, exacts a heavy toll on development in a country that is particularly vulnerable to external shocks. Apart from affecting trade, tourism, economic relations, and investment, it hinders aid, technical and other foreign assistance, as well as the capacity of the government to effectively utilize aid (see for instance McGillivray et al. 2008, 2010). While we experienced the fragility of development prospects first hand in Fiji, its situation is sadly far from unique. Indeed, as a lower-middle-income country, Fijians are still relatively better off than the more than 700 million people that live in the fifty 'least developed countries'. Here, the international development community is increasingly concerned about the ability and willingness of governments to promote the development of their citizens, even in the face of extreme vulnerabilities.

The examples of Fiji, Myanmar, and Somalia illustrate that while countries may be fragile and may be so for different reasons, the presence or prospect of conflict is often a common feature. Consequently, concerns about state fragility have inspired more and more attempts to address anxieties on global security. Moreover, it is now also recognized that the growing challenge of climate change will make these problems so much worse—as fragile states do not have the ability to mitigate the expected impacts, or assist in adaption. In the latter regard, there is great concern that fragile states will not be able to deal with the possibility of large increases in environmentally forced migration and the potential conflict over resources that this could entail.

Consequently, the concept 'fragile state' is now firmly established in the global development discourse. It forms the central theme of the first European Report on Development (2009), of the World Bank's 2011 World Development Report (on conflict and governance), and of an increasing number of donors' international development strategies. Despite this centrality, there is still a lack of scholarly publications dealing critically with the topic—particularly its central concerns: that of dealing with and ending conflict, and strengthening the effectiveness of aid. This book is an attempt to fill this gap.

---

[3] *FijiSun*, News Limited, 1 December 2006.

1.2 What This Book Is About

One of the major challenges of global development is to identify when states are fragile, understand in which dimensions they are fragile and why, and determine the costs of such state fragility as well as how the international community should respond to fragile states.

This book studies these causes, costs, and responses from two main perspectives. The first is the perspective of conflict. Many fragile states are ravaged by conflict, and have become failed states. Some have only recently emerged from devastating civil war and remain fragile. Others have histories of military coups or have been in serious political crisis. Others still are small states with limited resource endowments, high debts, and are subject to natural hazards and other external shocks that continue to raise the spectre of conflict. Hence we cannot properly study state fragility without giving substantial weight to the relationship between conflict and state fragility. How does conflict contribute to fragility and how can fragile states avoid falling into conflict? How can fragile states in conflict make the transition to peace?

A second perspective taken in this book is on the role of the international community. This community, in particular donors, has an important challenge to contribute towards a reduction in conflict and an improvement in the effectiveness of aid. Indeed, despite the prominence of conflicts in many fragile states there is still a lack of research on the economic dimensions of conflict, aid, and development in fragile states. How can aid flows to fragile states be made more effective?

The rest of this chapter provides some background and discusses the contributions of the individual chapters towards a better understanding of the causes and costs of, and responses to, fragile states. In the next section we critically interrogate the concept of 'state fragility', including its analytical basis, and ask 'when are states fragile?' Then we consider the costs of fragile states and finally we draw together some implications for international responses to fragile states.

1.3 The Causes Of State Fragility

We have so far, on purpose, not explicitly defined the term 'fragile state', preferring examples to suggest what we meant. This is despite the fact that a number of such definitions have entered the discourse on fragile states, especially in the donor community. The reasons for not having earlier provided a definition of fragile states are twofold. First, although the definitions of fragile states in use in the donor community are recent, the deeper notion of states as being 'fragile' or 'vulnerable' is in fact a much older one, and we believe it is instructive to consider ways in which the concept evolved from previous concerns to identify the 'poorest of the poor' among nations. Second, most definitions of fragile states are static, *ex post* definitions, defining fragility (or state failure) after the fact. In showing how the concept of the development status of countries has changed over time we consider it appropriate to discuss some of the causes of what can be termed state 'fragility'. In our view, four broad (but interrelated) causes stand out: *conflict, low development status, vulnerability*, and *the lack of a developmental state*. By discussing these, and the way in which they raise state fragility, we emphasize the need for a forward-looking definition and predictive measures of state fragility. We suggest that it is not unreasonable to conclude that all states are fragile to various degrees, in various domains, and over different time periods, consistent with the comment by Engberg-Pedersen et al. (2008: 7) that 'fragility is a matter of degree...higher and lower levels of fragility may coexist in a society, state or a given territory'. Moreover reductions in fragility require an understanding of a state's vulnerability (a forward-looking notion), require peace and security, and require a developmental state.

But first we discuss the four previously mentioned broad determinants of state fragility and show how, within the concept of a developmental state (in a sense the opposite of a fragile state), these determinants relate to existing definitions of fragile states.

1.3.1 *Conflict*

The *Oxford English Dictionary* (2nd edn., 1989) defines the word 'fragile' as meaning 'liable to break or be broken; easily snapped or shattered; in looser sense, weak, perishable, easily destroyed'. In the context of independent political states, or countries, the term 'fragile state' suggests states or territories whose very existence is under threat. In the extreme case, where states do cease to exist or function to any normal degree, they can even be labelled as 'failed states' (see e.g. Ghani and Lockhart 2008). Looking at the post-Cold-War reconfiguration of states, a number of cases stand out as obvious fragile states or territories. Examples include some of the cases that will be studied in this book, such as Iraq, Palestine, or Somalia, as well as other places where violence, political strife, and economic collapse have been making headlines, such as Afghanistan, Haiti, Sudan, Zimbabwe, and others. With hindsight, the former Yugoslavia and Zaire were extremely 'fragile' states, ultimately 'failing' and perishing in violent conflict.

A common factor in the fragility of the states and territories just mentioned is the presence of conflict, or the potential for conflict. Even without conflict, fragile states have been described as 'sites of potential violence and warfare' and 'potential sites of terrorist activity' (Putzel 2007: 1). Hence conflict is a central theme in this book.

The Political Instability Task Force (PITF), previously the State Failure Task Force, describes four types of conflict events that can push a fragile state into failure: revolutionary wars, ethnic wars, adverse regime changes, and genocides and politicides.[4] From these types of conflict the PITF has compiled a consolidated list of state failures over the period 1955 to 2006. Over this period they record no less that 139 'state failure events' across 107 countries. Although they note that the number of wars and civil conflicts in the world had declined since the end of the Cold War, there were still at least 18 countries that, by the end of 2006, were in a state of serious conflict or state failure. In Appendix 1.A1 we provide a list of these countries, taken from the PITF's consolidated list of state failure. From this list it can be seen that a disproportionate number of failing states in conflict are in Africa (about 40 per cent) and the Middle and Near East (50 per cent).

Many of the states that were in conflict previously, and which are now in a post-conflict reconstructive phase, remain in a precarious condition. One reason is that the possibility of a relapse into conflict is high—there is a 50 per cent risk of conflict renewal during the first five post-conflict years (Collier 2006: 19). Of the countries noted by the PITF at the end of 2006 there were at least 13 countries that had emerged from violent conflict in the preceding five-year period. These countries are listed in Appendix 1.A2. Taken together, the countries in Appendix 1.A1 and 1.A2 can be argued to constitute 31 extremely fragile states.

A second reason for continued fragility in conflict and recent post-conflict states is due to the economic impact of violent conflict on a country's development and development prospects. A growing literature has in recent years examined the costs of conflict, especially of civil war. Most estimates suggest that the impacts of civil war are substantial and long-lasting (Chen et al. 2007). These include the direct costs in terms of destruction of infrastructure, diverted (military) expenditure as well as the much higher indirect costs of disruption of markets and increase in risk and uncertainty. Collier (1999) found that civil conflict depresses growth rates by about 2.2 per cent per annum on average. Lopez and Wodon (2005) calculate that Rwanda's gross domestic product (GDP) could have been 25 per cent higher in 2001 if it had avoided the genocide of 1994. Civil conflict also has spillover effects reducing growth in neighbouring countries (Murdoch and Sandler 2002)—a theme that is taken up further in this volume by Lisa Chauvet, Paul Collier, and Anke Hoeffler (see Chapter 5).

---

[4] See <http://globalpolicy.gmu.edu/pitf/>.

Conflict, which undermines the authority and legitimacy of the state and limits prospects for development, is clearly a major cause of fragility, and of identifying countries as fragile. However, weak or fragile states, due to low development status, in themselves can lead to conflict and an ensuing vicious cycle from fragility to conflict, and from conflict to further fragility. Thus the causality between state fragility and failure and conflict is multi-directional.[5] In practice, given the complex nature of many conflicts, it is most often difficult to disentangle the various influences, especially when conflicts have persisted for many years. Indeed, in the chapters in this book, the relationship between conflict and state fragility is explored in greater depth.

In particular, Chapter 4 of this book, by Ghassan Dibeh, is entitled 'Resources, Conflict, and State Fragility: Iraq and Somalia'. It contrasts two forms of state failure in the context of violent conflict: on the one hand states may fail due to conflict over bountiful resources, such as in oil-rich Iraq. On the other hand, states may fail in resource-poor states, such as Somalia because no group has an interest in forming a central authority. To understand the relationship between resources, state structures, and economic growth, Dibeh provides an overview of the theoretical literature and a model of the relationship between resources and the demand for government. This is then applied to the situations in Iraq and Somalia. The chapter provides a useful reminder that it is often difficult to predict in advance whether or when a country might fail, and that the importance of good leadership in the context of strong governance institutions should not be underestimated. These lessons emerge from a historical overview of Iraq's economic development since the 1960s. Three periods are contrasted: the era before the first Gulf War (1991), the era of international isolation between 1991 and 2003, and the subsequent post-Saddam Hussein period following the 2003 USA-led invasion. In essence, the story of the rise and fall of Iraq is of a country failing due to avoidable external conflicts (the war with Iran and the occupation of Kuwait) and internal conflicts (failing to establish trust and cooperation between Sunni, Shiite, and Kurdish groups). The policy implications from this chapter are that efforts to end conflict in failed states will differ significantly depending on the availability and distribution of resources, and the resulting incentive structures facing conflicting parties: one-size-fits-all externally imposed solutions are not likely to bring lasting peace and development.

---

[5] Recently Goldstone et al. (2005: 2) studied the relation between state weakness and conflict, finding that 'regime type is overwhelmingly the dominant factor behind revolutions, ethnic wars, and adverse regime changes'. In particular they find partial democracies with internal factions to face the greatest risk of falling into conflict, and point out that it is often when autocratic regimes begin to reform and introduce partial democratic changes that internal factionalization poses the greatest threat.

1.3.2 *Low development status*

Conflict is a well-recognized source of fragility through its destructive impact on human development. Often, as was noted in the previous section, low development status fuels conflict and creates a vicious cycle of underdevelopment—a 'poverty trap'. It is therefore necessary to broaden the characteristics and determinants of state fragility to go beyond conflict, to include the development status of such states.

It is an intuitively derived conclusion that states are likely to be more fragile, following the definition of 'fragile', the less developed they are. Ever since the establishment of the United Nations (UN) and the Bretton Woods Institutions there has been a concern to identify states with a low development status. Therefore, to understand the current context for the labelling of some states as 'fragile' it is useful to consider the way in which various labels or classifications relating to a state's development status have been used, and how these have evolved from static, income-based classifications to classifications that are more concerned about broader human well-being, including as will be discussed below, vulnerability.

In broad terms, socioeconomic classifications distinguish between *developed* states, *developing* states, and *least developed* states. These broad classifications have generally come to replace the Cold War terms 'First', 'Second', and 'Third World States'. The distinctions between these broad levels of development are often made based on per capita incomes. Thus one of the most well-known of the economic classification of states is the World Bank's use of per capita income to identify between low-income (with per capita income less than US$905), lower-middle-income (US$906–3,595), upper-middle-income (US$3,596–11,115), and high-income (with per capita income exceeding US$11,116) states. Low- and middle-income countries are regularly described as 'developing countries'. If one would be concerned about which of these could be 'fragile', one could start by identifying the poorest of the developing countries. At present 53 states are classified as low-income countries, of which 34 (64 per cent) are located in sub-Saharan Africa. A list of these low-income countries is contained in Appendix 1.A3.

One reason why it may be argued that poor countries might tend to be fragile is that many of the low- and middle-income countries have substantial state debt. States with high debt burdens most often do not have the resources to respond to mitigation of poverty or the potential impacts of external shocks. The IMF and World Bank, since 1996, identify a category of states that are both poor and heavily indebted. The 'heavily indebted poor countries' (HIPCs) initiative aims to target debt relief and low-interest loans to states that are poor and heavily indebted. The IMF has identified 41 countries (80 per cent of whom are located in sub-Saharan Africa) to qualify or to potentially qualify as HIPCs (IMF 2007a). Appendix 1.A4 lists the HIPCs as identified by the IMF.[6]

Of course, it was recognized from early on that monetary measures alone are inadequate measures of development. An early effort to take this into account is the UNDP's Human Development Index (HDI), adding measures of education and health to per capita income. The IMF adopts a value of 0.9 for a state's HDI to classify it as either an 'advanced' economy or a developed economy—there are 31 advanced economies by this measure (IMF 2007). The HDI is widely used today, but it is also widely criticized, not least because of the significant correlation between the HDI and per capita income, which has lead to the HDI being described as 'redundant' in a statistical sense (McGillivray 2005).

Aware of the shortcomings of many development indicators the Economic and Social Council of the UN expanded on the use of income and the HDI in an endeavour to identify the 'least developed countries' (LDCs). It classifies the latter using income per capita (LDCs will have a gross national income (GNI) per capita of less than US$750), an index of human assets (consisting of indicators such as nutritional status, health, literacy, and school enrolment), and an index of economic vulnerability (which takes account of natural and trade shocks, exposure, smallness of the economy, and remoteness) (see UNCTAD 2006). There are at the time of writing 49 states identified as being amongst the 'least developed'. Appendix 1.A5 lists these 49 LDCs in 2007. Of these, 33 (about 67 per cent) are in sub-Sahara Africa, followed by ten in Asia, five in Oceania, and one in the Americas.

Within the vulnerability index of the UN the SIDS stand out as being particularly vulnerable to external shocks, in particular natural hazards and macroeconomic shocks. One reason for the vulnerability to natural hazards is due to particularly fragile natural environments. Environmental fragility/vulnerability is, however, relevant beyond just the SIDS, and has in recent years attracted increasing attention from international organizations and donors, because of the threats posed by climate change and the growing awareness of the importance of environmental quality for human well-being in general. Various measures have therefore been adopted to classify countries according to their environmental impact and sustainability. Two notable recent indices of environmental fragility include the Environmental Performance Index (EPI) of the Yale Center for Environmental Law and the Center for International Earth Science Information Network (see Esty et al.

---

[6] The World Bank identifies countries which are eligible for concessionary International Development Association (IDA) finance based on per capita income of less than US$1,065 and a lack of financial ability to borrow from it. The Bank currently identifies 65 countries as being eligible for IDA finance.

2008) and the Happy Planet Index (HPI) of the New Economics Foundation (NEF) (see NEF 2006). These indices may be helpful in identifying state fragility from an environmental perspective.

The EPI measures the environmental performance of countries using a composite of 25 different environmental indicators.[7] Appendix 1.A5 lists the bottom quintile of countries in this index; i.e. the countries which are most fragile from an environmental perspective. Of these, 23 (77 per cent) are located in sub-Saharan Africa. The HPI is an index based on three indicators, of subjective satisfaction with life, life expectancy, and the 'ecological footprint' of a country.[8] The bottom quintile of the ranking based on the HPI can be interpreted as countries with poor ecological efficiency. Appendix 1.A4 lists these countries. As in the other classifications discussed so far, countries from sub-Saharan Africa again dominate this list, with 22 of the 35 countries in the bottom quintile of the HPI (63 per cent) being located here. Appendix 1.A6 is instructive in that it contains in the list of countries with poor ecological efficiency and poor subjective satisfaction with life countries which may be classified as middle- or high-income countries (such as the USA, Russia, and EU countries such as Bulgaria, Estonia, and Latvia). As in the vulnerability index, it suggests that although per capita income is clearly important, the link between per capita income and potential sources of country fragility is not a perfect one and cautions against defining fragile states based solely on per capita income. It also suggests that it is important to identify vulnerable groups within countries, whether those countries are seen to be 'fragile' or not.

1.3.3 *Vulnerability*

From the criteria used to decide whether or not a state belongs to the LDC group, it was clear that using measures of 'vulnerability' is a recent advance that distinguishes it from previous classification schemes. Vulnerability differs from other measures of a state's development level in that it is a forward-looking (*ex ante*) concept, referring in most cases to a state's potential to be negatively affected by future changes (Guillaumont 2009a, 2009b; Naudé et al. 2009a, 2009b). In what follows it will be shown that there is indeed a close relationship between state fragility and vulnerability:[9] that states which are vulnerable to poverty or external shocks are more fragile, and that fragility is often a factor which raises households' vulnerability to poverty, natural

---

[7] For a discussion of these 25 indicators, see Esty et al. (2008: 18).

[8] See <http://www.happyplanetindex.org>.

[9] As Guillaumont and Guillaumont-Jeanneney (2009: 5) note 'Fragility and vulnerability are apparently close, but are in fact, strongly different concepts according to the present literature, each with its own history.'

hazards, and economic shocks—as was illustrated by the events in Myanmar following the impact of Cyclone Nargis in May 2008 and in Haiti after the earthquake of January 2010, to mention just two examples.

To understand the concept of vulnerability in relation to state fragility it is appropriate to define vulnerability. In two companions to this book, we deal in greater detail with the concept of vulnerability (see Naudé et al. 2009a, 2009b). For present purposes though we can mention that the use of apparently different definitions of vulnerability in different disciplines be they in economics, or environmental or social sciences, does not necessarily reflect conflicting views on the nature of vulnerability itself. As had been shown by Alwang et al. (2001), different scientific disciplines have definitions of vulnerability that differ in specifics because they focus on different components of risk.[10] Beyond these risk-specifics, most definitions of vulnerability now views it from the point of view of the vulnerability of a 'system', such as a household, region, or country, to 'specific perturbations that impinge on the system' or to the probability of a 'system' undergoing a negative change due to a perturbation (Gallopin 2006: 294). As examples, the International Strategy for Disaster Reduction (ISDR) defines vulnerability as 'the set of conditions and processes resulting from physical, social, economic, and environmental factors, which increase the susceptibility of a community to the impact of hazards' (ISDR 2004: 16).

In the context of the poorest countries, Guillaumont (2009a) provides an excellent overview of the work done by the UN Committee for Development Policy on designing an economic vulnerability indicator; see also Guillaumont (2009b). Naudé (2010) discusses the use of vulnerability and resilience indicators to measure the degree to which fragile states in Africa are at risk from a global financial crisis such as that of 2008–9.

De Léon (2006) offers an excellent summary of the development of the concept of vulnerability outside of the field of economics, from the work of Chambers (1989), which focuses on sustainable livelihoods of households, to the work sponsored by United Nations Department for Economic and Social Affairs (UN-DESA) which focuses on vulnerability of small island states and the work of the United Nations University's Institute for Environmental and Human Security (UNU-EHS).[11]

---

[10] De Léon (2006: 9–10) discusses the relationship between risks, vulnerability, and hazards, where 'risk' refers to the probability that a community or household or country may experience a particular loss due to the occurrence of a particular hazard. For a given hazard, the higher the vulnerability of a system, the higher the risk it faces.

[11] The UNU-EHS has pioneered the British Broadcasting Corporation (BBC) framework in the identification and management of vulnerability to natural hazards. In this approach, due to Bogardi and Birkmann (2004) and Cardona (1999), vulnerability is a dynamic process which consists of exposure, susceptibility, and coping capacity over various economic and social dimensions.

In economics, vulnerability has often been defined as the risk of households falling in or remaining in poverty due to either idiosyncratic hazards (due to characteristics of the individual household) or covariate/aggregate hazards (external to the household) (e.g. Chaudhuri et al. 2002). By focusing on hazards, and not just transient poverty but the probability of remaining in poverty (chronic poverty), it takes into account 'both exposure to serious risks and defenseless against deprivation' (Kamanou and Morduch 2004: 155).

From the common definitional elements, it is clear that vulnerability relates *to* an undesirable outcome (e.g., vulnerability *to* poverty, vulnerability *to* food insecurity, or vulnerability *to* natural hazards) and that such vulnerability is due to 'exposure to hazards', which cause 'perturbations' (Alwang et al. 2001: 6). These hazards can have many origins: from environmental, socioeconomic, and physical to political hazards. It is also clear that the 'system' can imply different spatial levels of analysis that exhibit vulnerability, from micro (household), to meso (regional) and macro levels (countries, the globe). In recent years the related concept of 'fragility' has been applied to the level of countries and regions and it has been argued that fragility is in fact a more proper concept to use on the aggregate level and that vulnerability is a more proper concept on the micro-level. Binzel and Brück (2007: 5) define fragility as 'the existence of persistent, systematic, significant and interrelated social, political and economic uncertainties'. In this sense, fragility need not replace vulnerability on the macro-level, as fragility can be seen as an important (covariate) source of household and country vulnerability.

One reason for the imperfect link between per capita income and fragility has been explored in the growing literature on countries', and in particular SIDS' vulnerability to natural hazards (see, e.g., Wisner et al. 2004). This literature is at pains to point out that a natural hazard only becomes a natural disaster if there is a vulnerable population group, and that populations are often vulnerable due to insufficient institutional support, such as weak government and community capacity—such as which would generally characterize a fragile state but which could also occur due to institutional weaknesses in states that appear on the face of it not to be fragile. There are thus elements of fragility which may put many people even in high-income countries at risk. This has led some to call for analysis of fragility on different spatial and administrative levels (Naudé et al. 2009b). Strong institutions are therefore a source of resilience which mitigates the possible adverse impacts of external shocks (and internal conflict) and as such is clearly an important factor to take into consideration in identification of fragile states or vulnerable groups.

Briguglio (2001) discusses a number of methods to compile a vulnerability 'index'[12]—these range from normalizing variables and taking their averages, to mapping variables on a categorical scale, and to using regression methods to estimate predicted values for an index. Various vulnerability indexes on the country level have been proposed since UN-DESA initiated work on the vulnerability of small island states in the early 1990s. For instance the Commonwealth Vulnerability Index (CVI) consists of three indicators: export dependency, export diversification, and susceptibility to natural disasters (Easter 1998). The Inter-American Bank developed a Prevalent Vulnerability Index (PVI) consisting of the averages of three composite indicators for exposure or physical susceptibility, fragility, and resilience. One of the most extensive vulnerability indexes is the Environmental Vulnerability Index (EVI) developed by UNEP and the South Pacific Applied Geoscience Commission (SOCAP) which uses over 50 indicators covering a large number of dimensions of vulnerability and resilience.[13] They classify countries, depending on how they score according to their indicators, as either resilient, at risk, vulnerable, highly vulnerable or extremely vulnerable to risks from their natural environment. Appendix 1.A7 contains the 35 countries classified in the EVI as extremely vulnerable. It is clear from this list that it is dominated by SIDS, and that it is not only the poor countries which are vulnerable; high-income countries such as Austria, Belgium, the Netherlands, and the UK are also seen as extremely vulnerable to environmental risks.

The brief review in the previous paragraphs has argued that states are fragile to the extent that they are in conflict or are likely to fall into conflict, and that this is related in a complex manner with a state's development status and its vulnerability. The former is most often measured using a country's poverty status (using some indicator of per capita income) but in recent years the concept of development status has been broadened to refer to human well-being. There is not an appropriate single indicator for human well-being without shortcomings. As a result various complementary measures are used. These include, as was discussed here, measures of human development, of economic and environmental vulnerability, of environmental sustainability and ecological efficiency and of subjective well-being. It was pointed out that there is increasing recognition in academic and policy-making communities that the quality of a country's institutions ultimately matter for its development status, but also for the degree to which it may be fragile or vulnerable even if its institutions result in a relatively high development status. This implies that a more nuanced and differentiated understanding

---

[12] Recent advances in the measurement of vulnerability is dealt with by the September 2009 special issue of the journal *Oxford Development Studies* which we guest edited. See Naudé, et al. (2009c).

[13] See <http://www.vulnerabilityindex.net>.

of the role of institutions, in particular of the state itself, is needed. In the next sub-section we argue that the opposite of a fragile state is a developmental state, and relate the main definitions of fragility to the concept of a developmental state.

1.3.4 *A non-developmental state*

While the classifications and measurements of the development status of countries as discussed above all capture some elements of fragility, they are not at all good precursors or complements to the identification of states that are fragile as per definition of fragility. They are imperfect measures for two main reasons. One, with the exception of the vulnerability index, all these measures are static, *ex post* measures of development outcomes. Two, the relationship between these measures and the underlying, ultimate determinants of state fragility is unclear. In this regard the discussion on the role of institutions in state fragility or robustness is paramount. More to the point, state orientation towards development has come to be seen as a crucial determinant of the role of the state in providing the necessary institutional foundations for development and for limiting fragility. The concept of the 'developmental state' has been coined to denote the ideal orientation and functioning required from governments to improve the development outcomes as measured by the various indicators discussed above (for an introduction see Woo-Cumings 1999).

During the 1980s and 1990s a debate raged in the development and international political economy spheres as to whether or not there is a role for the state in the economy. Viewpoints ranged from those espousing a minimalist role for the state (as 'night watchman') to the view that extensive state ownership and direction of production factors is required for development. A persuasive and influential view was (and still is) that governments are prone to failure and capture by interest groups, and need to be kept in check through various checks and balances. These needed to ensure 'good governance', associated with accountability, transparency, and economic freedoms (including economic liberalization) within a system of liberal democracy.[14] While the importance of liberal democracy, as a desirable outcome in itself, has received growing recognition in recent times, the view of a minimalist state concerned only with limiting political instability, corruption, and market distortions has received a more critical response. As a result the development community is

---

[14] A 'liberal democracy' refers to 'regular, free and fair elections, a bill of rights, separation of the powers of the executive, legislature and judiciary, a multiparty system and upholding of the rule of law' (Edigheji 2005: 7).

by and large gravitating to the view that states can fulfil a central role in development and that what is at stake is 'questions about commitment and capacity' (Fritz and Menocal 2007: 531). That the state could, and should do more was dramatically illustrated by the development success of Japan and the other East Asian 'miracle' economies (Hong Kong, Indonesia, Malaysia, Singapore, South Korea, Taiwan, and Thailand) (Stiglitz 1996) but also by the failure of development in most of sub-Saharan Africa (UNCTAD 2007).[15] In particular, the more activist role of the state in the former countries has led to the concept of the 'developmental state' being coined in the 1990s. More recently, in parallel with the growing concern with fragile states, the concept of the developmental state 'is back at the centre of the international policy debate' (Fritz and Menocal 2007: 531).

UNCTAD (2007: 59–60) defines development states according to their objective, which is 'to ensure sustained economic growth and development on the back of high rates of accumulation, industrialization and structural change'. However, a developmental state must go beyond objectives to being willing and able to implement the necessary initiatives to progressively realize these objectives (Edigheji 2005). Thus, in the words of UNCTAD (2007: 60) a developmental state 'has (or develops) the capacity to implement economic policies that effectively deliver development, which in turn gives it legitimacy'. It has been pointed out that many of the economically successful East Asian Miracle countries (as well as China to an extent) had in particular achieved a degree of legitimacy despite not being fully democratic states, through their capacity to deliver development outcomes. This lack of democracy is now seen not as a strength but as a source of vulnerability, exposing citizens of these countries to state misuse and abuse of power (Mkandawire 2001). A 'democratic development state' therefore includes in addition to the commitment to progressive implementation of development policies, a commitment to liberal democracy (Edigheji 2005; Robinson and White 1998). According to UNCTAD (2007: 60) such a democratic development state has a 'social anchoring that prevents it from the use of its autonomy in a predatory manner'. Chapter 4 by Ghassan Dibeh focuses in particular on the absence of such 'social anchoring' in Iraq and Somalia as a cause of widespread predation and conflict over resources.

From a donor point of view, democratic developmental states as defined above are effective states, where aid will be more effective in achieving its objectives. The opposite of a democratic development state, a fragile or failed

---

[15] As was shown earlier, sub-Saharan African countries make up a disproportionate number of the poorest, least developed countries in the world, suggesting that state fragility is disproportionately high in this region. A recent UNCTAD (2007: 83) report argues that 'The escape of sub-Saharan Africa from poverty…could yet be found in the development states paradigm.'

state, is then by implication a state where aid will be less effective. It is more than just a structural inability to absorb aid, but more to the point an inability to utilize aid or a lack of capacity or willingness on the part of the state. In this regard the UK's Department for International Development (DFID 2005: 7) defines a fragile state as a state where 'the government cannot or will not deliver core functions to the majority of its people, including the poor'. Core functions here include the provision of basic services such as education, health, safety, and security, often the focus of donor aid programmes.

Brown and Stewart (2007) propose a definition of fragile states that makes reference to the underlying reasons for the inability of states to deliver on their core functions. They define fragile states as 'states that are failing, or at risk of failing, with respect to authority, comprehensive service delivery or legitimacy' (2007: 5). Thus failure with respect to authority is seen to manifest in violent conflict, high crime, lack of safety and security; failure with respect to service delivery is seen as the inability to extend basic services (health, education, etc.); and failure with respect to legitimacy is seen to manifest in lack of democracy, freedoms, and civil liberties (ibid.: 5–6). They use data on political violence, on absolute and progressive service delivery, and on democratic governance to identify fragile states that are failing or seem to at risk of doing so, in each of these three dimensions. They identify 11 countries that are failing in at least two of these dimensions, with countries from sub-Saharan Africa again dominating the list: Angola, Congo (DR), Equatorial Guinea, Sierra Leone, Saudi Arabia, Mali, Burkina Faso, Niger, Burundi, Myanmar, and Iraq.

Various means have been proposed to identify fragile states based on these notions of a non-developmental state. Two of the foremost are the World Bank's (2005) classification based on the country policy and institutional assessment (CPIA) ratings,[16] and the Canadian International Development Agency's (CIDA) country indicators for foreign policy (CIFP) project (CIFP 2006). These two are dealt with in greater detail in Part I of this book.

In Chapter 2 entitled 'State Fragility: Concept and Measurement', Mina Baliamoune-Lutz and Mark McGillivray discuss the World Bank and OECD Development Assistance Committee approaches that classify a country as fragile on the basis of its perceived ability to use aid effectively for development purposes. Linking CPIA scores to this ability, both organizations define a country as fragile on the basis of threshold values of the CPIA. The World Bank, for example, considers a country to be a fragile state if it is a low-income

---

[16] For a clarification of the CPIA ratings, see the World Bank website: <http://web.worldbank. org/WBSITE/EXTERNAL/EXTABOUTUS/IDA/0,,contentMDK: 20941073~pagePK: 51236175~piPK: 437394~theSitePK: 73154,00.html>.

country with a CPIA score of 3.0 or less (these countries are also termed 'low-income countries under stress'—LICUS). Baliamoune-Lutz and McGillivray's contribution is to question the manner and methods in which fragile states are distinguished from non-fragile states. In particular they question the choice of a rigid CPIA score of 3.0 or less as a cut-off point for deciding whether or not a country is too fragile to use aid effectively. In their own words 'all countries are fragile to the extent that their ability to use aid differs. Some are simply more fragile than others'. In order to take into account that fragility differs along a continuum, they propose a framework that uses fuzzy-set theory, which allows for a more gradual distinction to be made between fragile and non-fragile states. They apply this to the 2005 CPIA scores from 76 countries, and conclude that using the traditional methods to classify countries may lead to some countries being incorrectly classified.

Chapter 3 continues in the vein of Chapter 2 to consider the measurement of state fragility. Whereas in Chapter 2 the authors took a pre-existing measure—the World Bank's Country Policy and Institutional Assessment (CPIA) and modified it to explicitly reflect the implicit ambiguity associated with CPIA scores, Chapter 3 by David Carment, Stewart Prest, and Yiagadeesen Samy entitled 'The Causes and Measurement of State Fragility' aims to build a new, more comprehensive measure of fragility.

The authors start by pointing out that despite the differing views on what constitutes a fragile state there is a number of areas of consensus on the approach to identify such states. One is that a large number of indicators should be used, and that use of a single or limited number of indicators, such as poverty, or conflict, is inadequate. Support for this requirement comes from the discussion in this chapter which has shown, with the assistance of the various appendices attached, how different methods and indicators of classifying countries result in different countries being highlighted. Second, chosen indicators must allow monitoring and indicate the causes of fragility. Third, measures must allow for different causes of fragility in different countries—we have seen earlier for instance how some of the high-income countries are particularly vulnerable to environmental risks and how many poor countries remain politically stable.

The CIFP Fragility Index attempts to meet these requirements, and locates the causes of fragility in threats to the authority (A), legitimacy (L), and capacity (C) of the state. These so-called authority, legitimacy, and capacity (ALC) components are used to gauge state performance across various dimensions, including the economic, governance, security and crime, human development, demographics, and environmental dimensions. They use this approach to compile a fragility index for countries over the period 1999–2005. Here it is only the degree of fragility which differs between countries. In Appendix 1.A8 the 40 most fragile states according to the CIFP project is listed. Comparison of the countries in this list with those of countries that are currently or recently in conflict (Appendix 1.A1 and 1.A2) and with the LDCs show some overlap, especially with regard to the predominance of states from sub-Saharan Africa. In the CIFP's Fragility Index 70 per cent of the 40 most fragile states are in sub-Saharan Africa (see Appendix 1.A9).

Despite the overlap with the 31 countries in or emerging from conflict, David Carment and co-authors argue in Chapter 3 that the 'security-instability-nexus' does not adequately put into perspective the fundamental causes and nature of state fragility which they argue should be seen as broader than just state failure due to violent conflict.

1.4 The Costs Of Fragile States

The costs of fragile states were mentioned at the outset of this chapter as one of the reasons for the greater concern of the international community with these states in recent years. For one, there is the realization that the global goals of development, as reflected in for instance the Millennium Development Goals (MDGs) of the United Nations, will not be achieved as long as a substantial number of states (home to almost a billion people) remain fragile and failing. Second, there is the realization that fragile and failed states have significant spillover effects onto the entire global economy, with adverse implications for global security and regional development and stability. And third, understanding the causes of state fragility and failure had become important for international assistance to recipient countries to be tailored to be more effective.

Part II of this book deals with these costs of fragile states. The major contributions of the chapters in this part are a quantification of the costs of failed and fragile states on a macro-level, and an illustration of the micro-level impact of state failure and fragility. Much of the existing literature on the costs of fragile states is limited to an assessment of the costs of violent conflict (war, civil war). 'The Costs of Failing States and the Limits to Sovereignty' (Chapter 5) by Lisa Chauvet, Paul Collier, and Anke Hoeffler estimates the full costs of a failing state. They argue that states can fail in three ways: by causing negative spillovers for citizens of neighbouring countries, by failing to provide basic security for their own citizens, and by failing to create and maintain an environment for the progressive and sustainable reduction of poverty.

The core argument here is that in these three ways, failing (or fragile) states impose costs, and that if large enough, may justify that their national sovereignty be overridden by international intervention. They calculate that the combined total cost of failing states (using the World Bank's classification of LICUS) is around US$276 billion per annum—more than twice what international aid flows would be if the OECD countries actually reach the UN target of giving 0.7 per cent of their GDP in aid. This suggests that there are significant benefits in solving the problems of fragile states.

In Chapter 6 the focus is on a country that has been in a long violent conflict: Palestine. Entitled 'Conflict and Fragility in Palestine: The Costs of the Closures Regime on West Bank and Gaza' this chapter by Sebnem Akkaya, Norbert Fiess, Bartlomiej Kaminski, and Gaël Raballand assesses the costs and consequences of Israeli border closures on the West Bank and Gaza (WB&G) economy. The chapter is an apt illustration of the causes and consequences of state fragility on conflict, and of conflict on state fragility and development. The chapter points out that Israeli security arrangements (such as checkpoints and external and internal closures of roads) have placed restrictions on the movement of goods and people to and from the WB&G, imposing significant economic costs, including contributing to a fragile Palestinian Authority. They use quarterly data from 1993 to 2005 in an autoregressive distributed lag model with the impact of closures proxied by the ratio of days worked net of closure to the number of potential working days. They estimate that one day of closure cost the WB&G about US$7 million in terms of lost income. In addition to these macroeconomic costs they also consider the impact of closures on remittances, employment, transport costs, external trade, and future economic activity. The loss in income of Palestinian workers in Israel between 2001 and 2003 is estimated to total more than US$693 billion, and the loss of export earnings as US$693 million. As the case of Palestine illustrates, conflict leads to isolation and fragmentation, which ultimately imposes huge economic costs, further weakening a state of authority's capacity to progressively address development.

While Chapters 5 and 6 were concerned with the macro-level costs and consequences of state fragility and failure, the remaining chapter in Part II takes a micro-level view, in particular to determine the costs and consequences of state fragility and failure on vulnerable groups such as women. Chapter 7, 'Gender and Ethnicity in Fragile States: The Case of Post-Conflict Kosovo' by Sumon Kumar Bhaumik, Ira Gang, and Myeong-Su Yun investigates whether female-headed households, particularly in relation to their ethnic group, suffer more after a conflict. They do this using household data on Serbian and Albanian households in the Balkan region of Kosovo, a region characterized by decades of political strife and outright armed conflict during most of the 1990s. They find that female-headed households did on average not suffer more than male-headed households, but that when ethnic affiliation is taken into consideration, the picture changes. Then they find that living standards of minority Serb households are lower than that of Albanian households, with female-headed Serbian households having the lowest standard of living in Kosovo. The authors conclude that 'we need to study welfare in fragile states, where conflicts among ethnicities or tribes or political ideologies are at the forefront, not only from the ethnicity/tribe/ideology perspective, but also from gender perspectives'. This is an important message for finding ways and means of mitigating the impact of violent conflict in fragile states, and in aiding post-conflict reconstruction.

1.5 International Responses

Part II of this book strongly urges, as does Ghani and Lockhart (2008: 25) that the 'neglect of fragile states is not an option'. Therefore, in the final section (Part III) of this book, we ask how can the international community assist fragile states, given what we know of their causes and costs.

A three-pronged approach seems now to be gaining ground in the literature. This approach is to narrow the focus on the most fragile states, second to 'broaden the instruments' (Collier 2007), and third to improve the effectiveness of these instruments, including the effectiveness of aid—see for instance the World Bank (1998) report and the 2005 Paris Declaration on aid effectiveness.

According to Collier (2007) the focus of the international community should be on the 'bottom billion'—which could be taken to imply the 30 to 40 most fragile countries as identified also in this chapter. Once these countries have been targeted, a broad and holistic approach is needed, requiring a broad range of interventions from the international community. Brown and Stewart (2007: 36) explicitly state that reducing state fragility 'requires a comprehensive approach and set of objectives' and Basu Roy and Jolly (2007: 4) point out that the inability of the international community to 'adopt holistic strategies' have been an important constraint in furthering development in fragile states. David Carment and co-authors' approach towards understanding the causes of state fragility (see Chapter 3) suggests that these objectives should include improving the authority, legitimacy, and capacity of the state to provide basic services. It is consistent with the notion of building democratic developmental states.

In achieving objectives such as these various instruments or tools exist. Maxwell (2006) identified six instruments that may be taken to assist fragile states. These are (a) dialogue, either bilaterally or multilaterally, (b) bypassing government by providing humanitarian aid and NGO development directly to affected groups, (c) to incentivize government by rewarding performance or extending conditional support, (d) to invest in state capacity, for instance by providing aid for governance and institutional building, (e) to invest in non-state capacity such as by strengthening NGOs and the business sector directly, and (f) to engage in military intervention. Maxwell (2006) notes that the selection of these instruments will depend on the international actors undertaking them, and will also be context and case specific.

In this regard Chauvet and co-authors have already suggested in Chapter 5 that national sovereignty be overridden in certain cases in order to limit the negative spillover effects that these states impose on neighbouring states. On a related note, Chapter 8 of this book, by Mansoob Murshed and Philip Verwimp entitled 'Enforcing Peace Agreements in Fragile States through Commitment Technologies' argues strongly for the vital role of international intervention and mediation in securing sustainable peace agreements. They point to the fact that it is difficult to sustain peace agreements following civil wars. Examples of failed agreements include the Addis Ababa Agreement (1972), the Arusha Agreement (1993), and the Angolan Peace Agreements (1991 and 1994). They recognize that 'most peace agreements between warring factions in contemporary developing country civil wars are not self-enforcing' and that 'most civil wars cannot be ended without outside intervention, including the use of aid, trade restrictions, and peacekeeping efforts'. They illustrate their arguments with a discussion of the fragile state of Rwanda, where the 1993 peace agreement failed, setting in motion events which lead to the massacre of at least 500,000 Tutsis. They construct an analytical 'signalling' model of peace agreements which shows why self-enforcing peace agreements are so difficult to achieve. Their model in particular shows that external intervention can work if it is credible, providing important food for thought for those concerned about the effectiveness of such intervention in the many of today's most enduring violent conflicts.

The third prong of the emerging international approach, besides narrowing the focus and broadening the instruments, is to be concerned with the effectiveness of international assistance—in particular international aid and humanitarian assistance. The concern about aid effectiveness has spawned a large literature, which is partly surveyed by Mark McGillivray in Chapter 9, but which has tended to neglect the case of fragile states. In this chapter, and the following chapter by Sanjeev Gupta, the question of how to improve aid effectiveness in fragile states is investigated. A challenge, as already noted by Mina Baliamoune-Lutz and Mark McGillivray in Chapter 2, is how to appropriately identify which countries are fragile, given that this might influence the volumes of aid flowing to these states—they are particularly concerned about the World Bank's (2005, 2006) definition of fragile states, which sees these states as 'low-income countries under stress' (LICUS) which are countries with scores smaller than 3.0 in the country policies and institutional performance assessment (CPIA) rankings. It is found for instance, by David Carment and co-authors in Chapter 3, that fragile states indeed tend to receive less than proportional aid—reflecting the fact that they are seen as not being able to use aid effectively, which may in turn further undermine their development prospects.

In Chapter 9, Mark McGillivray provides an overview of the issues involved in aid allocation and the position of fragile states. His chapter entitled 'Aid Allocation and Fragile States' reviews the extensive literature in (a) how aid should be allocated to developing economies and (b) how aid is in practice allocated to these countries. He shows that, despite the apparent view that fragile states use aid less effectively, there is little in the literature to substantiate this view. In particular, aid does not affect only growth (the focus of much of the economics literature) but is important in preventing instability and conflict, improving human rights, and preventing or limiting negative spillovers to neighbouring countries. Therefore, McGillivray is arguing for aid to fragile states, arguing that to the extent that there might be absorptive capacity constraints (as there will be to a lesser or greater degree in all countries—an issue taken up further in Chapter 10) these might be avoided by allocating aid via non-governmental channels.

In Chapter 10, 'Enhancing Effective Utilization of Aid in Fragile States', Sanjeev Gupta points out that the literature on aid spending absorption in fragile states is still in its infancy. He adds to this literature by discussing the macroeconomic implications of aid flows for fragile states, and in particular for post-conflict countries. He shows that this depends on the configuration between aid absorption and spending, that is, whether or not aid is absorbed and spent, or absorbed but not spent, or neither absorbed nor spent, or spent but not absorbed. Aspects which influence this decision are a country's macroeconomic position, its capacity to absorb aid, and the quality of its institutions. Two options for fragile states are explored: front-loading of expenditure, and expenditure-smoothing. Under the first, a country increases spending sharply as aid flows in, and reduces it again afterwards. Gupta suggests that this might be a relevant approach for post-conflict countries where returns to physical infrastructure investment is likely to be substantial. Under the second option, a country aims to keep its spending stable over time. According to Gupta this might be an appropriate strategy for fragile states which faces high uncertainty and only temporary access to aid. A challenge that remains if fragile states are to adopt these strategies successfully is the implementation of a supportive medium-term expenditure framework in fiscal planning. Currently such a level of planning is beyond the capabilities of many fragile states, and remains an area wherein in the international community can provide invaluable assistance.

1.6 Concluding Remarks

This book is structured in a manner that reflects the causes and costs of, and responses to fragile states. The remainder of the book consists of nine chapters divided into three parts. Part I deals with the causes of fragile states. Part II examines the costs of fragile and failed states. Case studies focus on some of the most troubled places in the world: the Balkans, Iraq, Palestine, and Somalia. Part III is concerned with international responses to fragile states—particularly to find ways to end conflict in fragile states and provide effective international support for security and development. The focus is on establishing peace and improving the effectiveness of aid.

The topic of fragile states is a substantial one extending beyond the focus on conflict and international responses taken in this book. Understanding and dealing with state fragility and failure and its consequences is a relatively newly emerging field, the success of which may very well define the nature of development in the first part of the twenty first century. Justice cannot be done to the entire field in a single book. However, it is hoped that this book could play a modest role in stimulating further research, thought, and action towards a crucially important challenge facing humanity.

APPENDIX

Table 1.A1. States in conflict, end 2006 (from consolidated state failure events)

Afghanistan	Iraq	Sri Lanka
Central African Rep.	Israel	Thailand
Chad	Myanmar	Turkey
Colombia	Pakistan	Uganda
Congo, Dem. Rep.	Philippines	Yemen
Côte d'Ivoire	Somalia	
India	Sudan	

Source: PITF, 2008 <http://globalpolicy.gmu.edu/pitf/pitftabl.htm>.

Table 1.A2. States recently emerging from conflict, 2001–6 (from consolidated state failure events)

Algeria	Guinea-Bissau	Russia
Angola	Indonesia	Rwanda
Burundi	Iran	Sierra Leone
Fiji	Liberia	Solomon Islands
Guinea	Nepal	

Source: PITF, 2008 <http://globalpolicy.gmu.edu/pitf/pitftabl.htm>.

Table 1.A3. Low-income countries according to the World Bank

Afghanistan	India	Rwanda
Bangladesh	Kenya	São Tomé and Principe
Benin	Korea, Dem. Rep.	Senegal
Burkina Faso	Kyrgyz Republic	Sierra Leone
Burundi	Lao, People's Dem. Rep.	Solomon Islands
Cambodia	Liberia	Somalia
Central African Republic	Madagascar	Sudan
Chad	Malawi	Tajikistan
Comoros	Mali	Tanzania
Congo, Dem. Rep.	Mauritania	Timor-Leste
Côte d'Ivoire	Mongolia	Togo
Eritrea	Mozambique	Uganda
Ethiopia	Myanmar	Uzbekistan
Gambia	Nepal	Vietnam
Ghana	Niger	Yemen
Guinea	Nigeria	Zambia
Guinea-Bissau	Pakistan	Zimbabwe
Haiti	Papua New Guinea	

Source: World Bank (2008).

Table 1.A4. Heavily indebted poor countries, 2007

Benin	Nicaragua	Congo, Rep.
Bolivia	Niger	Guinea
Burkina Faso	Rwanda	Guinea-Bissau
Cameroon	São Tomé and Principe	Haiti
Ethiopia	Senegal	Comoros
Gambia	Sierra Leone	Côte d'Ivoire
Ghana	Tanzania	Eritrea
Guyana	Uganda	Kyrgyz Rep.
Honduras	Zambia	Liberia
Madagascar	Afghanistan	Nepal
Malawi	Burundi	Somalia
Mali	Central African Republic	Sudan
Mauritania	Chad	Togo
Mozambique	Congo, Dem. Rep.	

Source: IMF (2007).

Table 1.A5. The least developed countries, 2007

Afghanistan	Guinea	Samoa
Angola	Guinea-Bissau	São Tomé and Principe
Bangladesh	Haiti	Senegal
Benin	Kiribati	Sierra Leone
Bhutan	Lao PDR	Solomon Islands
Burkina Faso	Lesotho	Somalia
Burundi	Liberia	Sudan
Cambodia	Madagascar	Tanzania
Central African Rep.	Malawi	Timor-Leste

Chad	Maldives	Togo
Comoros	Mali	Tuvalu
Congo, Dem. Rep	Mauritania	Uganda
Djibouti	Mozambique	Vannatu
Equatorial Guinea	Myanmar	Yemen
Eritrea	Nepal	Zambia
Ethiopia	Niger	
Gambia	Rwanda	

Source: UNCTAD.

Table 1.A6. Bottom 20 per cent of countries in the Environmental Performance Index, 2007

India	Zambia	Guinea-Bissau
Malawi	Rwanda	Yemen
Eritrea	Burundi	Congo, Dem. Rep.
Ethiopia	Madagascar	Chad
Pakistan	Mozambique	Burkina Faso
Bangladesh	Iraq	Mali
Nigeria	Cambodia	Mauritania
Benin	Solomon Islands	Sierra Leone
Central African Rep.	Guinea	Angola
Sudan	Djibouti	Niger

Source: Esty et al. (2008).

Table 1.A7. Bottom 20 per cent of countries in the Happy Planet Index, 2006

Ethiopia	South Africa	Chad
Bulgaria	Sudan	Turkmenistan
Nigeria	Uganda	Equatorial Guinea
Moldova	Kuwait	Lesotho
Burkina Faso	Latvia	Russia
Lithuania	Niger	Estonia
United States of America	Malawi	Ukraine
Côte d'Ivoire	Zambia	Congo, Dem. Rep.
Rwanda	Central African Rep.	Burundi
Sierra Leone	Belarus	Swaziland
United Arab Emirates	Qatar	Zimbabwe
Angola	Botswana	

Source: NEF (2006).

Table 1.A8. Extremely vulnerable countries/islands according to the Environmental Vulnerability Index

Austria	Pakistan	Guam
Belgium	Philippines	Macau
Cook Islands	Singapore	Maldives
India	Trinidad and Tobago	Malta
Israel	United Kingdom	Nauru
Italy	Samoa	Norfolk Island
Jamaica	Barbados	Northern Mariana Islands
Japan	Bermuda	Saint Lucia
Kiribati	UK Virgin Islands	Tongo
Korea	French Polynesia	Tuvalu
Lebanon	Micronesia	US Virgin Islands
Netherlands	Guadeloupe	

Source: <http://www.vulnerabilityindex.net/EVI_Results.htm>.

Table 1.A9. Most fragile states 1999–2005 according to the CIFP Fragility Index (in order from high to lower fragility)

Sudan	Nigeria	Djibouti
Somalia	Chad	Rwanda
Afghanistan	Sierra Leone	Niger
Burundi	Pakistan	Zimbabwe
Iraq	Guinea	Myanmar
Congo, Dem. Rep.	Nepal	Laos
Yemen	Mauritania	North Korea
Haiti	Guinea-Bissau	Iran
Liberia	Central African Rep.	Cameroon
Ethiopia	Uganda	Swaziland
Angola	Togo	Comoros
Palestinian Territories	Equatorial Guinea	Bangladesh
Côte d'Ivoire	Kenya	
Eritrea	Congo (Rep.)	

Source: Carment et al. (2007: 38).

References

Alwang, J., P. B. Siegel, and S. Jorgenson (2001). 'Vulnerability: A View from Different Disciplines', *Social Protection Discussion Paper 0115*, Washington, DC: World Bank.

Bakrania, S., and B. Lucas (2009). 'The Impact of the Financial Crisis on Conflict and State Fragility in Sub-Saharan Africa', *Issues Paper*, Governance and Social Development Resource Centre.

Basu Roy, D., and R. Jolly (2007). 'Bridging Security and Development', *ID21 Insights*, 66.

Binzel, C., and T. Brück (2007). 'Analyzing Conflict and Fragility at the Micro-Level', Paper presented at the UNU-WIDER Conference on Fragile States, Fragile Groups, Helsinki, 15 June.

Bogardi, J., and J. Birkmann (2004). 'Vulnerability Assessment: The First Step Towards Sustainable Risk Reduction', in Malzahn, D. and T. Plapp (eds), *Disaster and Society: From Hazard Assessment to Risk Reduction*. Berlin: Logas Verlag.

Briguglio, L. (2001). 'The Vulnerability Index', Paper presented at the AOSIS Workshop on Trade, Sustainable Development and SIDS, Montego Bay, Jamaica, 12–15 December.

Brown, G., and F. Stewart (2007). 'Fragile States', Paper presented at the UNU-WIDER conference on Fragile States, Fragile Groups, Helsinki, 15 June.

Cardona, O. D. (1999). 'Environmental Management and Disaster Prevention: Two Related Topics', in J. Ingleton (ed.), *Natural Disaster Management*. London: Tudor Rose.

Carment, D., S. Prest, and A. Suryahadi (2007). 'Determinants of State Fragility and Implications for Aid Allocation: An Assessment Based on the Country Indicators for Foreign Policy Project', Paper presented at the UNU-WIDER Conference on Fragile States—Fragile Groups, Helsinki, 15–16 June.

Chambers, R. (1989). 'Vulnerability, Coping and Policy', *IDS Bulletin*, 20(2): 1–8.

Chaudhuri, S., J. Jalan, and A. Suryahadi (2002). 'Assessing Household Vulnerability to Poverty from Cross-Sectional Data: A Methodology and Estimates from Indonesia', Discussion Paper No. 0102-52. Columbia University.

Chen, S., N. V. Loayza, and M. Reynal-Querol (2007). 'The Aftermath of Civil War', *Post-Conflict Transitions Working Paper* 4, Washington, DC: World Bank.

CIFP (Country Indicators for Foreign Policy) (2006). *Fragile States: Monitoring and Assessment, the Way Forward*. Ottawa: Carlton.

Collier, P. (1999). 'On the Economic Consequences of Civil War', *Oxford Economic Papers* 51: 168–83.

Collier, P. (2006). 'War and Military Expenditure in Developing Countries and Their Consequences for Development', *Economics of Peace and Security Journal* 1(1): 9–13.

Collier, P. (2007). *The Bottom Billion*. Oxford: Oxford University Press.

De Léon, J. C. V. (2006). 'Vulnerability: A Conceptual and Methodological Review', *SOURCE. 4/2006*, Bonn: UNU-EHS.

DFID (Department for International Development) (2005). *Why We Need to Work More Effectively in Fragile States*. London: Department for International Development <http://www.dfid.gov.uk/pubs/files/fragilestates.pdf>.

Dingman, S. (2009). 'Today in Piracy: Somali Buccaneers Finally Step in It, Grab an American Ship', *National Post*, 8 April.

Easter, C. (1998). 'Small States and Development: A Composite Index of Vulnerability', *Small States: Economic Review and Basic Statistics Annual Series 4*. London: Commonwealth Secretariat.

Edigheji, O. (2005). 'A Democratic Developmental State in Africa?' *Research Report 105*, Johannesburg: Centre for Policy Studies.

Engberg-Pedersen, L., L. Andersen, and F. Stepputat (2008). 'Fragile Situations: Current Debates and Central Dilemmas', *DIIS Report 2008: 9*. Copenhagen: Danish Institute for International Studies.

Esty, D. C., M. A. Levy, C. H. Kim, A. de Sherbinin, T. Srebotnjak, and V. Mara (2008). *2008 Environmental Performance Index*. New Haven: Yale Center for Environmental Law and Policy.

Fritz, V., and A. R. Menocal (2007). 'Developmental States in the New Millennium: Concepts and Challenges for a New Aid Agenda', *Development Policy Review*, 25(5): 531–52.

Gallopin, G. C. (2006). 'Linkages Between Vulnerability, Resilience, and Adaptive Capacity', *Global Environmental Change*, 16: 293–303.

Ghani, A., and C. Lockhart (2008). *Fixing Failed States: A Framework for Rebuilding a Fractured World*. New York: Oxford University Press.

Goldstone, J. A., R. H. Bates, T. R Gurr, M. Lustik, M. Marshall, J. Ulfelder, and M. Woodward (2005). 'A Global Forecasting Model of Political Instability', Paper presented at the Annual Meeting of the American Political Science Association <http://globalpolicy.gmu.edu/pitf/PITFglobal.pdf>.

Guillaumont, P. (2009a). *Caught in a Trap: Identifying the Least Developed Countries*. Paris: Economica.

Guillaumont, P. (2009b). 'An Economic Vulnerability Index: Its Design and Use for International Development Policy', *Oxford Development Studies* 37(3): 193–228.

Guillaumont, P., and S. Guillaumont-Jeanneney (2009). 'State Fragility and Economic Vulnerability: What is Measured and Why?', Background paper prepared for the European Report on Development.

IMF (International Monetary Fund) (2007a). 'Factsheet: Debt Relief Under the Heavily Indebted Poor Countries Initiative'. December. <http://www.internationalmonetary fund.org/external/np/exr/facts/hipc.htm> (accessed 6 February 2008).

IMF (International Monetary Fund) (2007b). *World Economic Outlook*. <http://www. imf.org> (accessed 6 February 2008).

ISDR (International Strategy for Disaster Reduction) (2004). *Living with Risk: A Global Review of Disaster Reduction Initiatives*. Geneva: ISDR.

Kamanou, G., and J. Morduch (2004). 'Measuring Vulnerability to Poverty', in S. Dercon (ed.), *Insurance Against Poverty*. Oxford: Oxford University Press, UNU-WIDER Studies in Development Economics, 155–75.

Lopez, H., and Q. Wodon (2005). 'The Economic Impact of Armed Conflict in Rwanda', *Journal of African Economies* 14(4): 586–602.

Maxwell, S. (2006). 'Six Approaches to Fragile States', ODI Blog, January <http://blogs. odi.org.uk/blogs/main/archive/2006/01/16/109.aspx>.

McGillivray, M. (2005). 'Measuring Non-economic Wellbeing Achievement'. *Review of Income and Wealth*, 51(2): 337–64.

McGillivray, M., W. Naudé, and A. U. Santos-Paulino (2008). 'Small Island States Development Challenges: Introduction', *Journal of International Development* 20(4): 481–5.

McGillivray, M., W. A. Naudé, and A. U. Santos-Paulino (2010). 'Vulnerability, Trade, Financial Flows and State Failure in Small Island Developing States', *Journal of Development Studies* 46(5): 1–13.

Mkandawire, T. (2001). 'Thinking about Developmental States in Africa', *Cambridge Journal of Economics* 25: 289–314.

Murdoch, J., and T. Sandler (2002). 'Civil Wars and Economic Growth: A Regional Comparison', *Defence and Peace Economics* 13(6): 451–64.

Naudé, W. A. (2009). 'Fallacies About the Global Financial Crisis Harms Recovery in the Poorest Countries', *CESifo Forum* 4: 3–12.

Naudé, W. A. (2010). 'Africa and the Global Economic Crisis: A Risk Assessment and Action Guide', RSCAS Working Paper No. 2010/27, Robert Schuman Center for Advanced Studies, European University Institute, Florence.

Naudé, W. A., A. Santos-Paulino, and M. McGillivray (2009a). *Vulnerability in Developing Countries*. Tokyo and New York: UNU Press.

Naudé, W. A., M. McGillivray, and S. Rossouw (2009b). 'Measuring the Vulnerability of Sub-National Regions: in South Africa', *Oxford Development Studies* 37(3): 249–76.

Naudé, W. A., A. Santos-Paulino, and M. McGillivray (2009c).'Measuring Vulnerability. An Overview and Introduction', *Oxford Development Studies* 37(3): 183–91.

NEF (New Economics Foundation) (2006). *The Happy Planet Index: An Index of Human Wellbeing and Environmental Impact* <http://www.happyplanetindex.org> (accessed 6 February 2008).

Putzel, J. (2007). 'Retaining Legitimacy in Fragile States', *ID21 Insights* 66, May.

Robinson, M. and G. White (eds) (1998). *The Democratic Development State: Political and Institutional Design*. Oxford: Oxford University Press.

Stiglitz, J. E. (1996). 'Some Lessons from the East Asian Miracle', *World Bank Research Observer* 11(2): 151–77.

UNCTAD (2006). *The Least Developed Countries Report 2006*. New York and Geneva: United Nations.

UNCTAD (2007). *Economic Development in Africa 2007: Reclaiming Policy Space, Domestic Resource Mobilization and Developmental States*. New York and Geneva: United Nations.

Wisner, B., P. Blaikie, T. Cannon, and I. Davis (2004). *At Risk: Natural Hazards, People's Vulnerability and Disasters*. Second edition. London: Routledge.

Woo-Cumings, M. (1999). *The Developmental State*. Ithaca: Cornell University Press.

World Bank (1998). *Assessing Aid: What Works, What Doesn't, and Why*. New York: Oxford University Press.

World Bank (2005). *Low Income Countries Under Stress: Update Operations Policy and Country Services* <http://siteresources.worldbank.org/INTLICUS/Resources/388758–1094226297907/LICUS_Update.pdf> (accessed 28 February 2008).

World Bank (2006). *IDA Resource Allocation Index 2008*. Washington, DC: World Bank.

World Bank (2008). Data and Statistics: Country Groups <http://web.worldbank.org/WBSITE/EXTERNAL/DATASTATISTICS/0,,contentMDK:20421402~pagePK:64133150~piPK:64133175~theSitePK:239419,00.html#High_income> (accessed 6 February 2008).

Part I
Causes

2

State Fragility: Concept and Measurement

Mina Baliamoune-Lutz and Mark McGillivray

2.1 Introduction

The international donor community has grave concerns about the effectiveness of aid to countries it classifies as 'fragile states'. The positive impact of aid
on growth and poverty reduction, and the ability to efficiently absorb additional inflows are thought to be significantly low in these countries compared
to other recipients. In some donor circles this impact is even thought to be
non-existent (Torres and Anderson 2004; McGillivray 2006). Donors insist
that unless aid can be made to work better in fragile states, the intended
developmental dividend from these increased flows will not be observed,
and the worldwide achievement of the much espoused Millennium Development Goals will not be possible in the foreseeable future, let alone by the
agreed target of 2015 (Branchflower et al. 2004).

A number of alternative fragile state classifications are employed by the
international donor community, each based on the World Bank's country
policy and institutional assessment (CPIA) ratings. CPIA ratings are prepared
annually by World Bank staff and consist of 20 criteria[1] related to the appro-
priateness of a country's economic policies and the performance of its public
institutions. Arguably, the most widely used classification deems a country as
fragile if it is a low-income country that has a CPIA score of 3.0 or less. These
are also the criteria that the World Bank uses to allocate a country to the low-

---

[1] Since 2004 the number of criteria has been reduced to 16. The CPIA overall score is obtained by
adding up the average scores from four clusters and assigning equal weight (25 per cent) to each.
The criteria within each cluster have equal weight.

income country under stress (LICUS) group. Forty-six countries were classified as fragile states according to this definition in 2004.[2]

This chapter questions the manner in which the donor community delineates fragile from non-fragile states. It develops a framework that uses fuzzy-set theory to deem a country as fragile. Fuzzy-sets allow for gradual transition from one state to another while also allowing one to incorporate rules and goals, and hence are more appropriate for measuring outcomes that are ambiguous or opaque. The chapter applies its framework to 76 low-income countries, for which the CPIA data are publicly available. The fragile state group that this framework provides is compared to the list which the international donor community would construct using the criterion of a CPIA score of 3.0 or less.

2.2 Donor Perception Of Fragility

As mentioned, the donor community equates state fragility with the inability of a recipient country to use aid inflows to achieve economic growth and poverty reduction. This community further equates this inability with a recipient country's CPIA score. The reason why the inability to efficiently absorb aid inflows for growth and poverty reduction is in effect measured by CPIA scores reflects an implicit consensus within much of the international donor community regarding aid effectiveness. That consensus is that the impact of aid on income growth, poverty reduction, and other developmental outcomes is conditional on recipient country policy regimes and institutional performance. Specifically, the consensus is that the more appropriate these regimes are from a developmental perspective and the better the performance of these institutions, the greater will be the incremental effectiveness of aid.

This consensus is based on the findings of the well-known and extremely influential aid-growth paper by Burnside and Dollar (2000) and subsequent papers by Collier and Dollar (2001, 2002). Burnside and Dollar (2000) estimate a growth model that includes a variable obtained by multiplicatively interacting a measure of policy and aid. The relationship between growth and this interaction was found to be linear, positive, and statistically significant at all levels of growth and the aid-policy interaction variables. Collier and Dollar found likewise, but for an interaction of the CPIA and aid.

---

[2] The international donor community's concerns over fragile states are easy to understand if one looks at the plight of these countries. According to the second classification, roughly one-third of the world's population who live in extreme income poverty, some 340 million people, reside in fragile states. Of the estimated 10.8 million children who died before their fifth birthday in 2002, just over 40 per cent lived in these 46 states (Branchflower et al. 2004). One should also acknowledge that, as is evident from this discussion, the term 'fragile state', as used in the donor community, might be misleading, to the extent that it is not used to delineate states only in terms of their likelihood of breaking-up or vulnerability to downside shocks.

Yet there seems to be no clear or obvious justification for the CPIA thresholds used to partition fragile from non-fragile states. Indeed, the results of the Burnside-Dollar and Collier-Dollar studies do not provide evidence that such partition actually exists. The results of these studies tell us that if we associate fragility with aid effectiveness, all countries are fragile to the extent that their ability to use aid differs. Some are simply more fragile than others.[3] Given this, and assuming that aid effectiveness does indeed vary among states according to their policies and institutional performance, how might one partition fragile from not-so-fragile states?

A number of approaches might be valid, but let us highlight two. The first would be to revisit the econometric research of Burnside-Dollar and Collier-Dollar, to seek to establish whether there has been a previously undetected statistically significant structural break in the aid-policy-institutions and growth relationship. The CPIA score at which this break occurs would then be used to partition countries on the basis of their perceived fragility. While this approach in principle might have appeal, there are two weaknesses associated with it. The first is that there is no guarantee that such a structural break actually exits. The second is that econometric studies subsequent to Burnside-Dollar and Collier-Dollar have not been able to find a robust relationship between policies and institutions and aid effectiveness (Easterly et al. 2004; McGillivray et al. 2006; Baliamoune-Lutz and Mavrotas 2009). This is not to say that policies and institutions do not matter for the impact of aid on growth. But what it does suggest is that it is difficult to find a robust relationship between these variables in the context of an econometric model.

The second approach is to simply accept the CPIA thresholds used by the donor community to partition fragile from non-fragile states but to acknowledge that such partitioning is not an opaque outcome, that differences in degrees of fragility among countries are not always crisp, clean, and unambiguous. It is not clear, for example, that a country with a CPIA score of 3.1 uses aid observably better than one with a CPIA score of 3.0 or 2.9. The case for assigning ambiguity to CPIA thresholds becomes stronger if one considers how CPIA scores are obtained. CPIA scores are based on subjective ratings provided by World Bank staff. Different staff rate different countries. Ratings are inter alia based on data for the countries being rated, but it is well-known that developing country data are subject to often large measurement and reporting errors. Each of these facts combine to suggest that one should not treat CPIA scores as clean, crisp outcomes that can be compared with terribly

---

[3] Note that Burnside and Dollar do indicate a level of their policy variable at which aid's impact on growth falls below zero. One might deem a country fragile if aid has no positive impact on growth. But there is no evidence that the donor community has done this, as there appears to have been no attempt to match this level with those of the CPIA used to deem a country fragile.

high degrees of precision.[4] This, of course, in turn means that one should treat the categorization of countries as fragile or non-fragile with a healthy degree of scepticism if they are close to the chosen CPIA threshold. It also means, however, that one should not use CPIA scores as reported by the World Bank to assign countries to these categories but use a fuzzy transformation of these scores. Such a transformation formally recognizes the ambiguity or opaqueness of CPIA scores and categorizations based on them. This chapter adopts this approach and outlines it in the next section.

2.3 Fuzzy Fragility

2.3.1 Method

Lotfi Zadeh (1965), widely credited with the conceptualization of fuzzy-set theory, defines fuzzy-sets as a class of objects with a continuum of grades of membership.[5] Degrees of membership in the set of achievements (or goals) are usually expressed by numbers belonging to the interval [0,1]. Fuzzy-sets allow for gradual transition from one state to another while also allowing one to incorporate rules and goals. Thus, fuzzy-sets are more appropriate for measuring outcomes that are vague or ambiguous. In the context of measuring state fragility, fuzzy-sets would allow us to examine changes in country ranking depending on the degree of vagueness and the level (threshold) at which performance changes from disastrous to average or good (depending on how we define the cutoff point).

To derive fuzzy CPIA scores, we follow Baliamoune-Lutz (2006) and Baliamoune-Lutz and McGillivray (2006) and use the following fuzzy membership function:

$$\mu(x_i) = \frac{1}{1 + e^{-\alpha(x_i - \beta)}} \tag{2.1}$$

This function is quite adequate for the purpose of determining, for example, whether the outcome is close enough to the goal for it to be considered a success or whether differences between two outcomes should be considered as relevant differences. Equation (2.1) is obtained by first noting that the distance ($d(x)$) between the actual outcome and the goal provides a measure of the extent of the success in attaining the goal. If the outcome is complete

---

[4] This was acknowledged in the study by the World Bank. That study called for the disclosure of CPIA ratings within confidence intervals and the flexible application and interpretation of these scores (World Bank 2004).

[5] Baliamoune-Lutz (2006) and Baliamoune-Lutz and McGillivray (2006) provide a discussion of the concept of fuzzy-set theory and its application. This section draws on these two studies. Readers wanting more background information on the application of fuzzy-set theory can consult these studies, the first in particular.

success, we have full membership, i.e., $\mu(x_i) = 1$, and the distance between the actual outcome and the goal is zero. Thus, $d(x) = 0$. For cases where $d(x) > 0$ we have $\mu(x_i) < 1$. Thus we may write the membership function μ as:

$$\mu(x_i) = \frac{1}{1 + d(x_i)} \tag{2.2}$$

Zimmermann (1987) points out that the relationship between physical objects and perceptions takes an exponential form. Thus, $d(x)$ can be expressed as: $d(x) = e^{-a(x_i - \beta)}$. Substituting in Equation (2.2) yields Equation (2.1).

It can be shown that the parameters α and β can be obtained as follows:

$$\alpha = \frac{\ln\left(\frac{\mu_h}{1 - \mu_h}\right) - \ln\left(\frac{\mu_l}{1 - \mu_l}\right)}{x_h - x_l}$$

and

$$\beta = \frac{x_l \ln\left(\frac{\mu_h}{1 - \mu_h}\right) - x_h \ln\left(\frac{\mu_l}{1 - \mu_l}\right)}{\ln\left(\frac{\mu_h}{1 - \mu_h}\right) - \ln\left(\frac{\mu_l}{1 - \mu_l}\right)}$$

where μ_h represents the membership degree of the highest achievement (x_h) of the goal, and μ_l represents the membership degree of the lowest achievement (x_l) of the goal (Baliamoune-Lutz 2006).

2.3.2 Results

Using the information from the above discussion and Equation (2.1), we derive fuzzy CPIA scores and report the results in Table 2.1. Assumptions regarding what constitutes high (best) or low (worst) achievement as well as the values for α and β are shown in Table 2.A1 in the Appendix. We should note that the parameter (slope) α can be used to represent the degree of vagueness or ambiguity and β may be used to represent the identification threshold, the score at which a country moves from a fragile to non-fragile state; see Zimmermann (1987: 205); Baliamoune-Lutz (2006).

It is important to note that deciding what constitutes the highest and the lowest achievement may be subjective but it is not arbitrary. Indeed, using substantiated rules we can build scenarios or ranges based on perceived degrees of ambiguity and the identification threshold. For example, we could define the CPIA score at which countries move from a fragile to non-fragile state. The donor community does something similar to this when it decides on the cutoff point. The main difference is that the use of fuzzy-sets allows us to incorporate relevant information about the extent of ambiguity and threshold levels. Given that empirical evidence on the positive impact of aid on growth

Table 2.1. IDA CPIA scores and *fuzzy* CPIA scores, 2005 (fragile states are those with a CPIA score of 3.0 or less)

IDA rank	Country[a]	CPIA Scores (1)	Fuzzy scores using the same alpha and beta for all clusters (2)	Fuzzy scores using different alpha and beta for each cluster (3) D (1)	(4) D (2)
1	**Armenia**	4.33	4.50	5.12	4.60
2	Cape Verde	4.09	4.28	4.97	4.53
3	Samoa	3.98	4.17	4.83	4.47
4	St Lucia	3.97	4.16	4.82	4.38
5	Tanzania	3.94	4.14	4.82	4.30
6	St Vincent and the Grenadines	3.92	4.11	4.74	4.14
7	Honduras	3.91	4.10	4.68	3.99
8	Uganda	3.88	4.08	4.58	3.86
9	Ghana	3.85	4.04	4.71	4.12
10	Georgia	3.83	4.03	4.68	4.03
11	Maldives	3.83	4.03	4.65	4.00
12	Bhutan	3.79	3.99	4.66	4.14
13	Dominica	3.78	3.98	4.57	3.92
14	India	3.77	3.96	4.64	4.05
15	Burkina Faso	3.76	3.95	4.58	3.93
16	**Senegal**	3.75	3.94	4.57	3.92
17	Vietnam	3.74	3.93	4.54	3.85
18	Nicaragua	3.72	3.91	4.53	3.83
19	Bolivia	3.71	3.90	4.42	3.69
20	Mali	3.71	3.90	4.54	3.89
21	Serbia and Montenegro	3.70	3.89	4.47	3.75
22	Grenada	3.69	3.88	4.52	3.93
23	Albania	3.68	3.86	4.35	3.63
24	Pakistan	3.66	3.85	4.24	3.53
25	Azerbaijan	3.65	3.84	4.29	3.59
26	Benin	3.65	3.84	4.37	3.65
27	Indonesia	3.65	3.84	4.30	3.59
28	Sri Lanka	3.62	3.80	4.41	3.71
29	Kenya	3.60	3.78	4.28	3.56
30	Bosnia and Herzegovina	3.59	3.77	4.29	3.57
31	**Madagascar**	3.54	3.72	4.29	3.57
32	Kyrgyz Republic	3.51	3.68	3.86	3.41
33	Lesotho	3.51	3.68	4.26	3.54
34	Moldova	3.50	3.68	4.16	3.45
35	Rwanda	3.48	3.65	4.19	3.47
36	Mozambique	3.46	3.63	4.08	3.37
37	Mongolia	3.44	3.61	4.14	3.42
38	Bangladesh	3.42	3.58	3.87	3.30
39	Ethiopia	3.38	3.55	3.96	3.29
40	Guyana	3.35	3.51	3.94	3.27
41	Malawi	3.35	3.51	4.10	3.38
42	Nepal	3.34	3.50	3.86	3.23
43	Tajikistan	3.34	3.50	3.64	3.25
44	Zambia	3.32	3.47	3.96	3.25
45	**Yemen, Rep.**	3.29	3.44	3.75	3.17
46	Cameroon	3.29	3.44	3.87	3.20
47	Niger	3.26	3.41	3.89	3.18
48	Mauritania	3.16	3.29	3.61	3.04
49	Kiribati	3.16	3.29	3.78	3.05
50	Djibouti	3.14	3.27	3.53	3.02

51	Nigeria	3.14	3.27	3.43	2.92
52	Vanuatu	3.14	3.27	3.69	3.02
53	Sierra Leone	3.12	3.25	3.50	2.93
54	Papua New Guinea	3.11	3.24	3.65	2.98
55	Cambodia	3.09	3.22	3.33	2.94
56	Gambia	3.08	3.21	3.52	2.94
57	Guinea	3.02	3.13	3.34	2.89
58	Uzbekistan	3.00	3.11	2.99	2.71
59	Lao, People's Dem. Rep.	2.98	3.09	3.06	2.73
60	São Tomé and Principe	2.98	3.08	3.49	2.81
61	**Burundi**	2.97	3.07	3.19	2.74
62	Tonga	2.93	3.03	3.20	2.75
63	Chad	2.88	2.98	3.02	2.74
64	Congo, Dem. Rep.	2.84	2.93	2.95	2.72
65	Solomon Islands	2.83	2.91	2.98	2.59
66	Congo, Rep.	2.79	2.87	2.89	2.50
67	Haiti	2.77	2.84	2.89	2.66
68	Guinea-Bissau	2.68	2.75	2.86	2.47
69	Sudan	2.59	2.64	2.64	2.36
70	Angola	2.58	2.63	2.63	2.35
71	Eritrea	2.50	2.54	2.33	1.82
72	Côte d'Ivoire	2.49	2.53	2.64	2.30
73	Togo	2.49	2.53	2.57	2.37
74	Comoros	2.42	2.45	2.23	1.99
75	Central African Rep.	2.39	2.42	2.32	2.12
76	Zimbabwe	1.82	1.82	1.52	1.37

Note: [a] Five IDA countries excluded since not rated in CPIA 2005 exercise (Afghanistan, Liberia, Myanmar, Somalia, Timor-Leste). For calculation of the cluster averages, all criteria are equally weighted within a cluster; IRAI is calculated as the mean of the score of four clusters. Scale: 1 = lowest, 6 = highest. Rankings are based on un-rounded data.

Source: See text. CPIA data taken from World Bank (2006).

and poverty reduction, and the effects of many of the components in the four clusters (see Appendix 2.A1) used to derive CPIA scores are ambiguous, the use of fuzzy-sets seems to be more appropriate than the way CPIA scores have been computed so far.

World Bank CPIA scores are shown in Column (1) of Table 2.1. There are according to these scores 19 countries that would be considered fragile owing to a score of 3.0 or less, starting with Uzbekistan and ending with Zimbabwe. Fuzzy CPIA scores, those that we have derived using fuzzy-sets, are shown in Columns (2)–(4). It is clear that once we take into account the ambiguity of the outcomes we get different scores from the World Bank's CPIA. In Column (2) we use the same level of ambiguity and the same threshold for all four clusters and find five countries would no longer be classified as fragile: Uzbekistan, Lao, São Tomé and Principe, Burundi, and Tonga.

Assigning the same ambiguity level to all clusters may not be appropriate. There appears to be no reason why a priori this is necessarily correct. To illustrate how scores would change once we allow for differences in the levels of ambiguity and thresholds, we derive scores assuming different values for α and β. We in particular assume, for illustrative purposes, a higher degree of vagueness and a *restrictive* (high) threshold for public sector management and institutions (cluster D). In Column (3) of Table 2.1 we assume a *high* level of ambiguity and high identification threshold (by assuming that the worst outcome is a score of 3), while in Column (4) we assume *very high* ambiguity and threshold (by assuming that the worst outcome is a score of 4). Under these two further scenarios there are an additional seven countries which would either be taken out of or added to the fragile state group. Under all three ambiguity scenarios there are 11 countries whose classification as either fragile or non-fragile changes as a result of providing a fuzzy transformation of the World Bank CPIA scores. These countries are shown in boldface in Table 2.1. The fuzzy scores shown in the table suggest that there is ambiguity over whether a country should be classified as fragile using World Bank CPIA scores if these scores fall between 3.12 and 2.88. Put differently, classifying a country with a score within this range as fragile is not robust with respect to the extent of ambiguity assumed in the analysis on which the fuzzy scores shown in Table 2.1 are based.[6]

2.4 Concluding Remarks

This chapter applies fuzzy transformations to the 2005 CPIA scores for 76 countries and tried to partition fragile from not-so-fragile states taking into account the inherent ambiguity in measuring policies and institutions, and assuming that aid effectiveness does indeed vary among states according to their policies and institutional performance. The fuzzy scores we derived are different from the CPIA scores. These differences imply that some countries, particularly the ones close to the border of their quintile (or close to the IDA cutoff points) may be incorrectly classified. Indeed, given the ambiguity assumptions assumed in this chapter, there are 11 countries whose classification as either fragile or non-fragile changes as a result of providing a fuzzy transformation of the World Bank CPIA scores.

The analysis of this chapter clearly points to the need for flexible application and interpretation of CPIA scores in not only determining whether or not a country should be classified as fragile but also in other applications of the CPIA. Beyond this it points to the need for more sophisticated measures of fragility. If, as the donor community has to date done, fragility is to be defined on the basis of the effectiveness of aid to recipient countries, then one

---

[6] An anonymous referee of this chapter perceptively noted that the correlation coefficients between all CPIA values shown in Table 2.1 (fuzzy and original) are very highly correlated, with coefficients greater than 0.90. While this is true, it follows from the above discussion that fragile state classifications can change even if correlation coefficients are unity.

approach would be to first develop a measure that assesses the effectiveness of aid across recipient countries, and then scientifically identify a threshold level of this measure at which this effectiveness is zero, negligible or unacceptably low. This threshold, from an aid effectiveness perspective, could be used to partition fragile from other states. And if there is ambiguity over this measure then fuzzy transformations of it should be used in this partitioning.

APPENDIX

Table 2.A1. Parameters for computing degrees of membership used in Table 2.1

Cluster[a]	Best outcome	μ_h	Worst outcome	μ_l	α	β
A	5	0.833	2	0.334	4.6049	0.4838
B	6	0.999	2	0.334	11.4135	0.3939
C	5	0.833	1	0.167	4.8259	0.500
D (1)	6	0.999	3	0.500	13.8412	0.500
D (2)	6	0.999	4	0.667	18.6969	0.6296

Note: [a] CPIA clusters:
A: Economic management (macro management, fiscal policy, debt policy);
B: Structural policies (trade, financial sector, business and regulatory environment);
C: Policies for social inclusion/equity (gender equality, equity of public resource use, building human resources, social protection and labour, policies and institutions for environmental sustainability);
D: Public sector management and institutions (property rights and rule-based governance, quality of budgetary and financial management, efficiency of revenue mobilization, quality of public administration, transparency, accountability, and corruption in the public sector).

Source: <www.iteresources.worldbank.org/IDA/>.

References

Baliamoune-Lutz, M. (2006). 'On the Measurement of Human Wellbeing: Fuzzy-set Theory and Sen's Capability Approach'. In M. McGillivray and M. Clarke (eds), *Understanding Human Wellbeing*. Tokyo: United Nations University Press.

Baliamoune-Lutz, M. and G. Mavrotas (2009). 'Aid Effectiveness: Looking at the Aid–Social Capital–Growth Nexus'. *Review of Development Economics*, 13(3): 510–25.

Baliamoune-Lutz, M. and M. McGillivray (2006). 'Fuzzy Wellbeing Achievement in Pacific Asia'. *Journal of the Asia Pacific Economy*, 11(2): 168–77.

Branchflower, A., S. Hennell, S. Pongracz, and M. Smart (2004). 'How Important are Difficult Environments to Achieving the MDGs?'. Poverty Reduction in Difficult Environments Working Paper No. 2. London: Poverty Reduction in Difficult Environments Team, Policy Division, DFID.

Burnside, C., and D. Dollar (2000). 'Aid, Policies and Growth'. *American Economic Review*, 90(4): 847–68.

Collier, P., and D. Dollar (2001). 'Can the World Cut Poverty in Half? How Policy Reform and Effective Aid Can Meet the International Development Goals'. *World Development*, 29(11): 1787–802.

Collier, P., and D. Dollar (2002). 'Aid Allocation and Poverty Reduction'. *European Economic Review*, 26(8): 1475–500.

Easterly, W., R. Levine, and D. Roodman (2004). 'Aid, Policies, and Growth: Comment'. *American Economic Review*, 94(3): 774–80.

McGillivray, M. (2006). 'Aid Allocation and Fragile States'. WIDER Discussion Paper 2006/01. Helsinki: UNU-WIDER.

McGillivray, M, S. Feeny, N. Hermes, and R. Lensink (2006). 'Controversies of the Development Impact of Aid: It Works; It Doesn't; It Can, But that Depends . . .'. *Journal of International Development*, 18(6): 1031–50.

Torres, M. M. and M. Anderson (2004). 'Fragile States: Defining Difficult Environments for Poverty Reduction'. Poverty Reduction in Difficult Environments Working Paper No. 1. London: Poverty Reduction in Difficult Environments Team, Policy Division, DIFD.

World Bank (2004). 'Implementing Performance-Based Aid in Africa: The Country Policy and Institutional Assessment'. Africa Region Working Paper Series, 77. Washington, DC: World Bank.

World Bank (2006). *IDA Resource Allocation Index 2008*. Washington, DC: World Bank.

Zadeh, L. A. (1965). 'Fuzzy-sets'. *Information and Control*, 8: 338–43.

Zimmermann, H. J. (1987). *Fuzzy-sets, Decision Making, and Expert Systems*. Boston: Kluwer Academic.

3

The Causes and Measurement of State Fragility

David Carment, Stewart Prest, and Yiagadeesen Samy

3.1 Introduction

'First-generation' perspectives on state fragility and failure focus on breakdown as caused by a single variable: violent intrastate conflict. Such perspectives and policies are understandable, since the 1990s were witness to a number of catastrophic failures tied to conflict, from Liberia, Somalia, and Sierra Leone in Africa, to Serbia and Bosnia in Europe. One may further divide such first-generation perspectives into two camps. The first group consists of more structurally oriented theories that focus on the 'root causes' of state weakness; those permissive conditions that 'allow' poverty or conflict to happen. The second group includes more agency-focused perspectives that emphasize how state and non-state actors, in pursuing competing political agendas, interact to produce conflict. Poverty is a key structural variable for the first camp, whether defined in absolute or relative terms, while the latter group looks at actor motivations, including both greed and grievance.[1]

---

[1] As a result, since the end of the Cold War, there have been several attempts to develop theoretical models (and empirical tests thereof) in order to explain state failure as a function of civil conflict. This literature has identified a number of causal mechanisms for civil wars including: environmental and demographic pressures (Homer-Dixon 1999; Diehl and Gleditsch 2001); greed versus grievance factors, where self-interest takes over justice-seeking behaviour; and the exploitation of natural resources to finance conflict (Collier 2000; Collier and Hoeffler 2004). Others such as Easterly and Levine (1997) point out the role of high levels of ethnic and religious fragmentation while Van Hear (1998) finds diasporas to have a high impact in the onset and course of a war. Such analyses of conflict can, to some extent, be transposed to an analysis of fragility because both internal wars and fragility are likely to be affected by (and affect) economic, political, and social environments. Furthermore both conflict and fragility result (implicitly or explicitly) from human interactions.

A focus on the security–instability nexus is legitimate, of course, if the underlying purpose is to develop policies on armed conflict in the most egregious cases of failure; however, to the extent that conflict is a symptom and not a cause of fragility and failure, it does not enhance our understanding of the phenomenon. As a consequence, a spotlight on conflict factors alone does not help us develop more effective policies to respond to or, ideally, to pre-empt the onset of fragility. All societies experience conflict, just as all societies are to some extent unequal. By the time either conflict or poverty becomes sufficiently extreme to spur the international community to action, it is usually too late to respond effectively except through costly operational responses such as military intervention, or painful economic structural adjustment.[2] Thus there is a need for proactive approaches that focus on long-term structural transformation.

Second-generation approaches differ in several respects. While acknowledging that background conditions are important, they recognize that factors such as poverty and conflict by themselves are not good measures of fragility; rather they are symptomatic of a host of more fundamental causal factors. It is true that many failed and fragile states are poor but they also suffer from unequal distribution, poor service delivery,[3] and weak governance, among many other problems.[4] For example, the World Bank (2005) claims that a typical low-income country under stress (LICUS) has a GDP per capita roughly half that of a stable low-income country. Similarly, Chauvet and Collier (2005) point out the negative effect that fragile states have on neighbouring

---

[2] This is not to suggest that analysts and policy-makers would be unwise to focus on the all important security dimensions. We know that fragile and failed states constitute a security risk in a number of important ways. First, they are a risk to their people because they lack capacity, resulting in a lack of basic security. They lack governance, resulting in the inefficient and inequitable distribution of public goods; and they lack control over violence within their territory, resulting in further division and weakness, and the diffusion of conflict into new jurisdictions. Failed and fragile states are also vectors for transnational threats and global problems—they lack capacity to prevent the transmission of diseases such as avian flu; they are unable to control the transmission of AIDS; they host base-camps for transnational criminal networks; their weak border control provides opportunities for human and drug trafficking, along with other forms of smuggling; and their internal conflicts create refugee flows that upset the demographic balance of neighbouring states. Finally, failed and fragile states are regional and international risks because they are more likely to engage in risky behaviour in violation of international laws, rules, and principles; they provide support for the diffusion of weapons of mass destruction; they engage in hostile interactions with their neighbours; their weakness attracts foreign intervention; and their diaspora groups may become conduits of conflict diffusion and contagion.

[3] Stewart and Brown (2007) employ the concept of 'progressive service delivery' as part of their definition of state fragility. In essence, states are considered fragile or failed if their service outcomes—rates of infant mortality, level of access to improved water, etc.—are substantially below the levels predicted by their income. Thus, some measure of country context is built into quantitative evaluation.

[4] These and other challenges are listed in the World Bank definition of low-income countries under stress (LICUS). See World Bank (2002).

countries, again illustrating the need to ground analysis in both a comparative and regional context, and not just in absolute terms.

A good example of a second-generation approach focusing on economic and institutional factors including poverty (rather than conflict) is the fragility model provided by Mina Baliamoune-Lutz and Mark McGillivray in Chapter 2 of this volume. Drawing on the World Bank's country policy and institutional assessment (CPIA) and LICUS assessments, the authors show that conventional World Bank criteria arbitrarily divide fragile and non fragile states. Applying the notion of a 'fuzzy CPIA', the authors produce a ranking of the most fragile states which is intuitively appealing in the same way our ranking of capacity-challenged states (provided below) highlights the importance of economic performance measures. In addition, the authors argue, as do we, that refinement and nuance in country rankings should result in better aid allocation decisions. However, whereas their point of departure is a focus primarily on economic factors embedded in their revised CPIA scoring methodology, our approach is to disaggregate country performance measures, using elements that reside outside CPIA and LICUS considerations in addition to them, such as security and legitimacy considerations.

In addition, second-generation approaches assume that fragility and failure tend to be 'multi-effective'. By this, we mean that the presence of a fragile or failed state carries implications not only for the security and livelihoods of state inhabitants and neighbouring countries, but for any efforts to ameliorate the situation. For example, McGillivray (2005) finds that growth in fragile states would have been lower in the absence of aid to them, that they face larger absorptive capacity problems relative to other countries, and that they are also under-aided.

We raise this issue because there are important differences among efforts to classify and organize fragile states and the Baliamoune-Lutz-McGillivray 'fuzzy CPIA' rankings are but one of several such efforts. In Appendix table 3.A1 we can see what happens when leading first and second-generation indices are regressed against the logarithm of GDP per capita (a measure of capacity) and the security cluster (which includes, among others, political violence among civilians, the intensity of armed conflict, military expenditure as a percentage of GDP and law enforcement). This table shows that the explanatory powers of these two variables are very different for each index used. In the case of GDP per capita, it explains 64 per cent of the variation in the USAID's Marshall-Goldstone State Fragility Index and only 43 per cent of the well-known Fund for Peace Index. On the other hand, for security, the corresponding numbers are 21 per cent and 35 per cent respectively. We have also added the Brooking's Institution weak states index, which bears a strong resemblance to our own (see Appendix table 3.A3).

The key point is that the Fund for Peace Failed States Index as a first-generation approach places greater emphasis on conflict outcomes than other indicators of fragility, and this explains why different rankings of countries are obtained. But it also confirms our suspicion that the Fund for Peace Index is dealing with conflict-related end states and not necessarily processes that lead to fragility. Further, the World Bank/LICUS approach—highlighted in Chapter 2 of this volume—is more biased towards economic factors given the nature of its underlying indicators; GDP per capita explains 11 per cent of the variation in that index but security hardly explains anything and is not significant. What we find is that different indices tend to have inherent biases, towards conflict, economic factors or stability factors. In brief, it is probably right to assume that per capita income and security are related to fragility in more complex ways and that they are both drivers and manifestations of fragility. Our chapter will clarify the strengths of these relationships.

The rest of the chapter proceeds as follows. In the section 3.2 we introduce our second-generation framework for assessing fragility, the Country Indicators for Foreign Policy (CIFP) Fragile States Project. In section 3.3, we validate our fragility index, and in section 3.4 we examine the implications of fragility for aid allocation using our authority, legitimacy, and capacity (ALC) framework. The final section concludes with directions for future research and implications for policy.

3.2 Towards Policy-Relevant Assessment Of Fragility

Notwithstanding the fact that state fragility as a theoretical construct has now become an important part of the international political discourse, it nonetheless remains an elusive concept for both academics and policy-makers.[5] There are a number of interpretations of state fragility, all of which appear to some extent in the international lexicon. Variously characterized as difficult partners (OECD 2001), difficult environments (Torres and Anderson 2004), collapsed states (Goldstone et al. 2000), LICUS (World Bank 2002), poor performers (AusAID 2002), weak performers (ADB 2004), failing and/or failed states (Rotberg 2004), and countries at risk of instability (PM's Strategy Unit 2005), the concept encompasses a number of partially overlapping, yet analytically distinct concepts regarding vulnerability. The OECD, for instance, defines fragile states as 'countries where there is a lack of political

---

[5] Though we do use subgroups of fragile states as part of our empirical analysis, in general we do not focus on a set number of fragile states; instead we identify state fragility as being primarily a question of degree, rather than of kind. While some countries are in fact failing or failed, in general, aspects of fragility can be identified in virtually all states.

commitment and insufficient capacity to develop and implement pro-poor policies' (Morcos 2005; Prest et al. 2005). The World Bank, on the other hand, focuses on some 30 LICUS that are characterized by very weak policies, institutions, and governance. The UK's Department for International Development (DFID) defines state weakness in broadly similar terms, focusing on states in which 'the government cannot or will not deliver core functions to the majority of its people, including the poor' (DFID 2005).

Despite disagreements regarding what a fragile state is, some points of consensus have nonetheless emerged among policy-makers. First, there are many states that would qualify as 'fragile', 'failed', 'failing', or LICUS; attempts to draw up a specific list normally end up with between 30 and 50 countries. Second, as reported by Chauvet and Collier (2005), the cost of disengagement from such states can be extremely high, proving more harmful in the long term to international peace and security than continued engagement. Third, many donor governments now believe that outside involvement must be coordinated at the strategic level.[6]

Similarly, there have been some attempts to reach a level of consensus on issues of vital importance to programming in failed and fragile states. The first area of consensus is that preliminary analyses must draw on the widest range of structural indicators. Single or limited factor analyses are inappropriate for complex fragile environments. A wide survey of performance indicators provides a sound basis for cross-state strategic-level comparative analysis, which is a prerequisite of a rational engagement policy. Second, programming must be grounded in an ongoing process of risk assessment and monitoring. Policy tools therefore must be able to identify countries at risk and provide guidance as to the type of engagement required. Monitoring must provide risk analysis to allow for policy deliberation and resource mobilization, vital prerequisites of timely and effective engagement. Even more than in other developing economies, a thorough understanding of context in fragile states is a prerequisite of effective and properly sequenced engagement; context is necessary to ensure that we understand the causal factors driving stakeholder behaviour, and changes in incentive structure necessary to produce positive outcomes.

In terms of our own approach, one crucial assumption we make is that fragile states show strengths and vulnerabilities in one or more areas based on the idea that all states possess three fundamental components of 'stateness', namely authority, legitimacy, and capacity (ALC) (Carment et al. 2006a). Weakness along one or more of these dimensions will impact on the

---

[6] Such efforts received official support as part of the Paris Declaration; see OECD (2005).

overall fragility of a particular country. *Authority* refers to the ability of the state to enact binding legislation over its population and to provide the latter with a stable and safe environment. *Legitimacy* refers to the ability of the state to command public loyalty to the governing regime and to generate domestic support for government legislation being passed and policies being implemented. *Capacity* refers to the power of the state to mobilize public resources for productive uses (Carment et al. 2008: 350). Typical proxies for authority include variables such as the level of corruption and contract regulation. Legitimacy is measured by variables such as regime type, human rights, and gender empowerment. Capacity includes measures such as GDP per capita, the trade balance and foreign aid. Each indicator is used for one dimension only, and decisions about the choice of indicators were arrived at based on consensus by a panel of experts (see Appendix B at the end of this chapter for further information).

As conceptualized in our research, capacity is in some ways similar to the focus on progressive service delivery suggested by Stewart and Brown (2007). However, the latter brings in elements of state authority, in that it attempts to capture not only the resources available to the state, but also the government's willingness to devote those resources to the delivery of essential services. In this sense, progressive service delivery as an evaluative concept is reminiscent of DFID's focus on state 'willingness' to pursue pro-poor outcomes, described in its fragile states strategy (DFID 2005).

The capacity problems that beset the fragile states of sub-Saharan Africa are distinct from the legitimacy and authority problems of the fragile states of Central and South Asia. For example, in our country rankings (<www.carleton.ca/cifp>), Pakistan and Sri Lanka exhibit poor performance on measures of authority and legitimacy, while middle performers in Africa such as Ghana, Kenya, and Tanzania are faced with capacity problems. Of course, those that show up repeatedly at the top of our rankings are those that face challenges across multiple categories. North Korea provides an intriguing example of how second-generation analysis can produce results that are both more intuitively satisfying and more useful to policy-makers than those emerging from a simple indexing exercise. In the 2007 CIFP fragility index, North Korea is ranked fifty-second overall. However, when fragility is measured in any one of the ALC dimensions, a much more nuanced picture emerges. Balanced against middling rankings for both authority and capacity, is an extremely weak legitimacy score; North Korea ranks as the third most fragile state in terms of legitimacy. Given North Korea's current status as international pariah, such a finding has a high level of intuitive appeal. With its low level of legitimacy, the regime might be termed brittle—endowed with sufficient authority and capacity to maintain control of state borders and territory, but highly vulnerable to exogenous shocks. The result thus conveys more useful information than a simple rank ordering of states according to the level of development, or presence of conflict-inducing factors, providing a spring-board to further discussion of policy options available to the international community.

Table 3.A2 in the Appendix provides a list of the top 40 fragile states based on data for the period 1999 to 2005, with Burundi being the most fragile state (see also Table 3.A3 for the scoring scales). It provides data for the overall fragility score, scores along the ALC components, scores for the different indicator clusters, with gender as a cross-cutting theme. What is striking in examining the most fragile states is that though they appear in more than one category, they rarely rank high on all three, an indication that fragility man-ifests itself in different forms that require different types of intervention. When broken down in terms of the six indicator clusters (e.g., for the top 20 fragile states), none appear on all six and only a few appear on four, again an indication that fragile states face different challenges.

3.3 Methodology And Empirical Results

The lack of a clear and universally accepted definition of fragility speaks to its multifaceted nature. Thus, in this section, we seek to validate our fragility index by examining its main determinants. As a first step, we identified the most significant indicators from each of the indicator clusters listed in Table 3.A2 through bivariate correlations in order to arrive at a parsimonious multivariate model of state fragility. For example, in the case of the economics cluster, we tested a number of indicators (GDP, GDP per capita, economic growth, inflation, inequality, unemployment, etc.) individually against the economics index, and chose the one with higher explanatory power. Inde-pendent variables that are highly correlated with each other were not chosen because they would basically pick up the same effect (for example, GDP per capita and GDP). This approach was applied to each of the six clusters as well as the cross-cutting theme of gender, resulting in the following baseline model for estimation:

$$fragility_i = \beta_0 + \beta_1 income_i + \beta_2 growth_i + \beta_3 demo_i + \beta_4 trade_i + \epsilon_i \qquad (3.1)$$

where 'fragility' is the CIFP fragility index described above[7]; 'income' refers to the logarithm of GDP per capita in purchasing power parity (PPP); 'growth'

---

[7] Only countries with a fragility score of 4 and above are considered, thus excluding OECD and other high-income countries that are typically not considered as fragile.

refers to the growth of GDP per capita, 'demo' refers to the level of democracy from the Polity IV dataset; 'trade' refers to trade openness, namely the ratio of the sum of exports and imports to GDP; subscript '*i*' refers to countries; and ε_i is the error term with the usual properties. This baseline model is thus controlling for economic and political factors, most of which can be found in the literature that relates economic growth to stability, as well as work of the Political Instability Task Force (PITF) that examined the threats that weak and failed states represented for their neighbours and the international system (Goldstone et al. 2000). It also allows us to move away from explanations or theories that rely on a single variable to a more realistic multivariate approach that controls for the effects of different variables.

Our sample consists of a maximum of 156 countries with a five-year average of most recent data until 2006 and Table 3.1 provides summary statistics of variables used in the empirical analysis. In addition to the variables of our baseline model, squared terms for democracy and trade are included in different specifications of the baseline model to take into account nonlinearities uncovered in Carment et al. (2006b). Dummy variables were added to the baseline model to control for regional effects, and other variables that appear in the literature such as the human rights empowerment index, the human development index (HDI), and ethnic diversity and ethnic risk were considered (see Table 3.A4 for correlations among different regressors). Even though these variables did not show up as the most significant predictors in bivariate correlations, they are included in order to test some of the common hypothesized causal factors identified in the conflict and fragility literature.

Table 3.A5 in the Appendix shows the results when the benchmark Equation (3.1) and its augmented versions are estimated using ordinary least

Table 3.1. Summary statistics

Variable name	Description	No. of observations	Mean	Median	Standard deviation
ETHDIV*	Ethnic diversity	128	0.39	0.42	0.26
ETHRISK*	Risk of rebellion	98	4.84	3.77	3.86
FRG	Fragility index	156	5.89	5.80	1.06
GDPG	Economic growth	148	3.46	3.56	3.11
HDI	HDI	148	0.65	0.72	0.16
HREM	Human rights empowerment	154	5.32	6.00	3.07
LDEM	Level of democracy	129	1.77	4.00	6.40
PPP	GDP per capita	134	5031	3867	4552
TRAD	Trade openness (% of GDP)	141	83.18	75.38	37.71

Note: *Data available for only one year.

Source: See text.

squares. For the benchmark equation, the logarithm of GDP per capita, which measures the level of development, is significant at the 1 per cent level and with the expected sign in column (1). Poorer countries tend to be more fragile than richer countries on average and this result continues to hold when a broader measure of development, the HDI, is considered in column (6). As for the other variables, countries that grew faster, countries that are more democratic, and countries that are more open to trade over the estimated period tended to be less fragile. Squared terms for the level of democracy, trade openness, and the human rights empowerment index were added to verify whether the relationships are nonlinear; this was true only for the level of democracy. In other words, the inverted 'U' relationship that several authors have uncovered between conflict and regime type is confirmed in the case of our fragility index. The human rights empowerment index is also significant (column (4)) with a negative sign indicating that countries with better human rights records tend to be less fragile. Finally, both variables for ethnic risk and ethnic diversity are significant and positively correlated with fragility.

Table 3.A6 in the Appendix shows the results when countries with fragility scores of 6 and above are considered. Even though the overall fit of the equations was lower than in Table 3.A5, the signs and significance of the independent variables did not change very much. The main difference is that trade openness is no longer significant, which can be explained by the fact that the most fragile countries tend to trade less in general. Growth is also not always significant; it is possible that fragile countries do not have high growth rates to begin with, and that any growth that does occur is not being distributed throughout the economy, or that the time period considered is too short to see any effect.

To verify whether our results are robust, we regressed lagged values (by five years) of the independent variables on the fragility index to reduce the possibility of reverse causality or endogeneity—for example, fragility may affect a country's level of development, its growth, its regime type or even the extent to which it trades. Our results did not change. We also considered instrumental variable estimation with lagged values of the independent variables as instruments. The level of development remained highly significant in explaining fragility but the other variables lost some of their significance or became insignificant.[8]

---

[8] These results, while interesting, warrant further investigation beyond the scope of this chapter. Given the possibility of endogeneity in our estimates, some of the factors discussed could be symptoms as well as causes of fragility.

3.4 Aid Policy And Fragility

Having validated our fragility index in the previous section, we now turn our attention to how fragility is related to aid allocation and aid effectiveness.[9] We use the insights from the previous section together with the ALC framework and events-based monitoring developed by CIFP to discuss aid policy and state fragility. Prior to Burnside and Dollar's (1997, 2000) seminal contributions to the literature on aid and growth, a number of empirical studies found that aid did not contribute to growth (see, for example, Mosley 1980; Boone 1996). Burnside and Dollar (1997, 2000) showed that aid works in good policy environments (meaning that, by definition, it will not work as well in fragile state ones) and their views continue to receive broad support despite criticisms by Easterly (2003). Other surveys of the literature by Hansen and Tarp (2000), for example, are more positive and argue that aid leads to increases in growth, regardless of the policy environment, effectively nullifying the micro–macro paradox (Mosley 1986) of aid. Other than its impact (or lack thereof) on growth, critics of aid have also cited fungibility, lack of donor coordination, too much tying of aid, lack of absorptive capacity and the failure of conditionality to buy reforms, among other factors determining aid effectiveness. The Burnside-Dollar argument that aid works in good policy environments, and concurrent findings that neglecting fragile countries may in fact worsen poverty and lead to a further weakening of the state, pose a dilemma for policymakers and analysts alike.[10] When making decisions on where and how to allocate aid, should they be sensitive to fragile state environments or not?

When measured in terms of aid per capita (Table 3.2), our calculations indicate that fragile states (top 20 or top 40) are under-funded relative to all aid recipients and the volatility of aid flows to fragile states has also increased over time.[11] Except for the 1969–78 period, aid to fragile states as a percentage of gross national income (Table 3.A3) has not changed significantly.[12] We also examine how aid flows change when considering states with specific sources of weakness—namely, weakness in authority, legitimacy, or capacity (see Tables 3.2 and 3.3). Though the general pattern still holds that fragile states receive reduced per capita funding when compared to all aid recipients, additional trends emerge. States with weak authority and legitimacy consistently

---

[9] We do not examine aid effectiveness in fragile states empirically here. For such studies, see for example McGillivray (2007) and Carment et al. (2008).

[10] Chauvet and Collier (2005) estimate the cost of a country falling into LICUS status to be US $80 billion on average.

[11] While underfunding is true for the overall samples (top 20 or 40) of countries considered fragile, there is significant variation when one examines individual countries: some are receiving far more than what they can absorb, and others are not receiving enough.

[12] The table assumes that the top 40 or 20 fragile states were the same over the whole period even though the fragility index used to rank countries is for the last five years up until 2005.

Table 3.2. Aid allocation to fragile states based on ALC (aid per capita, US$)

	1969–78	1979–88	1989–93	1994–8	1999–2003
			All aid recipients		
-average	22.4	51.5	56.7	106.4	80.8
-standard deviation	30.4	64.9	70.7	518.9	202.5
			Fragility index		
Top 40 fragile states					
-average	15.3	36.8	44.7	45.0	35.1
-standard deviation	23.8	42.2	46.1	44.6	47.8
Top 20 fragile states					
-average	8.3	22.4	29.8	37.2	37.7
-standard deviation	6.4	17.4	20.5	46.6	63.1
			Authority		
Top 40 fragile states					
-average	8.6	21.0	28.2	38.8	35.8
-standard deviation	7.3	19.3	22.9	51.3	55.1
Top 20 fragile states					
-average	7.7	22.7	30.2	36.4	32.9
-standard deviation	6.3	22.9	27.9	51.2	64.3
			Legitimacy		
Top 40 fragile states					
-average	12.1	20.7	30.4	28.6	29.5
-standard deviation	14.0	28.7	31.2	48.2	64.4
Top 20 fragile states					
-average	11.8	27.0	28.1	30.8	28.6
-standard deviation	14.5	32.1	34.0	39.2	48.3
			Capacity		
Top 40 fragile states					
-average	20.6	51.2	69.1	78.9	72.4
-standard deviation	29.5	54.5	73.2	143.0	153.7
Top 20 fragile states					
-average	22.5	49.7	66.1	64.6	49.6
-standard deviation	32.6	51.1	73.9	79.7	48.2

Source: Authors' calculations based on OECD-DAC aid statistics, and the CIFP Fragile States Index.

received lower amounts of aid per capita than states lacking capacity. Furthermore, the relative levels of aid to states lacking authority and legitimacy appear to have shifted over time, a finding that holds for analyses done on both the top 20 and top 40 fragile states in each area. While states with weak authority received less aid per capita than states lacking legitimacy in the periods 1969–78 and 1979–88, flows approached parity during 1989–93; since then, states lacking in authority have received higher levels of aid than those lacking legitimacy. Indeed, aid flows to states lacking legitimacy have remained relatively stagnant since the early 1980s. Clearly, such findings are in large measure a reflection on global trends occurring during the period of observation. Both the end of the Cold War and attempts to contain or control civil conflict throughout the 1990s likely played a role in the evolution of development priorities. Nonetheless, the findings are both striking and intuitively satisfying.

Table 3.3. Aid allocation to fragile states based on ALC (aid as a % of GNI)

	1969–78	1979–88	1989–93	1994–8	1999–2003
			All aid recipients		
-average	5.9	8.9	10.6	10.7	8.8
-standard deviation	6.8	10.5	14.7	16.7	11.9
			Fragility index		
Top 40 fragile states					
-average	6.9	11.5	13.8	14.1	12.1
-standard deviation	6.9	12.6	12.6	11.5	10.1
Top 20 fragile states					
-average	4.6	9.2	11.9	11.9	13.7
-standard deviation	4.4	12.0	11.8	7.7	11.0
			Authority		
Top 40 fragile states					
-average	4.7	8.3	10.7	12.4	10.5
-standard deviation	4.5	11.6	11.8	12.8	10.5
Top 20 fragile states					
-average	5.2	10.5	12.6	12.6	12.0
-standard deviation	5.2	15.4	16.1	14.6	11.4
			Legitimacy		
Top 40 fragile states					
-average	4.6	8.2	8.6	7.6	7.7
-standard deviation	5.2	11.7	12.2	8.0	9.5
Top 20 fragile states					
-average	3.7	8.5	8.6	5.1	4.7
-standard deviation	5.2	15.9	15.0	6.6	9.0
			Capacity		
Top 40 fragile states					
-average	8.1	15.5	25.0	23.6	19.5
-standard deviation	6.7	11.8	25.5	25.7	15.8
Top 20 fragile states					
-average	7.9	14.8	21.8	20.2	18.0
-standard deviation	5.5	11.5	20.2	20.9	15.6

Source: Authors' calculations based on OECD-DAC aid statistics, and the CIFP Fragile States Index.

Table 3.3 highlights the variation in aid allocation as a percentage of gross national income (GNI). When compared with all aid recipients, fragile states on average receive more aid as a percentage of GNI than all aid recipients, though not significantly so. States lacking in capacity receive considerably more aid than other types of fragile states—in the latter three observation periods, low-capacity states on average relied on aid flows for more than 20 per cent of their GNI, a figure that held for both the top 20 and top 40 states. If one were to follow selectivity (that is, rewarding countries with good policies with increased aid since they can presumably use it more effectively) this would work against fragile states which in all likelihood lack the right policies to begin with.

The Collier-Dollar selectivity model (2002), which builds on the Burnside-Dollar result does just that, namely allocate aid to poor countries with good policies instead of funding reforms, with poverty reduction as the main criterion. Collier and Dollar (2002) derived poverty-efficient aid allocations, where aid is allocated in such a way as to maximize the number of people that are lifted out of poverty. According to their model, poverty-efficient aid will be higher when poverty is higher, per capita income is lower, and the policy environment is better. However, the main argument for aid selectivity rests on the idea that aid effectiveness depends on the policy environment, being based on Burnside and Dollar (1997, 2000), and it ignores other factors such as history of past conflicts, the level of democracy or political regime type. We have in fact seen in the previous section that many factors potentially impact on fragility. Once these factors are taken into account, fragile states might end up with more aid than the selectivity model would provide them. Needless to say, policy-makers need to be also aware of diminishing returns to aid as examined in several aid-growth empirical studies.

Assuming aid is effective in fragile states, the ALC framework can be a guiding framework for thinking about the types of intervention that are required (for example, programme versus project lending, targeting poverty versus governance, or looking at absorptive capacities). As argued earlier, when we examine fragility in terms of the ALC framework (or the different indicator clusters) for, let us say, the top 20 fragile states, the same countries do not always show up at the top of all these categories. The fact that the most fragile countries rank differently in terms of their ALC components, correlations among the elements notwithstanding, is an indication that certain areas need to be emphasized more than others. Lack of capacity on the part of the state, which is confirmed by the empirical investigation in section 3.3, seems to be important. However, to the extent that this may be correlated with the other components, namely authority and legitimacy, and given that the data show that some countries are more deficient in those sectors, aid focusing more directly on governance or corruption may be more helpful, for example, than direct attacks on poverty. It is also important to note that the general results (or shortcomings) from the literature and experience of the last 50 years as to why aid has not yielded expected results such as the lack of enforcement of conditionality, the failure of aid to 'buy' reforms, the volatility of aid flows, lack of absorptive capacity, and fungibility can all be examined using the ALC framework as a guiding framework.

To provide sectoral and operational guidance, CIFP adds further dynamic elements to the analysis, thereby providing the contextual component necessary for true 'second-generation' fragile state analysis. Events data, external and internal stakeholder analysis, and scenario generation all combine to provide context necessary to understand the dynamic elements of state performance. Such analysis would seek to uncover and highlight for policy-makers the emergent trends within a given state (both positive and negative), identify how actors and stakeholders might react to such developments, and

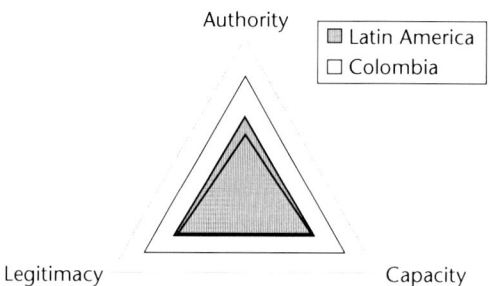

Figure 3.1. ALC comparative rank at a glance
Source: Wyjad (2007).

provide an evaluation of the possible consequences for policy and programming initiatives in the country. These dynamic data, when combined with initial structural findings, provide an assessment of both the underlying conditions and recent developments in a given country, thereby informing a more nuanced and ultimately more policy-relevant analysis of state fragility.

The following figures provide examples of the type of output that CIFP produces as part of its fragile state analysis, both taken from a recent fragility report on Colombia (Wyjad 2007). Figure 3.1 compares Colombia's ALC footprint to the regional average; as one might expect, the country suffers a gap in its level of authority as a result of long running conflict and the government's inability to exercise control over its territory and borders. State legitimacy and capacity remain comparable to regional averages however, providing entry points to international actors. Figure 3.2 combines structural and event data at the sectoral level. The overall level of risk is determined using CIFP's structural database, while the event barometers are produced using observations collected over a six month period extending from September 2006 to February 2007.

As part of its events analysis, CIFP observes and analyses all events reported on a given country from a variety of information sources—both domestic and international—over a given period, and uses that information to further the understanding of emerging trends in the country. The barometer indicates both the average score of events during the period, both aggregately and broken down by sector, as well as the event trend line for each cluster, defined as the slope of the ordinary least squares regression line of the weekly event average over the full observation period. Put simply, the arrow indicates whether events tended to become increasingly stabilizing or destabilizing over the period observed. In the case of security and crime, the news was bad and getting worse; in economics and human development the news was good and getting better; while in governance the status quo persisted. When combined with structural data, the resulting analysis provides a generally comparable, yet contextualized portrait of a given state's fragility.

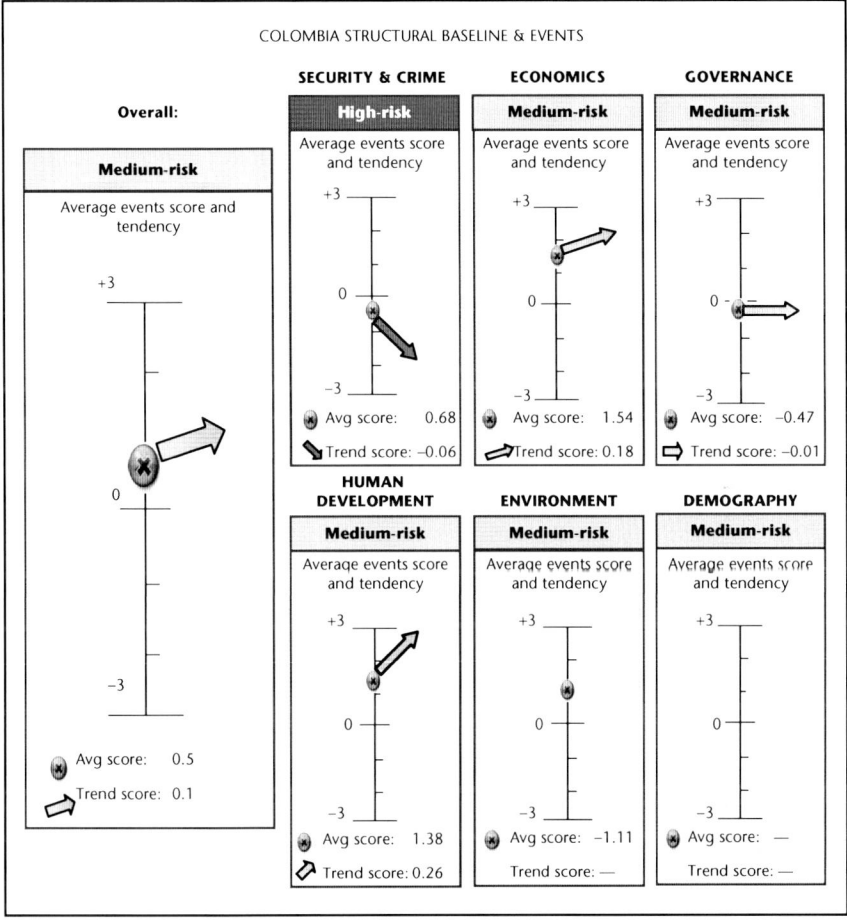

Source: Wyjad (2007).

Figure 3.2. Baseline and dynamic analysis

The CIFP state fragility assessment framework feeds into policy analysis at both the strategic and operational level. Strategically, such assessments allow policy-makers to evaluate the strengths and weaknesses of a given state, specify entry points where the international community might profitably direct its energy and resources, and provide a metric with which to measure fragile state performance over time in comparison to itself and others.

Second-generation analysis thus seeks to answer the following questions for policy-makers: What are the priority countries? Where can the international community respond most effectively? Which department(s) should lead/contribute to the response? How should resources be allocated? At the operational level, second-generation analysis provides a monitoring capability that informs operational goal-setting and measures policy effectiveness. Typical questions at the operational level include: Where/what are the primary sources of instability? How do recent events/trends affect policy formation and implementation? Are policies having an impact? Though both sets of questions may be answered using the same basic data, they require substantively different approaches to analysis.

3.5 Concluding Remarks

Compared to the literature on aid effectiveness, the literature on aid effectiveness *in fragile states*, and on the determinants of fragility, is comparatively much smaller, and deserves, in our view, further scrutiny. In this chapter, we have examined the determinants of state fragility by redefining the latter term around the notions of authority, legitimacy, and capacity of states. While this analysis yielded interesting results, it is our view that the search for better instruments to account for endogeneity, and a testing of different models highlighting the interaction effects of ALC components will yield useful results. While our results show that the main drivers of fragility are a combination of a number of factors (both economic and political) beyond conflict and economic dimensions, what we still need to know is how a combination of weaknesses in ALC structures influence fragility processes. We also examined the question of aid allocation to fragile states, basing our analysis on the empirical findings, the literature on aid selectivity, and the ALC framework, arguing that the latter could serve as a guiding framework for policy-makers and analysts by identifying country-specific patterns. As our project combines both structural and dynamic data an obvious next step will be to combine these into a framework to assess the impact of timing of aid interventions on fragility processes. In future research we will show how changes in a country's ALC components measured through dynamic data analysis are influenced by aid over time.

APPENDIX A

Tables

Table 3.A1. Fragility indices compared (developing countries, 2006)

	Marshall-Goldstone		Fund For Peace		Brookings		World Bank/LICUS		CIFP	
	1	2	3	4	5	6	7	8	9	10
Constant	37.00**	1.01	138.37**	45.88**	-0.79	9.01**	1.99**	3.61**	9.12**	3.69**
	[20.67]	[0.55]	[19.47]	[8.76]	[-1.27]	[17.68]	[4.70]	[15.57]	[29.75]	[14.27]
ln (GDP per capita)	-3.81**	—	-8.53**	—	1.01**	—	0.22**	—	-0.54**	—
	[-14.26]		[-8.13]		[11.11]		[3.16]		[-11.92]	
Security	—	1.88**	—	6.61**	—	-0.56**	—	-0.06	—	0.33**
		[5.71]		[7.09]		[-5.75]		[-1.38]		[6.22]
N	111	117	111	117	111	117	60	61	111	117
F Stat	0.00	0.00	0.00	0.00	0.00	0.00	0.01	0.17	0.00	0.00
Adj. R²	0.64	0.21	0.43	0.35	0.60	0.24	0.11	0.03	0.62	0.32

Note: (i) Except where indicated otherwise, the numbers n square brackets are robust t-values.
(ii) *(**) indicates 10(5) per cent level of significance.

Source: See text.

Table 3.A2. CIFP's top 40 fragile states, 2006 ranking

| Country | ALC scores | | | | Cross-cutting themes | Indicator clusters | | | | | |
	Fragility index	Authority	Legitimacy	Capacity	Gender	Governance	Economics	Security	Human development	Demography	Environment
Burundi	8.25	8.04	7.58	8.65	7.42	7.18	8.08	9.17	8.89	7.25	8.00
Congo, Dem. Rep. (Kinshasa)	8.11	7.93	7.58	8.49	7.72	7.67	6.93	9.15	9.70	7.35	5.47
Afghanistan	7.89	9.06	8.42	6.68	–	9.56	6.00	9.53	7.78	7.57	4.33
Somalia	7.86	7.53	8.41	7.82	–	8.90	8.42	7.18	8.51	7.34	7.13
Liberia	7.84	6.18	8.82	8.64	8.52	9.22	7.58	7.20	8.91	6.78	5.40
Chad	7.81	6.79	8.13	8.43	9.33	7.96	7.04	6.89	9.83	7.57	4.87
Ethiopia	7.81	7.58	7.14	8.31	7.47	6.59	7.44	8.07	8.83	8.35	6.40
Côte d'Ivoire	7.79	7.74	7.89	7.79	8.51	7.83	7.09	7.46	8.64	8.15	6.40
Angola	7.73	7.98	7.66	7.55	6.62	7.62	7.21	7.88	9.28	7.58	4.00
Eritrea	7.73	7.04	7.91	8.14	7.00	6.93	7.45	7.68	9.02	7.49	6.07
Haiti	7.72	6.81	8.53	7.94	7.27	8.32	7.24	8.05	7.95	6.90	7.67
Kenya	7.60	7.46	7.68	7.66	8.60	7.32	7.25	6.98	8.40	8.30	6.67
Rwanda	7.55	6.27	7.47	8.51	6.42	6.93	6.74	6.47	8.69	8.43	8.20
Zimbabwe	7.54	6.77	8.33	7.76	7.62	7.49	8.21	6.79	8.40	6.05	6.27
Guinea-Bissau	7.52	6.66	7.42	8.25	8.38	6.93	8.11	5.43	8.60	8.40	4.67
Sierra Leone	7.50	6.55	7.22	8.46	7.60	7.38	8.18	5.70	8.46	7.33	6.00
Congo (Braz.)	7.49	6.70	7.57	8.02	7.06	7.68	7.47	6.69	8.17	8.23	4.20
Sudan	7.48	7.83	7.58	7.21	7.82	7.13	6.38	9.22	8.22	6.95	6.00
West Bank / Gaza	7.41	6.69	10.33	7.50	8.30	6.85	9.08	8.16	4.78	7.00	9.00
Nepal	7.37	6.58	7.76	7.71	7.42	7.63	6.69	8.28	7.73	7.34	6.00
Nigeria	7.33	7.19	7.46	7.37	7.64	7.19	6.65	7.02	8.08	8.30	6.67
Niger	7.28	5.61	7.09	8.63	9.07	6.92	7.58	3.22	9.16	7.70	6.67
Yemen	7.27	6.59	8.32	7.31	8.93	8.00	6.56	7.44	7.20	7.63	8.33
Uganda	7.24	7.38	6.50	7.51	5.33	6.51	6.11	7.38	8.27	8.95	6.67
Central African Rep.	7.17	5.47	8.19	7.97	8.33	7.91	7.49	4.96	8.58	7.23	2.67

Mauritania	7.16	5.99	7.81	7.69	9.34	7.64	6.89	5.67	8.23	6.68	6.93
Guinea	7.15	5.97	7.56	7.92	7.40	7.40	7.36	4.87	8.94	6.90	4.93
Burkina Faso	7.00	5.50	6.39	8.28	7.90	5.61	7.16	3.25	8.94	8.40	5.00
Iraq	6.94	7.52	7.50	6.15	6.42	7.60	7.80	9.38	5.53	6.30	4.33
Tanzania	6.90	6.48	6.14	7.61	6.74	5.99	6.23	5.85	9.16	7.28	5.33
Malawi	6.89	5.87	6.29	7.90	7.42	5.78	7.84	3.52	8.45	8.43	7.00
Togo	6.83	5.50	7.54	7.48	8.17	7.56	6.56	4.26	8.21	6.98	6.33
Pakistan	6.82	7.08	6.43	6.83	6.11	6.47	6.01	8.58	6.44	7.34	6.73
Madagascar	6.81	5.06	7.24	7.83	7.94	6.68	6.88	4.89	8.15	7.74	5.00
Mozambique	6.79	5.53	6.12	8.05	6.80	5.05	7.23	5.05	9.20	7.15	3.67
Myanmar	6.79	6.96	7.15	6.47	6.25	6.75	6.96	8.81	6.75	5.20	4.73
Bangladesh	6.77	6.25	7.68	6.72	7.76	8.25	5.77	7.68	6.48	7.03	4.33
Cameroon	6.77	6.02	7.06	7.23	6.60	7.28	6.52	5.56	7.81	7.48	4.33
Mali	6.76	5.40	6.34	8.01	9.02	5.73	7.13	4.14	9.34	7.20	4.33
Laos	6.67	5.83	7.05	7.15	6.16	5.93	7.11	6.41	7.14	7.00	3.67

Source: See text.

Table 3.A3. Fragility index scoring scale

Score	Description
1–3.5	Country performing well relative to others
3.5–6.5	Country performing at or around the median
6.5+	Country performing poorly relative to others
Highest 5%	Country among worst global performers

Note: A few notes on methodology. First, this analysis draws on a methodology developed in 2001 for ranking countries using trend and volatility scores which has since been simplified for ease of use. Second, for the purpose of this analysis, we assume that fragility remains relatively constant over time, and use fragility scores calculated from 1999–2005 in the following analyses. In Carment et al. (2009), we conduct a similar analysis using a panel dataset for the years 1980–2006.

Source: See text.

Table 3.A4. Correlation matrix

	ETHDIV	ETHRISK	FRG	GDPG	HDI	HREM	LDEM	LPPP	TRAD
ETHDIV	1.00								
ETHRISK	0.13	1.00							
FRG	0.41	−0.01	1.00						
GDPG	0.05	0.14	−0.12	1.00					
HDI	−0.38	0.13	**−0.89**	0.04	1.00				
HREM	0.00	−0.04	−0.35	−0.35	0.24	1.00			
LDEM	0.07	0.24	−0.33	−0.32	0.28	**0.85**	1.00		
LPPP	−0.34	0.13	**−0.82**	−0.08	0.85	0.32	0.35	1.00	
TRAD	0.04	−0.25	−0.34	0.21	0.21	0.05	−0.05	0.17	1.00

Source: See text.

Table 3.A5. Determinants of fragility: Dependent variable, fragility index, 4 and above

Explanatory variables	(1)	(2)	(3)	(4)	(5)	(6)	(7)	(8)
Constant	11.71**	11.28**	11.80**	12.00**	11.72**	9.62**	11.11**	10.96**
	(24.04)	(22.22)	(23.52)	(25.86)	(24.67)	(38.43)	(20.76)	(19.43)
Log(GDPPC)	−0.66**	−0.59**	−0.66**	−0.66**	−0.64**	–	−0.64**	−0.60**
	(−12.26)	(−9.60)	(−12.14)	(−12.01)	(−11.70)		(−11.08)	(−9.54)
Growth	−0.05**	−0.04**	−0.05**	−0.04**	−0.04**	−0.05**	−0.05**	−0.05**
	(−2.96)	(−2.69)	(−2.78)	(−3.44)	(−3.27)	(−2.67)	(−2.98)	(−2.70)
Demo	−0.04**	−0.03**	−0.04**	–	–	−0.03**	−0.03**	−0.04**
	(−4.41)	(−4.03)	(−4.33)			(−3.07)	(−3.70)	(−4.09)
Demo*Demo	–	−0.01**	–	–	–	−0.01**	–	–
		(−1.97)				(−3.21)		
Trade	−0.01**	−0.01**	−0.01*	−0.01**	−0.01**	−0.01**	−0.01**	−0.01**
	(−3.38)	(−3.62)	(−1.74)	(−3.59)	(−3.51)	(−2.82)	(−2.20)	(−3.43)
Trade*Trade	–	–	0.01	–	–	–	–	–
			(0.64)					
Hrem	–	–	–	−0.10**	−0.02	–	–	–
				(−5.77)	(−0.44)			
Hrem*Hrem	–	–	–	–	−0.01	–	–	–
					(−1.55)			
HDI	–	–	–	–	–	−4.63**	–	–
						(−11.68)		

	(1)	(2)	(3)	(4)	(5)	(6)	(7)	(8)
Ethrisk	–	–	–	–	–	–	0.05**	–
							(3.68)	
Ethdiv	–	–	–	–	–	–	–	0.50**
								(3.08)
Afr	0.60**	0.59**	0.61**	0.70**	0.71**	−0.03	0.87**	0.68**
	(4.62)	(4.74)	(4.62)	(6.00)	(6.08)	(−0.25)	(6.02)	(4.82)
Lata	0.21	0.22**	0.20	0.29**	0.33**	0.10	0.28**	0.21
	(1.54)	(1.64)	(1.48)	(2.40)	(2.58)	(0.76)	(1.95)	(1.48)
Mena	0.07	0.02	0.08	0.02	0.03	−0.22	0.17	0.07
	(0.39)	(0.12)	(0.46)	(0.11)	(0.19)	(−1.39)	(1.34)	(0.43)
N	116	116	116	129	129	118	89	101
Adj. R^2	0.81	0.81	0.81	0.83	0.83	0.83	0.85	0.82

Note: Except where indicated otherwise, the figures in parentheses are the t-values. Standard errors are White-robust.
*(**) indicates 10(5) per cent level of significance.

Source: See text.

Table 3.A6. Determinants of fragility: Dependent variable, fragility index, 6 and above

Explanatory variables	(1)	(2)	(3)	(4)	(5)	(6)	(7)	(8)
Constant	10.86**	10.64**	11.51**	11.24**	10.94**	8.82**	9.99**	9.97**
	(14.50)	(14.09)	(14.39)	(17.63)	(15.33)	(25.27)	(11.11)	(11.26)
Log(GDPPC)	−0.53**	−0.48**	−0.56**	−0.55**	−0.53**	–	−0.49**	−0.44**
	(−5.94)	(−4.82)	(−6.35)	(−7.33)	(−6.53)		(−4.55)	(−4.51)
Growth	−0.04	−0.04	−0.05**	−0.03*	−0.03*	−0.05**	−0.03	−0.07**
	(−1.67)	(−1.64)	(−2.00)	(−1.93)	(−1.81)	(−2.29)	(−1.28)	(−2.64)
Demo	−0.04**	−0.04**	−0.03**	–	–	−0.03**	−0.04**	−0.04**
	(−3.14)	(−3.28)	(−2.57)			(−3.55)	(−2.52)	(−2.54)
Demo*Demo	–	−0.01**	–	–	–	−0.01**	–	–
		(−1.94)				(−2.58)		
Trade	−0.01	−0.01	−0.01	0.01	0.01	−0.01	−0.01	−0.01
	(−0.73)	(−0.23)	(−1.48)	(0.01)	(0.02)	(−0.70)	(−0.06)	(−0.61)
Trade*Trade	–	–	0.01**	–	–	–	–	–
			(1.17)					
Hrem	–	–	–	−0.12**	−0.01	–	–	–
				(−5.38)	(−0.08)			
Hrem*Hrem	–	–	–	–	−0.01	–	–	–
					(1.24)			
HDI	–	–	–	–	–	−3.02**	–	–
						(−4.88)		
Ethrisk	–	–	–	–	–	–	0.06	–
							(2.53)	
Ethdiv	–	–	–	–	–	–	–	0.39*
								(1.90)
Afr	0.30**	0.18	0.27	0.43**	0.43**	0.01	0.63**	0.52**
	(1.64)	(1.21)	(1.55)	(2.67)	(2.86)	(0.08)	(3.41)	(2.33)
Lata	0.30	0.24	0.26	0.56**	0.57**	0.26	0.31	0.40
	(1.27)	(1.16)	(1.15)	(2.35)	(2.40)	(1.55)	(1.31)	(1.26)
Mena	0.11	−0.15	0.13	−0.15	−0.11	−0.21	−0.08	0.13
	(0.46)	(−0.60)	(0.54)	(−0.75)	(−0.50)	(−0.64)	(−0.62)	(0.40)
N	55	55	55	57	57	56	38	42
Adj. R^2	0.51	0.56	0.52	0.64	0.65	0.58	0.67	0.57

Note: Except where indicated otherwise, the figures in parentheses are the t-values. Standard errors are White-robust.
*(**) indicates 10(5) per cent level of significance.

Source: See text.

APPENDIX B

About CIFP

Since 2005, the Country Indicators for Foreign Policy (CIFP) Project[13] has been conducting a second-generation analysis of fragile states, developing a methodology that combines dynamic event and stakeholder analysis with statistical information to produce context-rich country assessments that are nonetheless still comparable against the performance of peers. The analysis begins with a structural profile of the country, a composite index that measures overall country fragility along six dimensions or clusters: governance, economics, security, human development, demography, and environment. Each of these clusters is based on a number of indicators; for example, indicators under the 'economics cluster' include economic growth, gross domestic product (GDP), inflation, and unemployment, among others. The data are further analysed to provide insight into relative state strength and weakness along the three dimensions of 'stateness' referred to above, namely authority, legitimacy, and capacity. This multidimensional assessment methodology is a direct response to the multicausal nature of fragility and failure; states can weaken in any number of ways, such that any attempt to attribute fragility to a single deterministic set of causal variables inevitably remains underdetermined, capturing only a limited subset of all fragile states. Instead, CIFP adopts a more inductive approach, identifying areas of relative strength and weakness across all measures of state performance. It is this inductive and multifaceted approach to fragility and failure that distinguishes CIFP's database from conflict-driven first-generation projects such as the Fund for Peace failed states project.

Like its predecessor, the open-source CIFP conflict risk index (<www.carleton.ca/cifp>), the fragility index produced in collaboration with the Canadian International Development Agency (CIDA), employs a methodology of relative assessment. In ranking state performance on a given indicator, global scores are distributed across a nine-point index. The best performing state receives a score of one, the worst a score of nine, and the rest continuously distributed between these two extremes based on relative performance. More precisely, the global sample of countries is ranked from highest to lowest level of performance, divided into nine equal groups, and then assigned scores ranging from 1 to 9 for each indicator based on their rank position within the sample. In general, a higher score (7 to 9) indicates that the country is performing poorly relative to others while a lower score (1 to 3) indicates that the country is performing well relative to other countries. Given that relative country performance can vary from one year to another, global rank scores are averaged over a few years (up to a

---

[13] The current CIFP project builds on earlier iterations, dating back to 1997. Over that period, the CIFP project (together with the Canadian government, private sector, and nongovernmental organizations) has collected statistical information on a range of issues related to the political, economic, social, and cultural environments of countries around the world.

maximum of five years, given data availability) to mitigate against picking an unrepresentative year.[14]

References

ADB (Asian Development Bank) (2004). 'ADB's Approach to Weakly-Performing Developing Member Countries'. Paper prepared for the Asian Development Fund (ADF) IX Donors' Meeting, March. Available at: <www.adb.org/Documents/Reports/ ADF/IX/ weakly_performing.pdf>.

AusAID (2002). 'Australian Aid: Investing in Growth, Stability and Prosperity'. Available at: <www.ausaid.gov.au/publications/pubout.cfm? Id=6624_6294_3682_ 4822_1275>.

Bauer, P. (1981). *Equality: The Third World and Economic Delusion*. London: Weidenfeld.

Boone, P. (1996). 'Politics and the Effectiveness of Aid'. *European Economic Review*, 40(2): 289–329.

Burnside, C., and D. Dollar (1997). 'Aid, Policies and Growth'. World Bank Policy Research Working Paper No. 1777. Washington, DC: World Bank.

Burnside, C., and D. Dollar (2000). 'Aid, Policies and Growth'. *American Economic Review*, 90(4): 847–68.

Carment, D., S. El-Achkar, S. Prest, and Y. Samy (2006a). 'The 2006 Country Indicators for Foreign Policy: Opportunities and Challenges for Canada'. *Canadian Foreign Policy*, 13(1): 1–35.

Carment, D., S. El-Achkar, J. Gazo, S. Prest, and Y. Samy (2006b). 'Failed and Fragile States: A Briefing Note to the Canadian Government'. Country Indicators for Foreign Policy, Failed and Fragile States Project, Carleton University, Ottawa, Ontario.

Carment, D., Y. Samy, and S. Prest (2008). 'State Fragility and Implications for Aid Allocation: An Empirical Analysis'. *Conflict Management and Peace Science*, 25(4): 349–73.

Carment, D., Y. Samy, and S. Prest (2009). *Security, Development and the Fragile State: Bridging the Gap Between Theory and Policy*. London: Routledge.

Châtaigner, J.-M., and F. Gaulme (2006). 'Beyond the Fragile State: Taking Action to Assist Fragile Actors and Societies'. Document de Travail No. 4. Paris: Agence Française de Développement.

Chauvet, L., and P. Collier (2005). 'Development Effectiveness in Fragile States: Spillovers and Turnarounds'. Mimeo. Oxford: Centre for the Study of African Economics, Oxford University.

Collier, P. (2000). *Economic Causes of Civil Conflict and their Implications for Policy*. Washington, DC: World Bank.

Collier, P., and D. Dollar (2002). 'Aid Allocation and Poverty Reduction'. *European Economic Review*, 46(8): 1475–500.

---

[14] Excerpts of the above description are taken from Carment et al. 2009.

Collier, P., and A. Hoeffler (2004). 'Greed and Grievance in Civil War'. *Oxford Economic Papers*, 56(4): 563–95.

DFID (Department for International Development) (2005) *Why We Need to Work More Effectively in Fragile States*. London: DFID. Available at: <www.dfid.gov.uk /pubs /files/ fragilestates-paper.pdf>.

Diehl, P. F. and N. P. Gleditsch (2001). *Environmental Conflict*. Boulder, CO: Westview.

Easterly, W. (2003). 'Can Foreign Aid Buy Growth?' *Journal of Economic Perspectives*, 17(3): 23–48.

Easterly, W., and R. Levine (1997). 'Africa's Growth Tragedy: Policies and Ethnic Divisions'. *Quarterly Journal of Economics*, 112(4): 1203–50.

Fund for Peace (2007). 'The Failed States Index 2007'. *Foreign Policy*, July/Aug: 54–63.

Fund for Peace (2008). 'The Failed States Index 2008'. Available at: <http://www.fund-forpeace.org/web/> (accessed 4 January 2009).

Goldstone, J., T. R. Gurr, B. Harff, M. A. Levy, M. G. Marshall, R. H. Bates, D. L. Epstein, C. H. Kahl, P. T. Surko, J. C. Ulfelder, Jr., and A. N. Unger in consultation with M. Christenson, G. D. Dabelko, D. C. Esty, and T. M. Parris (2000). *State Failure Task Force Report: Phase III Findings*. McLean, VA: Science Applications International Corporation. Available at: <http://www.cidcm.umd.edu/publications/papers/SFTF% 20Phase%20III%20Report%20Final.pdf>.

Hansen, H., and F. Tarp (2000). 'Aid Effectiveness Disputed'. *Journal of International Development*, 12(3): 375–98.

Homer-Dixon, T. F. (1999). *Environment, Scarcity, and Violence*. Princeton: Princeton University Press.

Ignatieff, M. (2002). 'Intervention and State Failure'. *Dissent*, 49(1): 115–23.

Marshall, M., and J. Goldstone (2007). 'Global Report on Conflict, Governance, and State Fragility 2007: Gauging System Performance and Fragility in the Globalization Era'. *Foreign Policy Bulletin*, 17(1): 3–21.

McGillivray, M. (2005). 'Aid Allocation and Fragile States'. Background paper for the Senior Level Forum on Development Effectiveness in Fragile States. London, 13–14 January. Available at: <www.oecd.org/dataoecd/32/43/34256890.pdf>.

McGillivray, M. (2007). State Fragility and Aid Effectiveness: Classification Implications'. Paper presented at the UNU-WIDER Conference on Fragile States, Fragile Groups, Helsinki, 15–16 June.

Morcos, K. (2005). 'Chair's Summary'. Remarks presented at the Senior Level Forum on Development Effectiveness in Fragile States, London, 13–14 January. Available at: <www.oecd.org/dataoecd/32/43/34256890.pdf>.

Mosley, P. (1980). 'Aid, Savings and Growth Revisited'. *Oxford Bulletin of Economics and Statistics*, 42(2): 79–95.

Mosley, P. (1986). 'Aid Effectiveness: The Micro–Macro Paradox'. *Institute of Development Studies Bulletin*, 17: 214–25.

NSS (National Security Strategy) (2002). 'The National Security Strategy of the United States of America'. Available at: <http://www.whitehouse.gov/nsc/nss/2002/nss. pdf>.

OECD (Organisation for Economic Co-operation and Development) (2001). 'Poor Performers: Basic Approaches for Supporting Development in Difficult

Partnerships—Note by the Secretariat'. Paris: OECD-DAC. Available at: <www.oecd. org/dataoecd/26/56/21684456.pdf>.

OECD (Organisation for Economic Co-operation and Development) (2005). 'Paris Declaration on Aid Effectiveness: Ownership, Harmonisation, Alignment, Results'. Presented at the High Level Forum, Paris, 28 February – 2 March. Available at: <www. oecd.org/dataoecd/11/41/34428351.pdf>.

Prest, S., J. Gazo, and D. Carment (2005). 'Working out Strategies for Strengthening Fragile States: The British, American and German Experience'. Paper presented at the Fragile, Failed and Dangerous States Conference: Implementing Canada's International Policy Statement, Victoria, 25–27 November.

Prime Minister's Strategy Unit (2005). 'Investing in Prevention: An International Strategy to Manage Risks of Instability and Improve Crisis Response'. A Prime Minister's Strategy Unit Report to the Government of the UK. Available at: <www.strategy.gov. uk/work_areas/countries_at_risk/index.asp>.

Rice, S. E., and P. Stewart (2008) *Index of State Weakness in the Developing World*. Washington, DC: The Brookings Institution.

Rotberg, R. (ed.) (2004). *When States Fail: Causes and Consequences*. Princeton: Princeton University Press.

Severino, J.-M., and O. Charnoz (2005). 'Les mutations impromptues: état des lieux de l'aide publique au développement. Synthèse'. *Afrique contemporaine*, 213.

Stewart, F., and G. Brown (2007). 'State Fragility: Towards a Conceptual and Methodological Framework'. Paper presented at the UNU-WIDER Conference on Fragile States, Fragile Groups, Helsinki, 15–16 June.

Torres, M. M., and M. Anderson (2004). 'Fragile States: Defining Difficult Environments for Poverty Reduction'. PRDE Working Paper No. 1. London: DFID. Available at: <www.oecd.org/dataoecd/26/56/21684456.pdf>.

United States Government (2002). *The National Security Strategy of the United States of America*. Washington, DC: The White House. Available at: <www.whitehouse.gov/ nsc/nss.html>.

Van Hear, N. (1998). *New Diasporas: The Mass Exodus, Dispersal and Regrouping of Migrant Communities*. Seattle: University of Washington Press.

West, J. (2005). 'Concept Paper: Fragile States and Poverty'. Mimeo. Ottawa: CIDA.

Wolfensohn, J. (2002). 'Making the World a Better and Safer Place: The Time for Action is Now'. *Politics*, 22(2): 118.

World Bank (2002). 'World Bank Group Work in Low Income Countries Under Stress: A Task Force Report'. Washington, DC: World Bank. Available at: <www.worldbank. org/operations/licus/doments/licus.pdf>.

World Bank (2005). 'Fragile States: The LICUS Initiative'. Washington, DC: World Bank. Available at: <www.worldbank.org/servlets/ECR?contentMDK=20313429 &sitePK=388759>.

Wyjad, K. (2007). 'Fragile States Brief: Colombia'. CIFP (Country Indicators for Foreign Policy) Fragile States Brief No. 1, May.

4

Resources, Conflict, and State Fragility: Iraq and Somalia

Ghassan Dibeh

4.1 Introduction

Fragile states and conflict-ridden states are highly interrelated in the countries of the Middle East and North Africa region (MENA). This symbiotic and structural relationship forms an interesting area of study for policy-making in countries that are not necessarily poor and hence fragile, but rather are potentially rich and fragile (such as Iraq). In other countries in the area, such as Somalia and Sudan, fragility is a complex outcome of both conflict and poverty. However, the common factor in most fragile MENA states is state failure and governance structures that perpetuate civil conflicts and form the nexus of post-conflict reconstruction failures. According to classification by the UK's Department for International Development (DFID), fragile states in the MENA region include Somalia, Sudan, and Yemen. However, the *Foreign Policy* index of failed states classifies Lebanon, Egypt, Iraq, Sudan, Somalia, Saudi Arabia, Syria, Yemen, and Iran as failed, with the degree of failure ranging from 'borderline' to 'in danger' to 'critical'. This broader classification system which takes into account political determinants of fragility explains the tendency of some countries to become fragile states. For example, Iraq and Lebanon, two countries with a relatively high GDP per capita, are fragile states on the brink of civil strife and conflict that could transform them into the more traditional fragile states as per the DFID classification.

The analysis in this chapter assumes that there are two general types of fragile states: one type includes countries like Sudan, Somalia, and Yemen which fall under the more traditional concept of poor fragile states intensified by ethnic and tribal conflict. In the case of Somalia, the country is a de facto failed state divided amongst tribal warlords. In Sudan, despite the latest peace agreement, the country is divided between the Arab Muslim north and the mainly Christian African south. The nexus of tribalism, ethnic conflict, and poverty forms the basis for state failure in Sudan and Somalia. In the case of Somalia, as we see later in the chapter, the poor-resource attribute of the country makes it more amenable to chaos and anarchy. In the second type of state failure, on the other hand, state fragility is more related to the form of government established by potentially conflictive groups in a resource-rich economy (Iraq) or a middle-income state (Lebanon) with large financial wealth and debt-financed government expenditures. Through shared political space, the consensual or consociational democracy (since the independence in Lebanon and more recently in Iraq, following the USA invasion) is supposed to mediate the demands of the different sects and religious communities for resources. The underlying fragility-producing dynamics in these states is the process of state reconstruction and the failure of governance structures to produce stable political systems that distribute resources amongst different communities. These instabilities can cause either low-intensity conflict (Lebanon) or high-intensity conflict (Iraq) or devastating civil wars (pre-1990 Lebanon or perhaps future Iraq).

The chapter studies the political systems and economic development in two such conflict-states in the Middle East—Iraq and Somalia. Iraq is currently undergoing a social experiment during which a new form of government is being constructed after the passage of autocratic rule. Government is envisaged as a consociational democratic state, as it is designed a priori to serve as a political mechanism for the distribution of economic resources, mainly oil. Somalia, on the other hand, represents a stateless society bordering on complete anarchy. The incentives for power-sharing arrangements in Somalia are absent due to the lack of resources, the division of which various groups could potentially agree upon in any power-sharing arrangement. In this respect, Binningsbo (2005) shows in a theoretical and empirical study of post-conflict societies that consociational democracy as a power-sharing arrangement between different social groups increases the probability of stability and lasting peace in the post-war period. This chapter argues, however, that the consociational system may lead to rent-seeking confessional behaviour that could undermine the efficiency of state-led or private-sector-led economic development, particularly in post-war conflict societies rich in resources and with ethnic and religious divisions and, consequently, may lead to the prolongation of conflict or resurgence of political violence. The creation of a consociational democracy in Iraq in the post-invasion period has increased rent-seeking amongst the various ethnic and confessional groups and is fuelling the insurgency. The insurgency is attempting to improve its position within the consociational system that would eventually distribute the country's oil resources.

The chapter concludes that in relatively well-off fragile states, economic growth and development can be hindered by Olson-type rent-seeking coalitions. In addition, war when followed by a consociational political system can strengthen such coalitions (as happened in post-Saddam Iraq) rather than weaken them, as Olson had observed in the case of Germany after the Second World War (Eggertsson 1990). On the other hand, Somalia's evolution into anarchy after state collapse in 1991 is an example of the result of prolonged conflict in a resource-poor state. The development of what some called efficient anarchy (Leeson 2007) leads to a political-economic equilibrium where no group has an interest in forming a central authority.

The chapter is divided as follows: the next section discusses the various theories relating to resource availability, state structures, and economic growth. A prototype model is then developed to model the relationship between resources and the demand for government. Thereafter the economic development of Iraq until the Gulf War in 1991 is surveyed, followed by a discussion of the post-war reconstruction process in Iraq against the backdrop of the country's economic decline during the decade of economic sanctions in the 1990s. Iraq's political reconstruction process in the post-Saddam period is examined, given the relationship between oil resources and the political arrangements established. Then the model is applied to Somalia and the final section concludes.

4.2 A Model Of Government And Resources

Consociational democracy is one of the many forms of macroregulation of ethnic conflict within states. It is a system that distributes power amongst the constituent groups at the central level through 'a grand coalition government which incorporates the political parties representing the main segments of society (and) proportionality rules which apply throughout the public sector' (McGarry and O'Leary 1994). Hence, consociational democracy—in addition to being a system of distribution of political power between different ethnic or confessional groups as originally formulated by Lijphart (1969)—should also be analysed as a mechanism for dividing state-controlled resources. In Iraq, for example, this type of democracy must provide a distributional mechanism for the country's oil resources.[1] However, the necessary condition for establishing and successfully applying such a system is the existence of a resource

---

[1] The consociational system was successful in post-war Lebanon in distributing the proceeds of public debt and government expenditures, see Dibeh (2005).

threshold that permits the formation of a state. In the case of Somalia, this resource threshold is beyond reach, and resources in the economy do not permit the formation of a state nor, as a result, a constitutionally based distributional system amongst the different group and tribes. The alternative to this type of state distributional system is the abolition of the state and the creation of an anarchistic stateless society that mediates the production and distribution of resources. The theory can be summarized as follows: In an ethnically divided or tribal society, a consociational democratic state will arise if resources, R, are larger than some threshold value R^*. This theory arises from the rent-seeking society theories of the origin of the state (Olson) in contrast to the social choice theory where the state arises if the cost of government, G, is less than the private gain from the establishment of the state, PG. In this respect, the social choice theory advanced by Leeson (2007) applies to small primitive but homogeneous populations such as small African tribes.

The relationship between resource abundance and negative economic growth outcomes has been explained by three different theories—Dutch disease effects, predatory state, and conflict theories (Olsson 2007). The role of resources in engendering democracy or conflict has been modelled theoretically and investigated empirically in a number of studies. Aslaksen and Torvik (2006) extend the resources-democracy-conflict literature by developing an extended model in which conflict and elections arise endogenously from the interaction of players in a dynamic game. They find that the probability of conflict rises as the ratio of resources to productivity of labour increases. This implies that poor (low productivity) but resource-abundant countries have high risk of ending in conflict rather than democracy. Collier and Hoeffler (2005), utilizing an electoral competition model, show that resource-richness endangers democratic rule.

In addition to the relationship between resources and government, two important related questions are discussed in the literature: the relationship between resources and conflict, and the relationship between resource abundance and economic outcomes. From their study of civil wars over 1960–99, Collier and Hoeffler (2001) present empirical evidence for the hypothesis that the driving factor behind civil wars is the opportunity for economic gain or 'greed', and that ethnic divisions were insignificant. This agrees with the central thesis of this chapter that the political economy in post-Saddam Iraq is driven by expectations of resource gains from natural resources, whether achieved through outright conflict (if Iraq slips into civil war and subsequent breakup) or through consociational democracy which will provide the political space for their distributional arrangements. Torvik (2002) develops a theoretical model of natural resources and rent-seeking in which the abundance of natural resources triggers an increase in the number of economic agents

71

moving away from productive activities into rent-seeking behaviour. Moreover, Collier and Hoeffler (2005) find a negative relationship between resource-rich democratic countries and economic growth with autocratic resource-rich countries outperforming democratic ones.

In contrast to the models that rely mainly on game-theoretic or electoral models, the following section develops a new political economy model of government and resources in the tradition of Findlay (1989) and McGuire and Olson (1996).[2] The model sheds some light on the determinants of the size of government in a society with resources that can be used on their own (without government) to produce output. Findlay's (1989) seminal model introduces the role of government in society's production process as an externality that enhances the extraction of private production from private inputs. McGuire and Olson (1996) further develop a model of democracy and autocracy where output is a function of government or public goods needed by other resources (such as labour) for the production of output. In addition, literature on the optimal size of government has modelled government expenditures as input to the production function of society (Karras 1996). Tavits (2004) shows in an empirical study that government size is larger in consensus-type democracies than in majoritarian democracies. This is due to the increased role of the government in welfare provision in a consensus society. Let the production function of the economy be defined as:

$$y = Af(R, G) + Bg(R) \tag{4.1}$$

where R = resources; G = government size or institutions or public goods needed in co-operation with R for production of output. The production function assumes that resources are used for domestic production as developed in a variant of Hotelling resource extraction model developed by Heal (2007). Furthermore, the production function assumes that the economy can produce goods using a resource-only $g(R)$ and a combined government-resource channel $f(R, G)$. The latter is a variant of the productive role of government model introduced by Findlay (1989). The government plays a

---

[2] The model predicts possible outcomes as a function of resource abundance and the complementarities between resources and government in production. However, given the non-game theoretic and non-electoral nature of the model, it does not provide insight into the state-building process engendered by inter-group conflict and/or cooperation. For example, the concept of a minimum winning coalition, though relevant to the Iraqi case cannot be incorporated to the model. Eklund et al. (2006), however, have predicted that Kurdistan will not seek a minimum winning coalition tactic but a consensus path towards constitution building in Iraq. The multi-religious and multi-ethnic nature of Iraq, however, is amenable to the investigation of the types of electoral rules that 'activate' a specific dimension of ethnicity and hence to the formation of minimum winning coalitions as shown to be relevant in Africa by Posner (2005). Such minimum winning coalitions risk turning into 'permanent winning coalitions' such as a coalition between the Kurds and Shia in Iraq. Permanent coalitions can trump democracy (Horowitz, 1985) and can lead to instability. Indeed, such processes may have an impact on the success or failure of state construction in Iraq but cannot be captured in the current model.

productive role where a central government helps mobilize resources, protects property rights in these resources, enforces contracts, and invests in resource maintenance. The production function has the property that under 'anarchy', $y(0, R) \geq 0$. Let there be two groups in society with the following payoff functions[3]

$$\Pi_1 = \lambda(y - \gamma G - \theta pR) \tag{4.2}$$

$$\Pi_1 = (1 - \lambda)(y - \delta G - \theta pR) \tag{4.3}$$

where λ = share of group 1, γ and δ cost of government to groups 1 and 2 respectively, and θ = resource price.

The maximization problem with respect to G is then given by the following:

$$\frac{\partial \Pi_1}{\partial G} = 0, \frac{\partial \Pi_2}{\partial G} = 0, \tag{4.4}$$

which gives:

$$AR^\alpha \beta G^{\beta-1} - \gamma = 0 \tag{4.5}$$

$$AR^\alpha \beta G^{\beta-1} - \delta = 0 \tag{4.6}$$

Adding the two conditions we get:

$$AR^\alpha \beta G^{\beta-1} = \frac{\delta + \gamma}{2} \tag{4.7}$$

The maximization problem with respect to R is given by the following:

$$\frac{\partial \pi_1}{\partial R} = 0, \frac{\partial \pi_2}{\partial R} = 0, \tag{4.8}$$

The first-order conditions (4.8) give:

$$A\alpha R^{\alpha-1}G^\beta + \alpha BR^{\alpha-1} - p = 0 \tag{4.9}$$

Dividing first-order conditions (4.7) and (4.9) and rearranging terms we get:

$$R = \frac{(\gamma + \delta)\alpha(B + AG^\beta)G^{1-\beta}}{2A\beta} \tag{4.10}$$

Relationship (4.10) defines the $\frac{R}{G}$ intensity as a function of the various parameters of the model. The important parameter effects are as follows:

---

[3] In contrast, the model in McGuire and Olson (1996) has the property $y(G)$ so that $y(0)=0$.

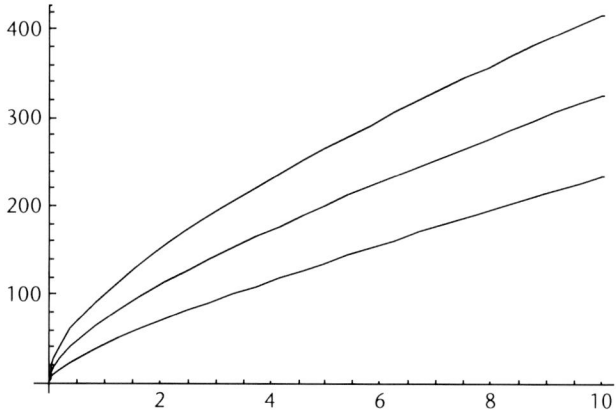

Figure 4.1. *R* versus *G* for parameter *B* values (*B* = 10, 20, 30)
Source: Author's simulation of (4.10) using MATHEMATICA.

- The higher β, the lower $\frac{R}{G}$. The higher β reflects the higher productivity and efficiency of the government, resulting in a larger government size or more effective institutions;

- The higher p, the lower $\frac{R}{G}$. The larger p reflects greater difficulty in extracting the resource, whether economic or otherwise. For example, an ethnic group attempting to secede (Kurds in Iraq or east region in Biafra) must take into account the possible resultant increase in p;

- The higher B, the higher $\frac{R}{G}$. If total productivity of the resource without government is high, then this results in a relatively smaller government size. Even in resource-poor economies, if B is very high, G can become very insignificant, a scenario that can represent stateless societies. In resource-rich economies, such as the oil-rich countries, G can be very minimal *if G is unnecessary for the exploration, extraction, and export of oil*;

- The higher α, the higher $\frac{R}{G}$. The higher the marginal productivity of the resource, the smaller is the relative government size.

As an illustration, Figure 4.1 shows a plot of *R* versus *G* for various values of the parameter *B*.

4.3 The Iraqi Economy Before The Invasion

The current state of Iraq, as a deeply divided country with a non-functioning polity and economy, is a phenomenon which was engendered by the economic crisis of the 1990s and intensified in the post-Saddam period. In this section, the Iraqi economy and its development in the period prior to the Gulf

War in 1991 are studied. It is shown that the economic developments during 1960–80 did produce a fairly developed economy and a central developmental state. In this respect, economic progress in Iraq during that period can be measured according to the criteria outlined in the Rostovian stages of economic development (Rostow 1960). Moreover, Iraq satisfied the Rostovian preconditions for takeoff with regard to social overhead capital and reactive nationalism. Furthermore, the country satisfied the other takeoff prerequisites such as: (i) investment comprised 10 per cent of GDP; (ii) advanced petrochemical industry had been developed; (iii) the political climate was favourable to modernization; and (iv) a capital-output ratio of 4:1 had been reached and an abundance of loanable funds created.

The economy had been guided by five-year plans since the 1958 revolution that overthrew the monarchy and signalled the beginning of the republican era in the history of Iraq. In 1976, the five-year plans were abandoned and replaced with indicative planning on an annual basis. The government was the most important actor in the economy, as it owned most of the means of production, in addition to the lifeline of the economy, the oil sector. Time-wise, the most important era in the Iraqi economy is the post-1973 period when, as a result of the Arab oil embargo and the subsequent rise in oil prices, oil revenue jumped from US\$1 billion in 1972 to US\$8.2 billion in 1975. This trend continued until 1980 when it was estimated that 'in the first nine months of 1980 (the war began on 22nd of September) oil export revenues were US\$25 billion or about US\$33 billion on an annual basis' (Kanovsky 1983: 5). This led to government expansion of its fiscal expenditures and investment programmes in an attempt to industrialize and diversify the structure of the economy that was becoming increasingly dependent on

Table 4.1. Investment programmes in Iraq, 1970–8

Year	1970–1	1973–4	1975	1977	1978
Total (millions of Iraqi dinar)	119	296	1,591	2,074	2,121
Industry (%)	23.4	15.2	43.9	46.5	32.2
Agriculture (%)	23.4	21.9	20.1	12.9	23.4

Source: EIU (1986/7).

Table 4.2. National accounts: trends in GDP

Year	1979	1984	1985	1986	1987	1988
Nominal GDP, in billions of US\$	38.6	47.6	46.8	54.3	68.4	91.0
Real growth, in billions of US\$	23.5	−8.0	−9.7	−4.7	−1.9	5.0

Source: EIU (1989/90).

oil. Table 4.1 summarizes the investment programmes for the period 1970–78; Table 4.2 provides national accounts, showing trends in GDP.

The objective was to allocate almost 70 per cent of oil revenues to investment programmes and in 1978, for example, 67 per cent of oil revenues were targeted to investment programmes. However, not all money allocated for these programmes was actually spent. Gross fixed capital formation, which reflects the efficiency of the government's implementation of the economic development plan, indicated tremendous growth rates from 1972 to 1976, followed by sluggish growth in 1976–81.

The developmental phase of the economy led, first, to the increasing importance of the oil sector, accounting for 67 per cent of GDP in 1980; and second, because of the huge oil revenues, increased public expenditures by the Iraqi government on social sectors such as education and health, as well as on industrialization and the military sector. Public employment became the source of national integration in Iraq. GDP per capita had increased to US $2,312 in 1979, on the eve of the Iran-Iraq war (Owen and Pamuk 1998).

During the post-boom industrialization drive of the 1970s to the war of the 1980s, the economy experienced upswings and downturns that left it both industrialized with comparatively huge financial resources, but also at the same time backward and indebted. The Iraqi economy suffered heavily from the Gulf War (1980–8); estimated costs of the conflict up to 1985 totalled US $226 billion at the 1980 dollar-level. Furthermore, by the end of 1988, when the value of oil exports had dropped to 50 per cent of their 1980 level, Iraq had accumulated an estimated US$60 billion in debts, costing around US$3 billion per year in debt servicing (Crusoe 1989). In addition, according to the Bank for International Settlements (BIS), foreign exchange reserves accrued by the government during the 1970s expected to reach US$25 billion in 1980 had dwindled to US$800 million by the end of 1983 (Crusoe 1989). The war also created extreme distortions in agriculture, the labour market, and capacity utilization—three major weaknesses of the pre-war economy. Closure of exporting facilities in the Persian Gulf caused Iraq's oil exports to decline considerably, dropping from 3.5 million barrels per day in 1979 to 2.6 million in 1988, and diminishing during 1984–5 to only 800,000–900,000 barrels. In 1987, fixed capital formation dropped to almost the pre-war era level. The Iraq-Iran war put an end to the growth in Iraqi GDP, which had averaged 27.9 per cent over the period 1968–78 (Khafaji 1983: 5).

In 1987, the economic climate began to change as a result of an increase in oil exporting capacity and higher oil prices. Expansion of the pipeline through Turkey increased oil export capacity by 500,000 barrels per day during the third quarter of 1987 and the pipeline flowing through Saudi Arabia increased it by an equal amount in September 1989. Furthermore, Iraq regained its traditional trade surplus position which had persistently experienced deficits during the years 1981–3 and 1986 (EIU 1986/7: 34; EIU 1989/90: 32).

4.4 Politics And Economy In Post-Saddam Iraq

We have shown that the Iraqi economy faced severe challenges at the end of the Iran-Iraq war. The decline in GDP per capita and the enormous foreign debt accumulated during the Iran-Iraq war (mainly to Arab countries) presented the most immediate problems. Arab advances to Iraq during this period have been estimated to have amounted to US$80 billion (Owen and Pamuk 1998). The decline in oil prices to around US$15–20 per barrel during this period prevented the Iraqi government from utilizing its oil exports—the traditional source of economic growth—to finance its way out of the crisis. The policy of the government staggered until the Iraqi regime invaded Kuwait in an effort to find a solution to its debt crisis. The first Gulf War in 1991 was a milestone in Iraq's subsequent decline: economic sanctions and embargo imposed on the country from 1991 to 2003 devastated the economy. Capital accumulation faltered as the government lost control of its oil revenues under the UN oil-for-food programme. The government, strapped for cash, initiated inflationary financial measures to pay government wages, causing hyperinflation in the 1990s. By 2001, GDP per capita at market exchange rate was around US$960 (Foote et al. 2004).

After the invasion, the Coalition Provisional Authority (CPA) led by Ambassador Paul Bremmer assumed responsibility for economic policy. The basic thrust of the economic policy was the enactment of free market reforms with foreign investment law, reforms in the banking sector, import liberalization strategy, and planned privatization of state enterprises as the main pillars (Looney 2004a). These reforms were to bring prosperity to Iraq, as it moved away from the statist economy to a free market one (Foote et al. 2004). However, four years after the invasion, the country has little to show in terms of economic progress, especially in the areas of public service such as electricity production and employment generation. These economic failures were intertwined with political and security developments. They should not, therefore, be perceived only at the economic level as traditional failure of neoliberal policies even though the incompatibility of such pro-market policies implemented in the Iraqi circumstances has been shown to be one of the main reasons for the failure of the post-war reconstruction programme (Looney 2006). In addition to the 'economic' failures of the neoliberal programme, developments in the post-Saddam governance structure, particularly the designs for the formation of a federal consociational democracy, led to growth-impeding political rent-seeking behaviour. The invasion by the USA did not trigger economic growth and prosperity as anticipated, but created instead a political economy of (re)distribution, that breeds sectarian violence, insurgency, and general economic collapse.

4.4.1 *Governance and state construction*

Many observers of Iraqi affairs have reached the conclusion that Iraq is at the crossroads between the establishment of a unified democratic state or disintegration and division across ethnic lines. According to Feldman (2006), the USA occupation of Iraq will be historically judged as a major upheaval whether towards a failed state or a 'reasonably democratic' one.

Failure to achieve an ethnic division of power has led some observers, such as Downes (2006), to suggest that the solution could be a territorial division of Iraq into three states—Sunni, Shiite, and Kurd, because power-sharing arrangements have failed to alleviate the mistrust among the groups. This was echoed in the *Iraq Study Group Report* issued in December 2006, i.e., the so-called Baker-Hamilton Report, which also warned of the dangers of regional breakup into three ethnic-based states.

Developments in the post-Saddam governance structure, especially the formation of a federal consociational democracy, were instrumental in creating this untenable political and ethnic-conflictive state. The neoconservative agenda for democracy in Iraq—envisaged as a beacon of good governance in the Middle East region—gave way to civil conflict, ethnic strife, and corruption on an unprecedented scale. Instead of the clean slate that neoconservatives assumed was being handed to them with the end of autocratic rule, the USA occupation authorities turned Iraqi politics into a denominational political system that hampered state reconstruction and nation-building in the post-war period.

The problem of nation-building in Iraq was immediately faced by the CPA and Paul Bremmer, the USA 'governor' of Iraq, and his actions during the first year of occupation sealed the fate of Iraqi political development in later years. According to a general consensus, the dismantling of the Iraqi army in May 2003, one month after the invasion, and the massive looting of Baghdad that occurred immediately after the invasion while USA troops watched helplessly sent out signals to the population that the transition from autocratic rule was fraught with insecurity. According to Feldman (2006), the rise of denominational politics was a way to create 'mutual protection associations' in the face of chaos. Although it is true to some extent that the rise of denominational politics was spontaneous, the deliberate USA design to create a multi-ethnic democracy was also instrumental in engendering this outcome. The nationalist development project of the Baath regime, although weakened by Saddam's personal and tribal politics in the 1980s and more importantly in the 1990s, was replaced with a political system based on the division of power explicitly between the ethnic and religious communities of Iraq. The establishment of the governing council (GC) in 2003 by Ambassador Bremmer immediately after the invasion was based on ethnic representation,[4] and laid the foundation for all subsequent governing bodies, appointed or elected, from parliament to government to be mirror-images of ethnic division. The GC was scrapped on 28 June 2004 when the CPA handed power to an interim government headed by secular Iyad Allawi—it was the start of the formal handover of power from the CPA to the Iraqis.

The pivotal point in the political construction of Iraq came in January 2005 when general elections were held due to pressure from Ayatollah Al-Sistani, the Shia highest religious authority in Najaf. USA authorities reluctantly agreed after massive demonstrations by the Shiites at the urging of Sistani (Chomsky 2006). The elections brought a Shia majority to power and led to the defeat of the pro-USA secular candidate, Iyad Allawi. They also paved the way for a constitution that institutionalized the confessional consociational democracy in Iraq. These political changes came in tandem with the intensified struggle over resources. The Iraqi economy had been dominated up to this point by international corporations involved in the USA-led reconstruction effort. The new political system started preparing the ground for a confessional division of the reconstruction spoils and of the benefits from increased oil prices that produced windfall profits to the state-owned sector. This explains the intensification of the Sunni insurgency in the post-elections period up to present day. In parallel to what can be called a normal political process, there were increasing tensions regarding the status of the important oil-rich Kirkuk region and these were turning oil politics into a new impetus for violence between the Kurds and the Sunnis. Moreover, the creation of the semi-autonomous regions (e.g. Basra in the south) that were forging economic ties across the border with Iran added fears within the Sunni minority of economic marginalization.

The USA plans for democratic progress in Iraq were diverted or controlled by pressure from Ayatollah Sistani. Sistani issued a series of *fatwas* from June 2003 onward. These *fatwas* stipulated that all constitutional and institutional formations be subjected to a public referendum. Given the majority of the Shia, this meant all such measures were subjected to the will of the Shias. Cockburn (2006) cites the incident of an Iraqi calling the results of the January 2005

---

[4] In a highly significant incident that attests to the role played by USA authorities in enshrining denominational politics into Iraq's new governance structure, Bremmer recalls in his memoirs that even the appointment of the communist party general secretary to the GC was done on confessional grounds in appointing him as a learned representative of the Shia community rather than a representative of the Iraqi communist party (Bremmer 2006).

elections for the constitutional assembly—which the Sunnis boycotted—the 'Sistani tsunami'. Cockburn (2006: 187) observes that in Iraq's pivotal first democratic elections, the 'Iraqis had voted almost wholly along ethnic sectarian lines'. Subsequently, the first elected government in post-war Iraq ushered in a new system of governance based on communal nature as a version of consociational democracy. But according to Anderson and Stansfield (2005), the effort was undermined by three negative aspects of the election: the marginalization of Sunni Arabs whose participation was estimated to be between 5–10 per cent; the dominance of Shiite religious parties in parliament; and the overrepresentation and empowerment of the Kurds.

In October 2005, the referendum for the Iraqi constitution—an important element in the confessional foundation of Iraqi polity in the post-Saddam period—was supported by the Shias and Kurds, and opposed by the Sunnis. The December 2005 parliament elections, although bringing a Sunni bloc to parliament, solidified the denominational political system of Iraq. Cockburn calls these events 'a series of misleading milestones...all the while the Iraqi state and society came even closer to dissolution' (2006: 222).

The democratic system established through denominational politics and early elections lacked a fundamental element of democracy: there was no competition for the inter-ethnic representation or uncertainly over election outcomes (Przeworski 1991; McGuire and Olson 1996). This is one of the reasons for the failure of democratic rule and the ensuing violent conflict. Both the eruption of violence against occupation forces and inter-communal fighting that intensified after the 2005 elections and constitutional year have left more than 600,000 dead (Burnham et al. 2006). The Sunni insurgents have imposed huge losses on the society, given the current political structures that would offer them little gain in the event of success in nation-building.[5]

4.4.2 *The geography and politics of oil*

Oil played a pivotal role in the Iraqi economic and political development before the Gulf Wars in the provision of resources for state expenditures, as we have seen in section 4.3. Stansfield (2005) observes that oil was perceived as a spoil of war in the post-Saddam period. The location of oil juxtaposed on Iraq's ethnic division based on three pre-independence *wilayat* (Mosul, Baghdad, and Basra) gives control of Basra and the southern fields to the Shia, and the northern fields of Kirkuk are dominated by the Kurds but highly contested by the Sunni. This interrelationship of geography and oil is one of the main defining elements of post-Saddam Iraq: centralized control over oil

---

[5] This type of behaviour in society is explained in McGuire and Olson (1996).

resources is eroding into a decentralized system embedded in the constitution adopted in October 2005 (Tsafos 2006). The constitution and the new hydrocarbon law proposal, however, were ambiguous on the extent of centralized versus decentralized mechanisms of oil production and distribution.

The consociational democracy currently being set up in Iraq is symbiotically related to the country's oil resources. In the post-invasion period, the development of the federal political system highlighted oil not only as a resource for national economic development or a source of contention between Iraq and colonial powers, as had been the case in the pre-nationalization phase, but as a resource contested by the different ethnic and religious groups for its revenue and 'rents'. Once the focus moved away from national economic development to distributional issues, the Kurds, Sunnis, and Shias realized from the outset that controlling oil was equivalent to controlling the main source of state revenue. There have been many calls by Iraqi observers for an oil distributional system based on individual allotments. Birdsall and Subramanian (2004) propose that a substantial part of the oil revenues be distributed directly to Iraqi citizens in an effort to avoid transforming Iraq into another oil-rich country with the usual economic ills with respect to Dutch disease, lack of incentives for the development of political institutions, and economic reform. If implemented, such a proposal would provide non-sectarian channels of distribution for oil resources that complement their usage for post-war reconstruction. More importantly, the proposal could break the confessional shackles on economic growth imposed by the new confessional system. Looney (2006) supports such a system, albeit with more attention being given to the usage of oil resources for reconstruction through the financing of public investments and in generating aggregate demand in a typical Keynesian strategy. An interesting feature of the proposal is that it is in part seen as promoting counter-insurgency tactics because individual allotments could encourage the Iraqis to protect oil assets from sabotage attacks and could mute the Sunni complaints about possible unequal distribution of the proceeds. In this respect, Feldman (2006: 44) observes that 'the Sunni insurgency wanted to convince the Shia and the Kurds that oppressing them or simply denying them a full share of state resources would be very costly'.

Although the distribution of oil proceeds is seen as crucial to success in rebuilding civil society (Zubeida 2006), all proposals for political and economic reform, including those concerning oil funds, add to the current destabilizing and centrifugal elements in Iraq. The 'distributional' element is given considerable weight in these proposals.

The new oil law draft was introduced in a furtive manner. The draft, yet to be approved by parliament, calls for the establishment of a Federal Oil and Gas Council that would approve all oil-sector contracts. Juhasz and Jarrar (2007) note that many Iraqi oil experts have called the law the 'split Iraq fund', as it paves the way for the three main ethnic groups/regions to claim their own oil production fields. However, the law is ambiguous enough to allow a strong central state to supersede measures by regional authorities. Hence, the application of the law will be an endogenous process depending on the power struggle among the central state, regions, and ethnic groups. At present, the latter has the upper hand. The consociational democratic government, if fully functional and operational with the inclusion of the Sunnis in the process, will eventually be the central mediator of regional/ethnic distribution of oil.

4.5 A Resource-Poor Economy: Somalia

Today, Somalia is considered to constitute a modern form of anarchy. The state collapsed in 1991 after the overthrow of Siad Barre, the last president of a unified Somalia. The country collapsed into a stateless existence, with Somaliland and Puntland as the two northern secessionist regions. This collapse outlasted USA and international military intervention in the early 1990s. Over the past few years, an attempt at unification was made with ideological underpinnings led by the so-called Islamic courts in an effort to extend central authority over most of Somalia. The efforts, however, were thwarted by an outright military intervention by Ethiopia in April 2007 which re-installed the provisional government. Despite such efforts at 'unification', the Somali state is far from escaping the trap of fragility, or worse, of failed state that has plagued the country for almost two decades.

The model presented above predicts that groups in a country like Somalia where resources are scarce have little incentive to create central government. In the language of the model, Somalia has the following parameters and endowments: low R, low β, high B. Somalia's main resources are pastoral production and crop farming, i.e., mainly agricultural resources.

The past record of Somalia's central government since the socialist phase of the 1960s and 1970s shows that, due to a low resource base, the government was either reliant on foreign assistance (the Soviet Union at the time) or highly inefficient with respect to economic policy (in the post-socialist period starting from 1980). Collapse of the state in 1991 and eruption of a civil war that continues unabated have shown that the country's various ethnic groups, tribes, and regions have limited interest in restoring central authority. Many observers note that the Somali economy has actually fared better during this period than under centralized rule (Mubarak 1997; Leeson 2006; Powell et al. 2006). For example, Powell et al. (2006) show that Somalia, in comparison with 42 other sub-Saharan African countries, has a comparable, if not better, level of progress in many economic and social welfare indicators. There has been economic progress despite the destruction of all public infrastructure such as electricity production, the spread of violence, and more importantly, the absence of central government or even a central bank.[6] Leeson (2006) has shown that for 18 key development indicators, Somalia has an improved record in 14 of them during the stateless period (2000–5) in comparison to the years 1985–90. Indicators such as life expectancy, maternal and infant mortality rates, immunizations, access to sanitation, and health have all improved. Many attribute this progress to the absence of the state or central authorities. For example, Mubarak (1997) shows that the collapse of the state led to regulations on urban commerce being lifted, and to the end of the negative effects of economic policies which had plagued Somalia in 1980–91. This allowed business in the cities to flourish, and pastoral and agricultural production to improve in rural areas. Currently Somalia is the biggest producer of cattle in the east African region (Powell et al. 2006). Moreover, the relative calm and stability of the breakaway state, Somaliland, have allowed the economy in the north to experience a relatively strong revival.

Various theories have attempted to explain the continuing resilience of anarchy in Somalia. One explanation is attributed to the ambitions of the warlords for national domination (Mubarak 1997). As Menkhaus (1995) observes, the inability of one group or alliance of groups early in the civil war to dominate the national politics prevented the return to central authority. Another theory is implicitly based on the benefits of anarchy in comparison to the predatory state that existed before 1991 (Leeson 2006). Finally, Menkhaus (2003) points to the zero-sum nature of state revival. Although the continued state of anarchy is beneficial to Somali development, anarchy generates mainly profitable opportunities in the private economy and a rise of prominence of economic actors such as businessmen and tribesmen. In this respect, the model in this chapter suggests that the benefits from central government in resource-poor Somalia would not create sufficiently greater material incentives for the warring factions and private actors to offset the huge costs of re-establishing central authorities after years of civil conflict. In Somalia, given the resource base and its low degree of complementarity with government form a 'disincentive' to the re-establishment of a central government.[7] Moreover, the experience of the breakaway region, Somaliland, in establishing a form of central authority shows that poor

---

[6] The central bank has been closed and stopped printing money after it was ransacked and destroyed in 1991 (Mubarak 1997).

[7] In Iraq, in contrast, conflicting groups have an intrinsic interest in establishing central authority because G is vital for the production and export of oil resources.

resources are the main obstacle to the continuation of the experiment (Mubarak 1997). This also applies to the assumption that currently state formation would be a zero-sum game whereby some players benefit from state construction, while others, as a result, correspondingly lose. This theory would be plausible if the newly formed state can be used as a redistributionary mechanism between groups in a zero-sum setting. However, and since resources in Somalia are very scarce and are mainly pastoral and agricultural, their extraction by the state would actually lower the benefits to all private actors, as has been witnessed during the socialist phase when the state supplanted the markets or even when Barre's government abandoned socialist policies for structural adjustment in the 1980s.[8] In addition, Somalia is one of three countries that are in arrears to the International Monetary Fund as of June 2009. The total value of arrears is 243 million SDRs. Somalia is also in arrears to the World Bank, African Development Bank with around 175 million SDRs (IMF 2009). This in addition to its total foreign debt that was estimated in 1990 to be 277 per cent of the GDP would put a burden on any future central government to raise taxes and revenues.

As the model in this chapter shows, groups in direct control of resources weigh the high costs of establishing a central government in Somalia against the benefits of the existing stateless set-up. Anarchy in Somalia, according to Samatar (1993: 35), is a return to the pre-colonial era when traditional ties based on Islam and kinship had 'an economic counterpart: nomadism and peasant agriculture. All households had access to productive resources'. Samatar (1993) further argues that the *petit bourgeoisie* was a new class that benefited from state power in the post-colonial period until 1991. This supports the argument of this chapter that in the presence of direct access to R (in the model represented by $y(0, R) \geq 0$) and due to the destruction of the *petit bourgeoisie* during the civil war, no group in Somalia has an interest in the resurrection of central state authority. This accounts for the fact that the recent attempts to unify Somalia originated from either a highly ideological group (the Islamic courts movement) or the Ethiopian military intervention that ousted the Islamic courts from Mogadishu.

---

[8] However, there are net social benefits to the restoration of central authority in Somlia, especially in the realm of public goods provision. For example, in education where two of its indicators (literacy rates and school enrollment) got worse during the stateless period, the prominence of for profit private activity excludes these benefits from being prominent in the various groups' welfare functions.

4.6 Concluding Remarks

Although the long-run relationship between democracy and economic development is viewed by many observers as positive (e.g. Olson 1993), it is governed by the design of specific institutions that prevent rent-seeking or violent behaviour on the part of individuals or groups (McGuire and Olson 1996). This chapter has shown that the level of resource availability plays a role in formulating the desire of groups for setting up state authority. In Iraq, the new government is being designed along the lines of a consociational democracy where all ethnic groups are represented through a government of national unity at least as of May 2006. According to our model, Iraq's abundance of resources and the high productivity of combining R and G make this attempt tenable.[9] However, the denominational politics generated by ethnic representation fails to produce stability because 'conflict' over resources is compounded by geography, and is thus usurping all plans for a stable consociational democracy.[10] In Somalia, on the other hand, the lack of resources, the direct access of producers to resources, and the low productivity and redistributional potential of combining R and G do not provide the various groups with adequate material incentive for the resurrection of central authority.

The theoretical model and country experiences introduced a central question with regard to the relationship between state failure, governance, and economic development in fragile multi-ethnic states. The failure to produce, either through inter-ethnic political or violent mediation and bargaining, a stable political and governance structure can have a negative impact on economic growth and development in the post-conflict period. In Iraq, the destabilizing force generated by ethnic rivalry over the control of resources (the Shia in the south, Kurds in the north, the conflict over Kirkuk, Sunnis in central region without acknowledged reserves) is threatening to break apart the country. The Baker-Hamilton Report observes that the 'Shia, Sunni and Kurdish leaders frequently fail to ... act in Iraq's national interest ... The result is an even weaker central government than the constitution provides' (2006: 13).

Formulation of a national economic development plan designed and implemented by a secular central government is necessary for transcending such divisions. Such a development plan need not resurrect autocracy in Iraq, nor

---

[9] The model predicted a process of building a consociational democracy in Iraq due to resource and government interdependency. It does not, however, consider the complexity involved in the bringing of such a project to fruition. Such a constitution-making process and its complexity, given the position of Kurdistan in a possible federal state, was studied by McGarry (2006), O'Leary (2006), and Eklund et al. (2006).

[10] It was noted by McGarry and O'Leary (1994) that federalism is not very successful in regulating conflict between ethnic groups in polyethnic states despite its attractiveness as a democratic solution to the problem of regulation of ethnic conflict.

introduce re-Baathification, even though it has been observed in the economic sphere that, at one time, there was a tendency on the part of the bureaucracy to revamp Baathist economic policy (Looney 2004b). The Iraqi question can be solved through the establishment of an all-encompassing democracy, as McGuire and Olson (1996) theoretically discuss. Such a system would ensure the elimination of inefficiencies and the growth-impeding politics of interest groups. The establishment of a developmental state is imperative for Iraq's economic progress, as is the necessity of secular national politics. In addition, integrating Iraq with the international economy necessitates the existence of a centripetal force, represented by strong central government, to counteract the centrifugal forces unleashed by the channels of economic exchange that have been established between the various ethnic groups and the global economy through state oil resources and foreign funds for post-war reconstruction.[11] In the Somali case, although anarchy seems to be working, it is an unstable system, as indicated by the recent chain of events, starting with the Islamic courts takeover to the Ethiopian invasion. The establishment of an all-encompassing democracy can also be a solution to the seemingly intractable Somali question.

References

Anderson, L. and G. Stansfield (2005). 'The Implications of Elections for Federalism in Iraq: Toward a Five-Region Model'. *Publius*, 35 (3): 359–82.

Aslaksen, A. and R. Torvik (2006). 'A Theory of Civil Conflict and Democracy in Rentier States'. *Scandinavian Journal of Economics*, 198 (4): 571–85.

Bhaduri, A. (2002). 'Nationalism and Economic Policy in an Era of Globalization'. In D. Nayyar (ed.), *Governing Globalization: Issues and Institutions*. Oxford: Oxford University Press for UNU-WIDER.

Binningsbo, H. M. (2005). 'Consociational Democracy and Post-Conflict Peace. Will Power-Sharing Institutions Increase the Probability of Lasting Peace after Civil War?' Paper presented at the 13th Annual National Political Science Conference, Hurdalsjøen, Norway, 5–7 January.

Birdsall, N. and A. Subramanian (2004). 'Saving Iraq from its Oil'. *Foreign Affairs* 83 (4): 77–89.

Bremmer, L. P. (2006). *My Year in Iraq: The Struggle to Build a Future of Hope*. New York: Simon and Schuster Trade.

Burnham, G., R. Lafta, S. Doocy, and L. Roberts (2006). 'Mortality after the 2003 Invasion of Iraq: A Cross-Sectional Cluster Sample Survey'. *The Lancet*, 368 (9545): 1421–8.

Chomsky, N. (2006). *Failed States*. New York: Henry Holt.

Cockburn, P. (2006). *The Occupation: War and Resistance in Iraq*. London: Verso.

---

[11] See a discussion on the theoretical relationship between globalization and national economic policy in Bhaduri (2002).

Collier, P. and A. Hoeffler (2001). 'Greed and Grievance in Civil War'. World Bank Policy Research Paper No. 2355. Washington, DC: World Bank.

Collier, P. and A. Hoeffler (2005). 'Democracy and Resource Rents'. Global Poverty Research Group Working Paper No. 016. Oxford: Global Poverty Research Group.

Crusoe, J. (1989). 'Iraq: MEED Profile'. *The Middle East Economics Digest*, February.

DFID (Department for International Development) (2005). *Why We Need to Work More in Fragile States*. London: DFID.

Dibeh, G. (2005). 'The Political Economy of Post-War Reconstruction in Lebanon'. WIDER Research Paper 2005/44. Helsinki: UNU-WIDER.

Downes, A. B. (2006). 'More Borders, Less Conflict? Partition and a Solution to Ethnic Civil Wars'. *SAIS Review*, 26 (1): 49–61.

Eggertsson, T. (1990). *Economic Behaviour and Institutions*. Cambridge: Cambridge University Press.

EIU (Economist Intelligence Unit) (various years). *Country Profile: Iraq 86–87 and 1989–90*. London: The Economist Publication Unit.

Eklund, K., B. O'Leary, and P. R. Williams (2006) 'Negotiating a Federation in Iraq'. In B. O'Leary, J. McGarry, and K. Salih (eds), *The Future of Kurdistan*. Philadelphia, PA: University of Pennsylvania Press.

Feldman, N. (2006). *What We Owe Iraq: War and the Ethics of Nation Building*. Princeton: Princeton University Press.

Findlay, R. (1989). 'Is the New Political Economy Relevant to Developing Countries'. World Bank Policy Research Working Paper No. 292. Washington, DC: World Bank.

Foote, C., W. Block, G. Crane, and S. Gray (2004). 'Economic Policy and Prospects in Iraq'. *Journal of Economic Perspectives*, 18 (3): 47–70.

Foreign Policy (2005). 'The Failed States Index Rankings by Foreign Policy and the Fund for Peace'. <http//blog.foreignpolicy.com/fsi_06/fsi06.html>.

Heal, G. (2007). 'Are Oil Producers Rich?' In M. Humphreys, J. D. Sachs, and J. E. Stiglitz (eds), *Escaping the Resource Curse*. New York: Columbia University Press.

Horowitz, D. (1985) *Ethnic Groups in Conflict*. Berkeley: University of California Press.

IMF (International Monetary Fund) (2009). 'Review of the Fund's Strategy on Overdue Financial Obligations', 18 August. New York: IMF.

Iraq Study Group (2006). *Iraq Study Group Report*. Washington, DC: Iraq Study Group.

Juhasz, A. and R. Jarrar (2007). 'Oil Grab in Iraq'. Federation of Property Information Providers Commentary, 22 February. Available at: <http://www.informationclearinghouse.info/article17193.htm>.

Kanovsky, E. (1983). *The Iran–Iraq War: Its Economic Implications*. Tel Aviv: Shiloah Center for Middle Eastern and African Studies.

Karras, G. (1996). 'The Optimal Government Size: Further International Evidence of the Productivity of Government Services'. *Economic Inquiry*, 34: 193–203.

Khafaji, I. (1983). *Al Dawla Watatawor al-Rasimali fi al-Iraq: 1968–1978*. Tokyo: United Nations University.

Leeson, P. (2006). 'Better Off Stateless: Somalia Before and After Government Collapse'. Working Paper. Fairfax. Department of Economics, George Mason University. Available at: <www//papers.ssrn.com/sol3/papers.cfm?abstract_id%20=879798>.

Leeson, P. T. (2007). 'Efficient Anarchy'. *Public Choice*, 130 (1–2): 41–53.

Lijphart, A. (1969). 'Consociational Democracy'. *World Politics*, 21: 207–25.

Looney, R. (2004a). 'Neoliberalism in a Conflict State: The Viability of Economic Shock Therapy in Iraq'. *Strategic Insights*, June, 3 (6): 1–11.

Looney, R. (2004b). 'A Return to Baathist Economics? Escaping Vicious Circles in Iraq'. *Strategic Insights*, July, 3 (7).

Looney, R. (2006). 'The Economics of Iraqi Reconstruction'. *Strategic Insights*, May, 5 (5).

McGuire, M. and M. Olson (1996). 'The Economics of Autocracy and Majority Rule: The Invisible Hand and the Use of Force'. *Journal of Economic Literature*, March, 34: 72–96.

Menkhaus, K. (1995). 'The Stateless'. *Africa Report*, May–June, 22–5.

Menkhaus, K. (2003). 'State Collapse in Somalia: Second Thoughts'. *Review of African Political Economy*, 30 (97): 405–22.

McGarry, J. (2006) 'Canadian Lessons for Iraq'. In B. O'Leary, J. McGarry, and K. Salih (eds), *The Future of Kurdistan*. Philadelphia, PA: University of Pennsylvania Press.

McGarry, J. and B. O'Leary (1994) 'The Political Regulation of National and Ethnic Conflict', *Parliamentary Affairs*, 47(1): 94–115.

Mubarak, J. (1997). 'The "Hidden Hand" behind the Resilience of the Stateless Economy of Somalia'. *World Development*, 25 (12): 2027–41.

O'Leary, B. (2006) 'Power Sharing, Pluralist Federation and Federacy'. In B. O'Leary, J. McGarry, and K. Salih (eds), *The Future of Kurdistan*. Philadelphia, PA: University of Pennsylvania Press.

Olson, M. (1982). *The Rise and Decline of Nations*. New Haven: Yale University Press.

Olson, M. (1993). 'Dictatorship, Democracy and Development'. *American Political Science Review*, 87 (3): 567–76.

Olsson, O. (2007). 'Conflict Diamonds'. *Journal of Development Economics*, 87 (2): 267–86.

Owen, R. and S. Pamuk (1998). *A History of Middle East Economies in the Twentieth Century*. London: I. B. Tauris.

Posner, D. N. (2005). *Institutions and Ethnic Politics in Africa*. New York: Cambridge University Press.

Powell, B., R. Ford, and A. Nowrasteh (2006). 'Somalia after State Collapse: Chaos or Improvement? Independent Institute Working Paper No. 64. Oakland: Independent Institute.

Przeworski, A. (1991). *Democracy and the Market*. New York: Cambridge University Press.

Rostow, W. W. (1960). *The Stages of Economic Growth*. New York: Cambridge University Press.

Samatar, A. I. (1993). 'Structural Adjustment as Development Strategy? Bananas, Boom, and Poverty in Somalia'. *Economic Geography*, 69 (1): 25–43.

Stansfield, G. (2005). 'The Transition to Democracy in Iraq: Historical Legacies, Resurgent Identities and Reactionary Tendencies'. In A. Danchev and J. McMillan (eds), *The Iraq War and Democratic Politics*. London: Routledge, 134–59.

Tavits, M. (2004). 'The Size of Government in Majoritarian and Consensus Democracies'. *Comparative Political Studies*, 37 (3): 340–59.

Torvik, R. (2002). 'Natural Resources, Rent Seeking and Welfare'. *Journal of Development Economics*, 67 (2): 455–70.

Tsafos, N. E. (2006). 'Geography and Oil Politics in Iraq'. *SAIS Review*, 26 (1): 63–4.

Zubeida, S. (2006). 'Sood wa Inhiar Al-Mujtamaa Al-Madani fi Al-Iraq'. In *Iraqi Society: Sociological Inquiry into Ethnicity, Confessions and Classes* (in Arabic). Beirut: Center for Strategic Studies, 93–117.

Part II
Costs

5

The Cost of Failing States and the Limits to Sovereignty

Lisa Chauvet, Paul Collier, and Anke Hoeffler

5.1 Introduction

In this chapter we estimate the costs of a 'failing state'. Such costs are of evident interest because they are a necessary first step towards a cost–benefit analysis of remedies. However, the costs of a failing state may also have a more fundamental significance. If state failure produces large spillover costs to neighbours there may be good reason to rethink the conceptual foundations of sovereignty, shifting some sovereignty from the nation to the region, and in the process empowering international intervention.

The most basic role of the state is to provide physical security to its citizens through maintaining a monopoly of organized violence within the society. Where the government fails to do this and rival organizations of violence emerge, the state descends into civil war. However, in the modern world the demands legitimately placed upon the state extend beyond this basic function of security. Governments in all modern societies play some role as regulators of private economic activity, and as suppliers of public goods such as transport infrastructure, health, and education. The quality of regulation and public goods is important for the capacity of citizens to earn a living. Increasingly, as globalization makes economic activity more mobile between countries, the quality of government matters in a relative rather than an absolute sense: governments that are much worse than others are likely to lose economic activities and this will rebound upon their citizens. Hence, a state can fail because its government provides a quality of regulation and public goods which is markedly worse than that provided by other governments. Throughout this chapter we are agnostic as to *why* states fail and concentrate on estimating the costs of state failure.

Some of the costs of failure arise from organized violence. Such costs are likely to be different from the costs arising from a failure of governance. In addition to these costs we also consider spillover effects to neighbouring countries. In the next section we consider these three distinct costs in more detail and the following three sections quantify each of these costs in turn. We conclude by drawing out the implications.

5.2 Failing States And Sovereignty

States can 'fail' in three distinct ways: they can hurt citizens in neighbouring countries, they can fail to provide basic security for their own citizens, and they can fail to provide an environment in which poverty reduction is feasible. We take these in turn.

In an inter-connected world, social and economic catastrophe in one country spills over onto neighbours. This contrasts with the state of the world when the concept of national sovereignty was formulated in the seventeenth century. Then, both a nation's economy and its society were very largely independent of other nations. Sovereignty as traditionally formulated thus does not take into account the costs that catastrophe inflicts on other countries. If these costs are 'large', the governments of such countries have a reasonable claim to the right of intervention in order to reduce them. Regardless of the rights of governments to inflict costs on their own citizens, it would be a radical extension of the concept of sovereignty for them to have the right to inflict large costs on neighbours. The magnitude of spillover costs is critical. Since all states inflict *some* costs on neighbours, only if they occasionally exceed a high threshold can such costs constitute an operational qualification to sovereignty.

The second basis for a dilution of sovereignty is the global concern to mitigate social catastrophe in any country. This may primarily be a response to the globalization of television news coverage. In September 2005 the UN unanimously endorsed the *Responsibility to Protect*, which creates the right to intervene if a government relinquishes its responsibility to protect, whether by lack of will or lack of capacity.[1] 'Responsibility to protect' is defined as protection of citizens from large-scale violent conflict that the government is either unwilling to prevent or incapable of preventing, but which international intervention could feasibly curtail. While international concern is

---

[1] The full text of UN Resolution A/RES/60/1 can be found at: <http://www//daccessdds.un.org/doc/UNDOC/GEN/N05/487/60/PDF/N0548760.pdf?OpenElement>.
The responsibility to protect populations from genocide, war crimes, ethnic cleansing, and crimes against humanity is set out in paragraphs 138 and 139.

recent, the concept of the state as providing security to its citizens through the possession of a monopoly on violence is at the root of the traditional conception of what constitutes a state. Governments that do not provide such a monopoly are thus 'failing' in this fundamental sense.

The third basis for a dilution of sovereignty is a counterpart to the responsibility proposed by the UN to provide aid to assist poverty reduction. Underpinning the norm that the governments of OECD countries should contribute 0.7 per cent of GDP as aid, is that in the extreme conditions of low-income countries, poverty reduction is not exclusively a national responsibility. Implicit in this responsibility of OECD countries to provide finance was a counterpart responsibility of the governments of low-income countries to manage their affairs in such a way as to be conducive to poverty reduction. These twin responsibilities of aid and governance were formally recognized in the *Monterrey Consensus* of 2000. Just as some OECD states are failing to provide the level of aid judged to be adequate for poverty reduction, so some governments of low-income countries are failing to provide policies and governance judged to be adequate and this failing inflicts avoidable poverty on their citizens. The threshold of policies and governance necessary for poverty reduction is intrinsically less clear cut than that for aid. Nevertheless, there is now a reasonable internationally generated threshold, namely that used by the World Bank to define low-income countries under stress (LICUS). LICUS are defined using the annual global rating of policies and governance known as the country policies and institutional assessment (CPIA) (World Bank 2002). Despite limitations, the CPIA is a serious professional attempt to provide a rating that is comparable both between countries and over time. Nor is the concept of an identifiable class of countries in which the government is failing to provide an adequate environment for poverty reduction confined to the World Bank. The Development Assistance Committee of the OECD, which represents all bilateral aid programmes, adopted the closely equivalent concept of *Difficult Partnerships*. An identifiable group of governments of low-income countries can thus reasonably be described as failing to provide an adequate environment for the attainment of the objective of the reduction of severe poverty. In turn, the international community has judged this objective to warrant international pressure for governments to meet target norms. Just as international pressure for the governments of OECD countries to meet a norm of aid finance is legitimate, so potentially it is legitimate to bring pressure on those governments that fail to meet a norm of policies and governance. Whether a governance threshold should be treated as a responsibility equivalent to an aid threshold depends again upon the scale of the costs inflicted by failure. If the costs of such failures of government are modest relative to aid, then the interventions implicit in concerns about them would be unwarranted interference.

There are thus three distinct types of cost that might define a failing state. Costs inflicted on neighbouring citizens, violence avoidably suffered by the state's own citizens, and poverty avoidably suffered by the state's own citizens. Where any of these costs are large there is a basis for qualifying sovereignty because they would either breach the rights or trigger the responsibilities of other states.

In the following sections we quantify these three types of cost: neighbourhood spillovers, internal violence, and poverty. We show that not only is each of these costs large, but the same conditions generate all three costs. The results have two important implications. One is that because the costs are large, international intervention that shares or even overrides the claims of sovereignty is likely to be justified. The second is that all three criteria support a common working definition of failing states: a definable class of governments should not be regarded as being fully sovereign.

The first cost we quantify is the poverty generated by policies and governance that are below the threshold set by the criteria for LICUS. We begin here because to a considerable extent the problem of large-scale internal violence, which is the second cost we quantify, turns out to be a by-product of this persistent poverty. Hence, the same conditions generate both persistent poverty and a high risk of violence. The third cost, spillovers to neighbours, turns out to be generated by both the stagnation common to LICUS, and large-scale violence.

5.3 The Cost To Citizens Of Failing States Of Weak Policies And Governance

Economic policies and governance differ massively between countries. Chauvet and Collier (2006) examine the opportunities for reform in failing states and provide some evidence that the most commonly found binding constraint is 'political will' due to a clash between elite interests and those of wider society. A further possibility of the underlying reasons for state failure is the lack of capacity to reform. However, in this chapter we are not primarily concerned with the question of why states fail or what can be done about it but which costs they inflict on their citizens and those of neighbouring states.

As suggested by Chauvet and Collier (2006), poor policies and governance are themselves the consequence of other factors such as particular configurations of interest groups. These deeper factors may reduce growth directly as well as via policies and governance. As a result, an apparent improvement that is divorced from underlying change may have only modest effects on growth. For example, interest groups may use other instruments to achieve their objectives and these may also be detrimental to growth. The poor policies and governance that define failing states should thus probably be regarded as the observable manifestations of a dysfunctional society. They can be thought of as lying on a continuum determined by their likely consequences for growth and poverty reduction. Potentially, a government fails if it adopts policies and governance that persistently fall below some low threshold and so inflicts slow growth or even absolute economic decline on its citizens. We adopt the World Bank criterion for LICUS as defining such a threshold and combine it with a concept of *persistence* of such poor policies and governance. To meet our criterion of persistence a country must fall below the LICUS threshold for a continuous period of at least four years. This is designed to exclude from the category of failing states those that merely suffer a temporary crash. Analogously, we wish to retain in the category of failing states those that having been below the LICUS threshold temporarily or weakly improve policies and governance a little above the threshold. A country exits the category of failing state only if it achieves a decisive improvement, by which we mean sustaining a level of policies and governance clearly above the threshold for at least three years. So defined, during the period 1998–2001 there were 23 such failing states which collectively accounted for only 7 per cent of the population of the developing world. We should note, however, that some countries that are evidently failing states on this criterion have been omitted due to missing data. Data are systematically more likely to be lacking if the state is failing. The most notable such omissions are Afghanistan and North Korea. Hence, the figure of 7 per cent is liable to be an underestimate with the true figure perhaps around 10 per cent.

A likely, though not inevitable, consequence of this level of policies and governance is that there is a failure in the normal growth process. Over the period 1990–2001 the average per capita growth rate of non-LICUS countries was 2.8 per cent whereas that in LICUS was only −0.06 per cent, in other words zero. The exceptions to this presumption of stagnation are generally associated with natural resource discoveries: for example, Equatorial Guinea has been able to have a high rate of GDP growth despite very weak policies and governance because off-shore oil production has come to dominate its small economy. Such stagnation only becomes critical in conjunction with both initially low income and the prolonged persistence of the inadequate policies and governance. The combination evidently results in persistent poverty. The same weak policies and governance in a country that was already at middle-income levels would not have such serious consequences. Hence, it is not that the international community should attach value to 'adequate' policies and governance in themselves, but rather that they become significant in the context of initially low income. In practical terms, policy-induced stagnation in the Middle East is of far less concern for the objective of global poverty reduction than policy-induced stagnation in Africa.

Our criteria of persistence have excluded by definition both temporary crashes that swiftly rebound and temporary improvements that quickly collapse, but they do not necessarily imply that the phase of inadequate policies and governance is prolonged. Chauvet and Collier (2005) use a logit regression to estimate the probability that a failing state will achieve a decisive exit from the condition. A few characteristics make exit significantly less likely: a small population and a low incidence of secondary education. In effect, turnaround is made harder if there are in absolute terms few well-educated people in the society. Compared with other developing countries the typical failing state indeed has both of the characteristics that predict persistence. The typical failing state has a population of only 15 million as compared with 42 million for elsewhere, and a far lower proportion of its population has completed secondary education: 3 per cent against 12 per cent for other developing countries. At the mean of failing state characteristics the predicted annual probability of exit is a mere 1.7 per cent. In turn, this probability can be converted into the mathematical expectation of the duration of being a failing state: in effect, how long the typical failing state will remain in the condition. The expectation is 59 years. Hence, the typical low-income failing state will indeed experience a prolonged period in which policies and governance are inadequate and so a high incidence of poverty is likely to be prolonged.

During the period 1998–2001 despite accounting for only 7 per cent of the population of the developing world, the LICUS countries accounted for 15 per cent of the number of people globally living in absolute poverty of less than one dollar per day: their incidence of poverty was 40 per cent as compared to only 20 per cent in the other developing countries. However, this radically understates the importance of LICUS for global poverty. As stressed by Wood (2008), the challenge of global poverty must be understood in a dynamic context. Essentially, the objective is to minimize the number of person-years in poverty. Because the non-LICUS developing countries are generally growing quite rapidly, even though they currently have considerable poverty this is not likely to be persistent. If the growth rates noted above persist, then by 2015 per capita income will have increased from 2004 levels by 47 per cent in non-LICUS countries while being unchanged in LICUS. The elasticity of headcount poverty with respect to mean per capita income is around -2.0 (Ravallion and Chen 1997; Bourguignon 2000). Hence, the incidence of poverty can be expected to decline by approximately 5.6 per cent per year in non-LICUS countries while remaining constant in LICUS. By that time the LICUS countries would account for around 29 per cent of poverty instead of 15 per cent as of 2001. If these different growth rates persisted for a further decade, then in 2025 LICUS would account for around 42 per cent. Recall that these are likely to be underestimates because of the omission of countries such as Afghanistan and North Korea. While such a projection to 2025 is evidently fraught with uncertainties, the past extreme persistence of the condition of being a failing state suggests that it is not completely unreasonable. As Wood discusses, quite how poverty is aggregated over the future depends upon choices such as the discount rate. However, on any reasonable discounting of the future it is clear that LICUS are a major part of the poverty challenge. Further, the very fact that so much poverty is concentrated in a few countries offers the potential for a highly focused strategy for poverty reduction. Growth in these countries is going to become increasingly effective relative to growth in other developing countries in reducing poverty.

The OECD is currently providing aid to developing countries of the order of US$80 billion. Were all OECD countries to meet the UN target of 0.7 per cent of GDP, aid would be increased by around US$135 billion. How do these figures compare with the costs inflicted on the citizens of failing states by poor policies and governance? To establish the latter we adopt the approach previously followed by Chauvet and Collier (2005), but using numbers specific to the present problem.

First, in Table 5.1 we introduce a dummy variable for failing states into a growth regression covering a global sample of developing countries over the period 1974–2001. Because we wish to have a single regression which can be used for all the costs to be considered, we confine the present concept of failing states to those which are at peace, and introduce a second dummy for those which are also in civil war. We also include dummy variables for neighbourhood spillovers. These other dummy variables will be discussed in subsequent sections. Our core regression is Ordinary Least Squares (OLS). However, to check the robustness of the results we repeat the regression using GMM. The results of both regressions are reported in Table 5.1. Our key result is confirmed: being a failing state at peace significantly reduces the growth rate by 2.6 per cent relative to being at peace with adequate policies and governance.[2] Note that this estimate of the loss of growth is very close to the difference cited above between the average failing state and the average for other developing countries during the period 1990–2001. The 90 per cent confidence interval around this estimate, which we can use to provide confidence intervals around our estimates of cost, is also shown in the table. In Appendix 5.A1, we also provide some robustness checks on the specification by adding controls for education and investment, which are conventional growth determinants, and a measure of the degree of democracy. Note that we do not introduce either policy variables such as openness, inflation, and the

---

[2] The coefficients on income and the non-failing state at war dummy are no longer significant, however these variables have no impact on our cost of state failure. The coeffient on the proportion of neighbours being FS at war is larger in the GMM estimation. We use the OLS coefficient for our calculations, resulting in conservative cost estimates.

Table 5.1. Growth effect of failing states, 1974–2001

		OLS		SYS-GMM
	(1)	90 per cent confidence interval		(2)
Income per capita, t-4	−0.008 (3.50)***	−0.012	−0.005	−0.005 (1.08)
Dummy non-failing states countries at war	−0.013 (3.02)***	−0.021	−0.006	−0.008 (0.83)
Dummy failing states at war	−0.042 (4.87)***	−0.056	−0.028	−0.033 (2.56)**
Dummy failing states at peace	−0.026 (6.96)***	−0.032	−0.020	−0.024 (3.64)***
Proportion of neighbours being FS at war	−0.018 (2.20)**	−0.032	−0.005	−0.062 (3.09)***
Proportion of neighbours being FS at peace	−0.018 (3.70)***	−0.026	−0.010	−0.021 (1.94)*
Constant	0.105 (4.89)***	0.070	0.140	0.077 (2.22)**
Observations	600			600
R-squared	0.17			
Number of countries	105			105
Hansen test of over-identification (p-value)				0.79
Number of instruments				116
AR(1) (p-value)				0.001
AR(2) (p-value)				0.507

Notes: Regression (1) is estimated with OLS. Regression (2) is estimated with System-GMM (Blundell and Bond 1998). All right-hand side variables are instrumented. Robust t statistics in parentheses.

* significant at 10%;

** significant at 5%;

*** significant at 1%. Dependent variable: growth rate of real income per capita, Penn World Tables 6.1. All regressions include time dummies.

Source: See text.

budget surplus, or institutional variables such as corruption and the rule of law, since these are already subsumed in the concept of a failing state and so incorporated into our dummy variable. None of these variants alters the results: the level of significance is sometimes reduced but the coefficients are always close to those of our baseline regression.

We then combine this loss of growth with our estimate of the probability of a decisive turnaround from the condition, namely 1.7 per cent per year. For example, if a failing state is very fortunate, in the first year it will lose 2.6 per cent of GDP relative to the counterfactual of adequate policies whereupon it will achieve a decisive turnaround.

The ultimate costs of having been a failing state then depend upon what is assumed about post-turnaround recovery. At one extreme, growth post-turnaround is merely the same as if the country had always had adequate policies. In this case the loss is perpetual: every year in the future the country is 2.6 per cent worse off than if it had not had the phase of inadequate policies and governance. We adopt the more hopeful, and probably more reasonable, assumption that during the recovery phase growth is unusually rapid: the economy recovers to where it would have been without the failing state phase, and the recovery takes as many years as that phase has lasted. The cost of having been a failing state is then the loss of GDP in each year until the economy attains the level it would have reached had it not been a failing state, discounted to the present. We adopt a discount rate of 5 per cent. We allow for the possibility of turnaround in each year, weighted by the probability that a turnaround will occur in that year, and sum across all of these possible paths of development. This generates the mathematic expectation of the discounted present value of the cost of being a failing state, viewed from the first year in which the country enters the condition (see Appendix for details).[3] Our central estimate of the costs of the typical LICUS-at-peace is US$28 billion, with the 90 per cent confidence interval from the growth regression giving a range of US$23 billion to US$32 billion. Table 5.2 summarizes these results.

Even when we limit our analysis to those countries for which we have complete data there are 23 such states. Thus, our central estimate of the present value of the cost of failing states from the loss of GDP implied by inadequate policies and governance is 23 times the cost per country, namely US$640 billion. Since this is a stock, to convert it into a sustainable flow comparable to global aid we again use a 5 per cent interest rate. Thus, were all failing states to achieve decisive change the gain would be approximately equivalent to a permanent income stream of US$32 billion per year. The likely correction for the omission of countries which lack data would increase this to around US$40 billion. Recall that this compares to aid levels of around US$80 billion. Since the gain would accrue exclusively to states with the highest incidence of poverty, it would be much better targeted than aid, much of which accrues to middle-income countries. Hence, were failing states to improve their policies and governance to the level prevailing in other developing countries, the pay-off, though less than the value of current aid flows, would be of the same order of magnitude. Thus, on the criterion of global poverty reduction these costs of failing states are sufficiently commensurate with aid to warrant a broad normative equivalence between the responsibility of OECD countries to provide aid and the responsibility of developing countries to provide adequate environments for economic development. Indeed, whereas aid has an evident opportunity cost in terms of the diversion of OECD government revenues from other uses, the reform of policy and

---

[3] The convergence term in the growth estimations creates an inconsistency between the way we calculate the cost in the Appendix—which does not account for any convergence—and our growth estimations. To check the robustness, we estimated regressions (1) and (2) of Table 5.1 without the convergence term. The results are very similar to those with the term. We thank Henrik Hansen for this comment.

Table 5.2. Cost of failing states

	NPV as a proportion of initial income that is lost due to failure	NPV of loss for typical FS/typical neighbour, in terms of the average GDP of FS at peace (US$5.5bn)/neighbour of FS (US$39.7bn)	NPV of losses of all neighbours of typical FS (n = 3.5)	NPV of losses generated by global total of FS (n = 23)
	(in %)	(in billion US$)	(in billion US$)	(in billion US$)
Failing state				
Growth loss = −0.026	506	27.8		640[a]
Growth loss = −0.032	585	32.2		740
Growth loss = −0.020	416	22.9		526
Violence				
Growth loss	64.4			70
DALYs				74
Total loss				144[b]
Neighbours				
Growth loss = −0.006 [1]	148	59	206	4,732[c]
Growth loss = −0.009 [2]	206	82	287	6,598
Growth loss = −0.003 [2]	86	34	119	2,727
Total NPV (a) + (b) + (c)				5,516
Cost per year				276

Notes: Shaded cells: calculations using the 90% confidence interval results of Table 5.1.
[1] Coefficients given in Table 5.1 (0.018) multiplied by the average proportion of neighbours that are failing states (0.33).
[2] Calculated from the confidence interval for the proportion of neighbours that are FS at peace (0.026*0.33 and 0.010*0.33).

Source: See text.

governance, while it might damage some interests, has no equivalent broad social cost.

5.4 The Cost To Citizens Of Failing States Of Large-Scale Violence

We now turn to the second cost of a failing state, namely an enhanced risk of large-scale internal violence. For this we base our approach on that of Collier and Hoeffler (2004a), but again using numbers specific to the present problem.

We continue to define a failing state on the basis of our previous criteria, except that now we confine the analysis to those states that are at war instead of those that are at peace. From the regressions reported in Table 5.1, the incremental loss to growth of a failing state that switches from peace to war is a further reduction in growth of 1.6 per cent. The typical civil war lasts around seven years (Collier et al. 2004). As with failing states at peace, the costs depend critically upon what is assumed about subsequent recovery. There is reasonable evidence that in the typical post-conflict situation the economy has a phase of above-normal growth (Collier and Hoeffler 2004b), and based on this we assume that the economy fully recovers its pre-war growth path over a ten-year recovery period, with supra-normal growth of 1.1 per cent per year. Hence, purely in terms of loss of GDP, many of the costs of war occur after it is over: income is lower than it would have been for a prolonged period. We then discount these annual costs incurred during and after the war back to the time of war onset and express it as a present value. So measured, the loss of GDP consequent upon a civil war in a country that is in any case a failing state due to poor policies and governance, is US$4.8 billion.

We next estimate the incidence of civil war among failing states. For this we rely upon a model that estimates the risk of civil war developed by Collier and Hoeffler (2004c). Based on global data for the period 1965–99 they analyse the onset of 54 civil wars in terms of characteristics observable prior to the conflict and predict the risk facing each country for each five-year period. Among these characteristics, three that are distinctive features of failing states are significant. These are low per capita income, slow growth, and a small population. Keeping other characteristics constant at the mean for all low-income developing countries, we use the model to predict the risk of civil war, first with the characteristics of failing states, and then with the alternative characteristics for the average of other developing countries. The risk for the typical failing state is 15.9 per cent per five-year period, as compared to only 7.8 per cent for other developing countries. Thus, with 23 failing states and an average five-year risk of 15.9 per cent, in the typical year 0.73 civil wars can be expected to break out, with an average cost of US$4.8 billion. Hence, the cost of civil war in failing states, purely in terms of the loss of GDP in those states, is around US$3.5 billion per year.

Of course, these economic costs of civil war do not fully capture the cost as perceived by the international community. Countries that contribute to the very high level of international peacekeeping forces are in general not motivated primarily by a desire to avoid these economic costs, but rather by the desire to reduce mortality within the affected countries. Civil wars substantially increase mortality. Only a small part of this is due to deaths directly caused by combat. Most mortality is due to the increased incidence of disease. This in turn is caused partly by the weakening of public health systems, for example, it may no longer be possible to conduct vaccinations in combat areas. Additionally, civil war generates refugees, and the mass movement of refugees across territories in which they lack acquired immunity to infection, spreads disease. Since these effects are highly persistent, much of the mortality attributable to civil war occurs once it is over. Taking these effects into account, Collier and Hoeffler (2004a) estimate that the value of the loss of life caused by the typical civil war is around US$5 billion. We should note that in making this estimate they use a very low valuation of a year of life of only US$1,000. As, in the typical year, 0.73 civil wars can be expected to break out, the annual value of the loss of life caused by war is US$3.7 billion. Adding US$3.7 billion to the cost of the typical civil war estimated above increases the estimate of the annual cost of war from US$3.5 billion to US$7.2 billion. Since these are annual flows we accumulate them into a total stock, assuming as previously a discount rate of 5 per cent. Thus, the net present value of the cost of violence is calculated at US$144 billion. Even with this additional layer of costs, the costs of civil war to citizens of failing states do not come close to the costs of poor policies and governance. To the extent that the welfare of the citizens of failing states is the motivating concern for international intervention, it is therefore not enough just to ensure that these societies are peaceful. If intervention is warranted on these grounds, its primary concern must be to change policies and governance.

While failing states are not the only source of civil war, they account for a disproportionate amount of it, just as they account for a disproportionate amount of poverty. The incidence of civil war in developed countries is negligible, so for practical purposes the costs of civil war are generated entirely in developing countries. Although failing states account for only 7 per cent of the population of developing countries, based on the differential risks discussed above, they account for half of the civil wars. Just as the challenge of poverty reduction needs to be considered in a dynamic context, so does the reduction of the incidence of civil war. The growth that other developing countries are on average experiencing is cumulatively further reducing their risk of civil war because higher levels of income reduce risk. Repeating the calculation of section 5.3, by 2015 the increase in per capita income in other regions of 47 per cent will have reduced the risk of conflict in those countries by 29 per cent, whereas if the failing states continue to stagnate, the risks will remain at their present high level. The share of global civil war accounted for by the failing states will rise to 60 per cent. On the same basis, by 2025 failing states would account for two-thirds of all civil wars.

Evidently, the distinctively high risk of civil war in failing states is attributable to their distinctive attributes. The stagnation that is a consequence of poor policies and governance prevents risks declining as a result of growth. However, risks are also heightened because the typical failing state has a much smaller population than other developing states. The risk of civil war is considerably increased if a region is divided into many small countries. An interesting counterfactual that captures this effect is to estimate the incidence of civil war treating all failing states as if they were a region, and then changing the characteristics of the 'region' to those prevailing in other developing regions. To complete the thought experiment, we start all countries from peace and consider the number of wars that begin during the first five-year period. The 'failing region' experiences 3.7 outbreaks of civil war, whereas in a developing region with the same total population but the characteristics of other developing areas the incidence would be halved to 1.8 outbreaks. Note that part of this higher incidence is due to the small population of failing states. Thus, the sovereignty of failing states may need to be called into question not only because the choices of their governments have such important consequences, but because part of the solution may be to pool sovereignty with neighbours, who may themselves be failing states, to generate larger nations.

5.5 The Costs To Neighbours

We now turn to the third cost, namely that inflicted on neighbours. Neighbours suffer a variety of costs from failing states, but here we concentrate upon the economic losses. Globally, growth spills over onto neighbours. On average, if all of a country's neighbours grow at an additional one per cent, the country's growth rate is increased by 0.4 per cent (Collier and O'Connell 2007). Since being a failing state reduces growth, we would therefore expect neighbours to suffer reduced growth. We estimate the costs to neighbours by introducing the proportion of neighbouring countries that are failing states into the growth regression of Table 5.1. We distinguish between whether the state is failing only in the sense of having poor policies and governance, or whether it is also at civil war. In the OLS regression, in each case being the neighbour of a failing state significantly reduces growth. Potentially, the dummy variables may be proxying geographic effects that are common to failing states and their neighbours rather than indicating a causal relationship. We therefore investigate the robustness of the result through GMM. We continue to find significant effects of the same magnitude.

First, we consider the spillovers from failing states that are at peace. Having such a neighbour significantly reduces the growth rate. From the OLS regression the loss, were all the neighbours to be failing states, would be 1.8 percentage points. Next, we consider the cost to neighbours if a failing state has a civil war. The growth loss for a country surrounded by failing states at war is the same as that for one surrounded by failing states at peace, namely 1.8 per cent, although taking into account the confidence intervals, this need not imply that the costs are literally the same. Combining the two effects, on average 33 per cent of neighbours are failing states.[4] Thus, on average this adverse neighbourhood effect reduces growth by around 0.6 percentage points. This reduction in growth persists for as long as the neighbouring state continues to fail. We thus repeat the calculation of section 5.3 in which each year the failing state faced some probability of turnaround.

The growth reduction of 0.6 per cent for neighbours of a failing state is larger than would be expected from the more general results on how a country's growth is affected by that of its neighbours. Recall that a 1.0 per cent change in the growth rate of the neighbours on average changes the growth of the country by 0.4 per cent. Since the typical failing state suffers a growth reduction of 2.6 per cent, if all the neighbours were failing states this would imply a growth loss of around 1.0 per cent. Since only a third of neighbours are typically failing states the implied growth loss is around 0.3, or about half of the estimated loss of 0.6 per cent. This suggests that the routes by which a failing state reduces the growth of its neighbours extend beyond the reduced opportunities to trade due to slower growth of GDP. For example, trade opportunities may be further reduced due to the policies of the failing state such as high tariffs or poor transport routes. Some channels of transmission need have nothing to do with trade. For example, the failing state may give the neighbourhood as a whole a bad reputation with foreign investors. Neighbours might also have to divert public expenditures into containing some of the social or political problems that spill over, such as heightened risks of disease consequent upon the migration of refugees, or the need for a higher level of military spending.

We next use the loss of growth to estimate the cost that neighbours bear from a failing state. While the reduction in the growth rate of the neighbour is considerably less than that of the failing state itself, the typical failing state has 3.5 neighbours and the GDP of neighbours is on average considerably higher

[4] Twenty-six per cent of neighbours are failing states at peace and 7 per cent are failing states at war.

than that of a failing state itself. These two effects more than offset the smaller loss on the growth rate so that in aggregate the cost to neighbours, at US$206 billion, considerably exceeds the cost to the failing state itself. As previously, with 23 failing states, the total cost to neighbours is thus 23 times the cost per state, or US$4732 billion. Since this is a present value, we again convert it into a flow using a 5 per cent interest rate, so that the cost per year is US$237 billion.

Failing states also inflict costs beyond their direct neighbours: these neighbours themselves have neighbours. If, as in the global average, each 1.0 per cent of a country's growth spills over to 0.4 per cent on the growth of its neighbours, then the loss of growth echoes across the region. The direct neighbours of a failing state lose 0.6 per cent off their growth rates, their neighbours lose around 0.2 per cent, and their neighbours will lose around 0.1 per cent despite being separated from the failing state by two intervening countries. While such distant repercussions may seem implausible, Murdoch and Sandler (2004) show that the reduction in growth caused by a civil war extends for a radius of around 800 kilometres. Some costs may even spread globally. For example, failing states are liable to become havens for international crime. This follows directly from their poor governance which gives them a comparative advantage in criminal activities. In those failing states in civil war the government loses control over part of its territory and this makes the environment well-suited for the cultivation of hard drugs. Around 95 per cent of the global production of hard drugs is estimated to come from such environments. Similar safe haven concerns arise with respect to terrorism. Finally, the international community is increasingly intervening in civil wars to restore and maintain peace. For governments to send their soldiers on such missions is politically hazardous. All these effects beyond that of lost growth for immediate neighbours, such as more distant growth effects, crime, drugs, terrorism, and peacekeeping duties are important costs that we have not attempted to quantify. They imply that our figure for the cost to citizens outside failing states is an underestimate.

One concern with our neighbourhood analysis is that state fragility and conflict are geographically clustered. This spatial auto-correlation could be a potential source of bias. Ward and Gleditsch (2002) address this problem of spatial dependency. They find that taking spatial interdependence into account results in a larger influence of the neighbours' conflict risk on the country's own conflict risk. Thus, their results suggest that our estimates of neighbour influence are likely to be an underestimate.[5]

---

[5] Ward and Gleditsch (2002) use cross-country data for a single year and their model is parsimonious. It is beyond the scope of this chapter to extend their methodology to our panel data investigation and a more complicated explanatory model.

5.6 Implications And Conclusion

We now have estimates of the three distinct costs of a failing state: the costs to citizens of such states of poor policy and governance, the costs to these citizens of civil war, and the cost of both these types of failure to neighbours. The costs are summarized in Table 5.2. Both the combined total and its composition are revealing.

The combined total cost of failing states is around US$276 billion per year. This far exceeds expenditure on global aid programmes and is indeed double what would be generated were the OECD to raise aid to the UN target level of 0.7 per cent of GDP. One implication is evidently that the problem of failing states should already be at the core of the development agenda. The entire global aid effort, with its supporting cast of multilateral and bilateral agencies, is substantially less than what would be contributed by turning around failing states. Evidently, the present aid effort has not proved capable of achieving these turnarounds. If doubled aid would do so it would be well worth it.

However, other instruments may be needed to address the distinctive problems of failing states and are likely to be complementary to the aid effort (Collier 2007). When the USA helped Europe post-1945 it combined aid through the Marshall Plan with the provision of security; enhanced trade opportunities; and standards and peer pressure for improvements in economic and political governance. A similar combination is likely to be more effective for Africa than exclusive reliance upon aid. While there are evident difficulties in developing and coordinating these additional instruments, the high pay-off to solving the problem of failing states suggests that the costs of surmounting them may be worthwhile.

The deployment of some of these instruments would raise issues of sovereignty. However, the high cost of failing states also has implications for whether overriding sovereignty is warranted. Were the governments of failing states willing and able to improve policies and governance to the level prevailing in other developing countries, the contribution to development would be of broadly similar magnitude to that were the OECD countries collectively to meet the 0.7 per cent of GDP target for aid. This suggests that the case for overriding sovereignty in order to overcome the free-rider problem in aid provision in the countries of the OECD is roughly commensurate with that for inducing reform in failing states.

The predominant component of the cost of failing states is the effects on other countries, especially neighbours: failing states are costly primarily because they inflict externalities on others. This in turn suggests that the ethical case for overriding the sovereignty of the governments of failing states may be better based on the rights of other governments to protect their own citizens, rather than the duty of other governments to protect the citizens of failing states.

Since the costs inflicted by failing states upon other nations accrue predominantly to neighbours, this suggests that sovereignty over a failing state should be vested regionally or sub-regionally. For example, the sovereignty of an African failing state might be shared between the country's government and the African Union. Evidently, this would not transfer any sovereign rights to the governments of donor countries. However, a regional organization that acquired partial sovereign powers could, for example, empower international agencies to act on its behalf.

APPENDIX

Table 5.A1. Robustness checks

	(1)	(2)	(3)	(4)	(5)
Income per capita, t-4	−0.008	−0.007	−0.010	−0.011	−0.009
	(3.50)***	(2.32)**	(2.72)***	(4.46)***	(3.62)**
Dummy non-failing states countries at war	−0.013	−0.013	−0.013	−0.011	−0.011
	(3.02)***	(2.75)***	(2.67)***	(2.49)**	(2.48)*
Dummy failing states at war	−0.042	−0.036	−0.036	−0.033	−0.040
	(4.87)***	(3.35)***	(3.42)***	(4.18)***	(4.71)**
Dummy failing states at peace	−0.026	−0.021	−0.020	−0.022	−0.024
	(6.96)***	(4.86)***	(4.87)***	(6.17)***	(6.27)**
Proportion of neighbours being FS at war	−0.018	−0.015	−0.014	−0.013	−0.012
	(2.20)**	(1.61)	(1.46)	(1.68)*	(1.53)
		$p = 0.11$	$p = 0.11$		$p = 0.13$
Proportion of neighbours being FS at peace	−0.018	−0.019	−0.016	−0.012	−0.016
	(3.70)***	(3.12)***	(2.78)***	(2.50)**	(3.24)**
Primary education		−0.0001			
		(0.97)			
Secondary education			0.0002		
			(1.23)		
Investment rate				0.001	
				(6.30)***	
Democracy					0.0004
					(0.82)
Constant	0.105	0.094	0.105	0.095	0.106
	(4.89)***	(3.70)***	(3.76)***	(4.82)***	(4.99)**
Observations	600	463	463	598	552
R-squared	0.17	0.13	0.13	0.22	0.16

Notes: Regressions estimated with OLS. Robust t statistics in parentheses.
* significant at 10%;
** significant at 5%;
*** significant at 1%. Dependent variable: growth rate of real income per capita, Penn World Tables 6.1. All regressions include time dummies.

Source: See text.

Calculation of the cost of being a failing state
(Chauvet and Collier 2005)

Let g be the annual growth rate and r the discount rate. If a country starts out as a failing state from an initial GDP of 1, its GDP at the end of year one will be $[1 - (1 - g)]$. If this country has a turnaround at the end of year one, then it will recover its initial level of GDP during the second year, meanwhile losing again $(1 - g)$ of its initial GDP. Thus, the loss of GDP if a turnaround occurs at the end of year 1 is:

$$C(1) = \frac{1 - (1 - g)}{r} + \frac{1 - (1 - g)}{r^2} + \frac{g}{r} + \frac{g}{r^2} = g\left(\frac{1}{r} + \frac{1}{r^2}\right).$$

$t=1$:

If, instead of having a turnaround in year one, the country has a turnaround in year 2, then it will lose $[1 - (1 - g)]$ in year one and $[1 - (1 - g)^2]$ in year 2. If the turnaround occurs at the end of year two, the country will start to recover, but meanwhile continues to lose $[1 - (1 - g)^2]$ in year 3 and $[1 - (1 - g)]$ in year 4. The loss of GDP if a turnaround occurs at the end of year 2 is:

$$C(2) = \frac{1 - (1 - g)}{r} + \frac{1 - (1 - g)^2}{r^2} + \frac{1 - (1 - g)^2}{r^3} + \frac{1 - (1 - g)}{r^4}$$

$t=2$:

$$= \frac{g}{r} + \frac{1 - (1 - g)^2}{r^2} + \frac{1 - (1 - g)^2}{r^3} + \frac{g}{r^4}$$

$$= g\left(\frac{1}{r} + \frac{1}{r^4}\right) + \left(\frac{1}{r^2} + \frac{1}{r^3}\right) - (1 - g)^2\left(\frac{1}{r^2} + \frac{1}{r^3}\right).$$

The same reasoning applies for year 3:

$$C(3) = \frac{g}{r} + \frac{1 - (1 - g)^2}{r^2} + \frac{1 - (1 - g)^3}{r^3} + \frac{1 - (1 - g)^3}{r^4} + \frac{1 - (1 - g)^2}{r^5} + \frac{g}{r^6}$$

$t=3$:

$$= g\left(\frac{1}{r} + \frac{1}{r^6}\right) + \left(\frac{1}{r^2} + \frac{1}{r^3} + \frac{1}{r^4} + \frac{1}{r^5}\right) - (1 - g)^2\left(\frac{1}{r^2} + \frac{1}{r^5}\right) - (1 - g)^3\left(\frac{1}{r^3} + \frac{1}{r^4}\right)$$

We end up with the following general formula for the loss of GDP if a turnaround occurs at the end of year t:

$$C(t) = g\left(\frac{1}{r} + \frac{1}{r^{2t}}\right) + \sum_{k=2}^{k=2t-1} \frac{1}{r^k} - \sum_{k=2}^{k=t}(1-g)^k\left(\frac{1}{r^k} + \frac{1}{r^{2t-k+1}}\right).$$

So taking into account the probability that each of these scenarios will occur, we end up with the following total cost from being a failing state:

Total loss from being a failing state =,

where $p(t)$ is the probability of turnaround in year t: $P(X=t) = p(t) = (1-a)^{t-1}\,a$.

References

Blundell, R. and S. Bond (1998). 'Initial Conditions and Moment Restrictions in Dynamic Panel Data Models'. *Journal of Econometrics*, 87 (1): 115–43.

Bourguignon, F. (2000). *The Pace of Economic Growth and Poverty Reduction*. Paris: DELTA.

Chauvet, L. and P. Collier (2005). *Policy Turnarounds in Fragile States*. Oxford: CSAE. Available at: <http://www//users.ox.ac.uk/%7Eeconpco/research/pdfs/policy-turnarounds.pdf>.

Chauvet, L. and P. Collier (2006). *Helping Hand—Aid to Failing States*. Oxford: CSAE. Available at: <http://www//users.ox.ac.uk/%7Eeconpco/research/pdfs/Helping-Hand-AidtoFailing States.pdf>.

Collier, P. (2007). *The Bottom Billion: Why the Poorest Countries are Failing and What Can be Done About It*. New York: Oxford University Press.

Collier, P. and A. Hoeffler (2004a). 'Conflict'. In B. Lomborg (ed.), *Global Crises: Global Solutions*. Cambridge: Cambridge University Press.

Collier, P. and A. Hoeffler (2004b). 'Aid, Policy and Growth in Post-Conflict Societies'. *European Economic Review*, 48 (5): 1125–45.

Collier, P. and A. Hoeffler (2004c). 'Greed and Grievance in Civil War'. *Oxford Economic Papers*, 56 (4): 563–95.

Collier, P., A. Hoeffler, and M. Söderbom (2004). 'On the Duration of Civil War'. *Journal of Peace Research*, 41 (3): 253–73.

Collier, P. and S. O'Connell (2007). 'African Growth: Opportunities and Choices'. In B. Ndulu, R. Bates, P. Collier, and S. O'Connell (eds), *The Political Economy of Economic Growth in Africa, 1960–2000*. Cambridge: Cambridge University Press.

Murdoch, J. C. and T. Sandler (2004). 'Civil Wars and Economic Growth: Spatial Dispersion'. *American Journal of Political Science*, 48 (1): 138–51.

Ravallion, M. and S. Chen (1997). 'What Can New Survey Data Tell Us about Recent Changes in Distribution and Poverty?' *World Bank Economic Review*, 11 (2): 357–82.

Ward M. D. and K. S. Gleditsch (2002). 'Location, Location, Location: An MCMC Approach to Modeling the Spatial Context of War and Peace', *Political Analysis*, 10: 244–60.

Wood, A. (2008). 'Looking Ahead Optimally in Allocating Aid'. *World Development*, July, 36 (7): 1135–51.

World Bank (2002). *Low-Income Countries Under Stress. Report of a Task Force*. Washington, DC: World Bank.

6

Fragility and Conflict in Palestine: The Costs of the Closures Regime on West Bank and Gaza

Sebnem Akkaya, Norbert Fiess, Bartlomiej Kaminski, and Gaël Raballand

6.1 Introduction[1]

The signing of the peace treaty under the Oslo accord in 1993 generated high expectations for the economic development of Palestine (World Bank 1993). Peace and stability were seen as key for domestic economic activity to attract foreign direct investment and to foster regional coordination and integration. In addition, a broad commitment by the international community to underwrite part of the cost of the Palestinian reconstruction programme was seen as supplying much needed capital and foreign exchange. The Protocol on Economic Relations (the Paris Protocol) signed in 1994 set the stage for a higher level of economic integration than that implicit in a standard customs union.[2] The Paris Protocol aimed to correct some of the development disparities by eliminating Israeli trade barriers on Palestinian agricultural products; removing restrictions on economic activities; developing financial institutions; creating a legal and regulatory framework; and reducing political and economic uncertainty.

Unfortunately, these hopes have never fully materialized. The tensions in Israeli–Palestinian relations have led to the emergence of the closures regime,

[1] The authors are grateful to Alex Kremer and Nithya Nagarajan, as well as Claus Astrup, Irina Astrakhan, Hussam Abu Dagga, Zenaida Hernandez, Kathy Khuu, Sami Miaari, and John Nasir for their valuable inputs to this chapter. The chapter also benefited from comments and suggestions from Sebastien Dessus, Dipak Dasgupta, Farrukh Iqbal, Samuel Otoo, Mustapha Kamel Nabli, Vincent Palmade, Elizabeth Ruppert Bulmer, Sweder van Wijnbergen, and John Wetter. The authors would also like to thank participants at the UNU-WIDER conference on Fragile States, in Helsinki in June 2007, for helpful comments. All errors are of course our own. Opinions expressed in this chapter are those of the authors alone and do not necessarily correspond to any affiliated organization.
[2] Arnon and Weinblatt (2001) provide a summary of the Paris Protocol negotiations.

which is the multi-faceted system of restrictions on the movement of goods and people both within the West Bank and Gaza (WB&G) and through Israel to the rest of the world. This has prevented any serious movement toward reconstruction and development of the Palestinian economy (Cobham 2001; Fisher et al. 2001). The second Palestinian Intifada that began on 28 September 2000 prompted a re-invasion of most of the West Bank by the Israeli Army in March 2002 as well the intensification of a highly restrictive closures regime, reinforced by Israel's construction of the 'separation barrier'.

The closures regime has created barriers to trade and to labour mobility for Palestinian workers into Israel; it has also prevented foreign providers of technical services from entering WB&G. These barriers stem from external closures combined with fixed and mobile security checkpoints inside the West Bank; the tightening of Israeli permit policies and the security risks of travelling to WB&G to provide services on site. Together they inflict substantial economic costs, both current and future. The closures regime has further led to increased fragmentation of the West Bank economy. WB&G is effectively a landlocked economy today. In the case of Gaza this is solely due to political arrangements following the Israeli disengagement in September 2004 that has restricted external access to land-crossing points. The economic space of the West Bank has become divided into small pieces via an elaborate system of internal fixed and mobile checkpoints. Checkpoints and internal closures within the West Bank in particular hurt rural communities and the agricultural sector. Rural communities in the West Bank have traditionally depended on urban areas for trading, employment, food and household supplies, and for access to services. Closures have affected these ties and their negative impact is particularly visible in transportation costs and price differentials for perishable agricultural goods.[3]

Closures are exerting both a direct and an indirect effect on Palestinian income. Closures reduce labour incomes; they also disrupt trade flows, investment, and domestic production and hence increase the extent of fragility. The economic cost of the closures regime, which amounts to the 'policy-induced' fragmentation of the WB&G economic space, has been the subject of several studies. Diwan and Shaban (1999) and Fisher et al. (2001) demonstrate the devastating impact of the closures regime on the Palestinian economy. While Fisher et al. (2001) show that both external and internal factors have contributed to the disappointing performance of the Palestinian economy in the first five years after the Oslo Agreement (1994–9), they argue that among external factors accountable for the poor performance the closures regime dominates. Fisher et al. (2001) considered the variations in labour income

---

[3] Arnon and Weinblatt (2001).

and put the economic costs of closure (in terms of GDP) between 9.7 per cent in 1994 and 1 per cent in 1995.

Following the outbreak of the second Intifada in 2000, both the frequency and duration of closures increased dramatically. This motivates us to attempt a more comprehensive analysis of the economic costs of closure.

The combined negative impact of barriers to trade and to movement of people is more than their simple sum. The direct loss of income by Palestinian workers in Israel can be approximated through restrictions in permits issued to Palestinian workers, but other effects are more difficult to estimate. The loss of income by Palestinian workers indirectly affects the economy through reduced expenditure on total production. Security concerns often prevent specialists from Israel and other countries from providing essential services. Similarly, in the absence of barriers to trade in goods and services, downward pressure on both wages and prices of non-tradable goods should have created new business opportunities for exports and should also have enhanced international competitiveness. In the presence of barriers, these opportunities cannot materialize.

The objective of the chapter is to assess the combined impact of closures on the WB&G economy. In contrast to earlier studies, we take a comprehensive approach combining econometric modelling with estimates derived from the fall in the number of work permits; increased transportation costs; and deviations from trends in foreign trade, etc. Using unpublished data, we quantify the impact of closures on WB&G economy. Due to the absence of a counterfactual as well as lack of data, estimating the costs of closures is difficult and we acknowledge that our estimates are likely to be highly conservative as they abstract from multiplier effects. At the same time, our analysis corroborates earlier results which demonstrate a negative impact of the closures regime on the growth dynamics of the WB&G economy.

The remainder of this chapter is organized as follows. Next we document trends in closures and the resulting fragmentation and greater fragility of the WB&G economic space. Then we estimates linkages between closures and growth using a dynamic macroeconometric model. Thereafter we quantify losses due to the contraction in labour flows and workers' remittances from employment in Israel. This is followed by identification of the impact of current restrictions on movement of goods and services, followed by a discussion of areas of economic activity that the closures regime effectively precludes.

6.2 The Closures Regime

6.2.1 *The extent of closures*

The closures regime has its roots in the Six-Day War of 1967, when the West Bank and the Gaza Strip were declared closed military areas. In 1972 Israel issued general exit orders, allowing free mobility into Israel and East Jerusalem, as well as between the Gaza Strip and the West Bank outside the morning hours of 01:00 and 05:00. In June 1989, Israel introduced a magnetic card system for border crossing which excluded released prisoners, former administrative detainees, or residents who had been detained but not charged.

General exit permits were revoked in January 1991 (at the time of the first Gulf War) and replaced with a personal exit permit scheme. Following a series of stabbings in 1993, Israel introduced a system of general closure, which effectively sealed off access to Israel and East Jerusalem to non-permit holders. Enforced by a series of checkpoints both at the border to Israel as well as inside the Occupied Territories, this system is still in place today. In response to the violence, Israel has also at times imposed total closure, where even permit holders are not allowed to clear internal or external checkpoints.

Israel's closures policy consists of:

- Internal closures: free mobility inside the West Bank and Gaza is restricted.

- External closures: access from West Bank and Gaza to Israel and East Jerusalem is restricted.

- External international closures: access from West Bank to Jordan and access from Gaza to Egypt is restricted.

Data from OCHA oPt (2005) for November 2004 illustrates the extent of the closures regime. During that month, free movement of goods and labour in the West Bank was restricted by more than 600 physical barriers (more than 10 per square kilometre), consisting of 61 full-time and 6 part-time staffed checkpoints, 102 roadblocks, 48 road gates, 374 earth mounds, 28 earth walls, and 61 trenches. Physical mobility was further restricted by the construction of the 'separation barrier' and the creation of a network of 'forbidden roads', which only allows access to Jewish settlers.

Closures have been a constant feature of the WB&G's economy since they were first introduced back in 1993. Since the outbreak of the Second Intifada in September 2000 the frequency and duration of closures have dramatically increased (Figure 6.1). Between September 1997 and September 2000 closures were rare and occurred on average only once every three months. The probability of a closure lasting at least one day per month increased from 33 per cent in pre-Intifada times (1997Q1 to 2000Q2) to 78 per cent after the outbreak of

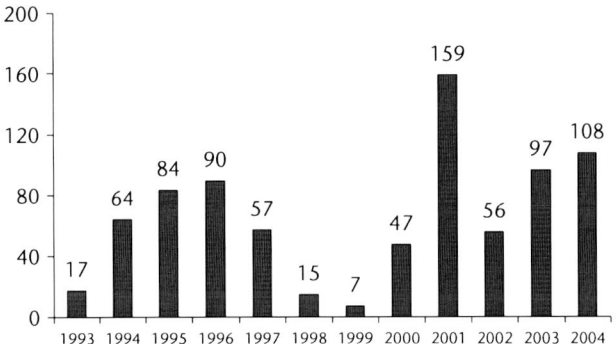

Figure 6.1. Effective closure days (1993–2004)

Source: UNESCO database on closures.

the Intifada.[4] During the pre-Intifada years between 1997 and 2000, there was only one single incidence of a month long closure, however since September 2000, closures have lasted a full month on twelve occasions.

6.2.2 Fragmentation and fragility of economic space

Closures, Jewish settlements, and the construction of the 'separation barrier' have contributed to a significant fragmentation of the economic space in WB&G. The WB&G are today a *de facto* landlocked country as Gaza's port and airports were bombed and the only crossing point between Gaza and Israel, Karni, is frequently closed for days and sometimes weeks at a time. Internal fixed and mobile checkpoints have chopped the economic space of the West Bank into small pieces.

The economic costs of fragmentation are clearly visible in price differentials between local mini markets in the West Bank. A price comparison of selected agricultural products in several localities in the West Bank on 15 February 2006 reveals substantial price differentials. As closures were not particularly severe on that particular day, these price gaps are indicative of the extent to which agricultural markets in the West Bank have been subject to the uncertainties of closures.

Figure 6.2 shows that differences between the highest and lowest retail price for tomatoes, eggplants, squash, cucumbers, and bell peppers ranged between 215 and 400 per cent. Prices in Ramallah were on average 79 per cent

---

[4] During the 48 months between September 2000 and September 2004, there were only ten months in which closures did not occur, whereas during the period 1997–2000, 32 months were unaffected by closures.

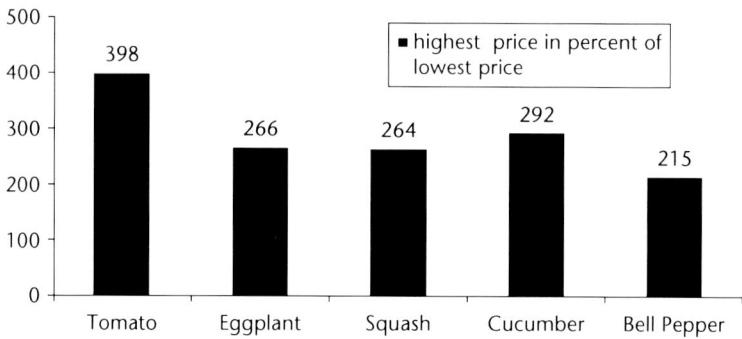

Figure 6.2. Retail prices per kg on 15 February 2006 in 11 towns and cities in West Bank (in %)

Source: World Bank.

higher than in Nablus, even though Ramallah and Nablus are only about 40 kilometres apart.

Due to communication technology, traders are well aware of these price differences. However, they do not act on this information as the risks of a shipment being tied up at an internal crossing point outweigh any benefit of price arbitrage. The stakes are highest for fresh produce, as the whole shipment could spoil if not delivered on time. Although transport costs also affect these price differentials, the uncertainty of closures is clearly the dominant factor. According to the Ministry of Agriculture, transport costs ranged from 4 per cent and 17 per cent of the retail value of vegetable consignments in February 2006. Even the cost of transporting a consignment from Bethlehem to Gaza amounted to only 13 per cent of its retail value. Had transport costs been the only factor taken into account by traders, they clearly would have moved products between markets lowering price differentials in the process. While transportation costs pale in comparison to the uncertainties of closure, altered transport costs have changed geographical patterns of internal trade. Higher transportation costs, together with the prohibition on Israeli traders to buy directly from Palestinians within the West Bank, in addition to other internal restrictions, have led to a relocation of wholesale agricultural trade from Nablus to Beta, Farah, and Badan in the West Bank.

6.3 Closures And Growth Dynamics

Economic activity in WB&G is heavily influenced by external factors. WB&G has been one of the largest recipients of foreign aid; in addition, 'imposed, incomplete economic integration' (Arnon and Weinblatt 2001) with Israel ties it closely to economic activity there and to developments in Israeli–WB&G security relations, as reflected in the closures regime.

To investigate the impact of the closures regime on growth dynamics in Palestine more formally, we model growth in WB&G, ΔY_{Pa}, as an autoregressive process adding a measure of closure alongside other variables controlling for internal and external determinants of growth. The impact of the closures regime is proxied by the ratio of days worked net of closure (effective working days) to the number of potential working days, eff/pot. The rate of unemployment in the West Bank and Gaza, U_{Pa}, GDP growth in Israel, ΔY_{Isr}, and international aid flows, Aid_t, are included to control for internal and external determinants of growth. The latter two variables account for Palestine's close dependency on Israel and on international aid flows.

We explore the behaviour of growth in Palestine starting from the following log-level specification

$$\ln Y_{PA,t} = \alpha_0 + \alpha_1 \ln U_{PA,t} + \alpha_2 \ln Y_{Isr,t} + \alpha_3 \ln eff/pot_t + \alpha_4 \ln Aid_t + \epsilon_t \qquad (6.1)$$

The model is estimated via the autoregressive distributed lag (ARDL) approach of Pesaran et al. (2001) based on quarterly data from 1993Q1 to 2005Q4. The ARDL approach has a number of appealing features. For one, it is applicable independent of whether the underlying variables are stationary, non-stationary and/or mutually cointegrated. This makes the ARDL approach less restrictive than comparable approaches. The ARDL also produces robust results in small samples (Pesaran and Shin 1999), which is highly appealing in our setting. In addition, the inclusion of a significant number of lags resolves the endogeneity problem, and finally, a dynamic error correction model (ECM) can be derived from the ARDL to integrate short run dynamics with the long run relationship without losing any long run information.

An ARDL representation of (1) is formulated as

$$\Delta \ln Y_{PA\,t} = \beta_0 + \beta_2 \ln Y_{PA,t-i} + \sum_{i=1}^{n} \beta_2 \Delta \ln X_{t-i} + \sum_{i=1}^{n} \beta_1 \Delta \ln Y_{PA,t-i} + \epsilon_t \qquad (6.2)$$

where X is a vector of exogenous variables consisting of U_{Pa}, Y_{Isr}, eff/pot and Aid.

The ARDL procedure involves bounds testing of (6.2). These bounds tests involve an F-test on the joint null hypothesis that the coefficients on the level variables are jointly equal to zero (see Pesaran and Shin 1999; Pesaran et al. 2001). Instead of the conventional critical values, these tests involve two asymptotic critical value bounds, depending on whether the variables are I(0) or I(1) or a mixture of both. If the test statistic exceeds their respective upper critical values, then there is evidence of a long run relationship. If the test statistic exceeds its upper bound, then the null of no cointegration can be rejected regardless of the order of integration of the variables. Inference is only inconclusive if the test statistic lies between the bounds.

If cointegration cannot be rejected, the conditional long run model is then produced from the reduced form solution of (6.2), when the first-differenced variables jointly equal zero. The long run coefficients and error correction model are estimated by the ARDL approach to cointegration, where the conditional ECM is estimated using Ordinary Least Squares (OLS) and the lag structure for the ARDL specification of the short run dynamics is determined by the Schwarz–Bayesian criteria.

Our econometric analysis of WB&G growth dynamics confirms that the level of economic activity in WB&G are closely tied to economic activity in Israel, foreign aid, and developments in Israeli–WB&G security relations, as reflected in the closures regime (Table 6.1). The impact of foreign aid on the GDP, as captured in our growth equation, is positive, but smaller than that of closures: a 10 per cent increase in aid raises the real GDP of WB&G around 0.9 per cent.

Based on the coefficient estimates of our model, we estimate that a ten percentage-point increase in the ratio of effective to potential working days—equivalent to about 30 more days worked due to the removal of closure restrictions—increases the real GDP by 1.2 per cent, or about 0.17 per cent per day worked. In other words, one day of closure is estimated to cost WB&G about US$7 million in terms of lost income. These estimates are broadly in line with UNSCO estimates, which put the economic costs of one day of closure at around US$8 million to the WB&G economy.

While estimates in this section are based on an econometric macromodel, the following sections provide microevidence of the direct and indirect impact of closures on three distinct channels: workers' remittances, current restrictions on movement of goods and services, and future capacity to export.

Table 6.1. Key determinants of WB&G economic activity

ARDL			Error correction representation		
Dependent Variable: $lnY_{PA,t}$			Dependent Variable: $\Delta\, lnY_{PA,t}$		
Regressor	Coefficient	T-Ratio[Prob]	Regressor	Coefficient	T-Ratio[Prob]
$lnY_{PA,t-1}$	0.53831	3.7100[.003]	$\Delta\, lnY_{IS,t}$	0.95832	3.8419[.002]
$lnY_{IS,t}$	0.95832	3.8419[.003]	$\Delta\, U_{PA,t}$	−0.91289	−2.8304[.015]
$lnY_{IS,t-1}$	−0.73068	−3.3034[.007]	$\Delta eff/pot_t$	0.05466	1.9169[.079]
$U_{PA,t}$	−0.91289	−2.8304[.016]	ΔAid_t	0.03914	1.8290[.092]
eff/pot_t	0.05466	1.9169[.082]	$Ecm(-1)$	−0.46169	−3.1820[.008]
Aid_t	0.03914	1.8290[.095]			
Constant	0.91322	.41379[.687]			

Note: With error correction term, $Ecm, = lnY_{PA,t} -.493*\, lnY_{IS,t} + 1.9773*\, U_{PA,t} -.118*\, eff/pot_t -0.0848*\, Aid -1.97$.

Source: See text.

6.4 The Impact Of Closures On Workers' Remittances

Israel's security policy impacts the WB&G labour market via a reduction in work permits and direct closures. Both have reduced the number of days that Palestinians can work in Israel and have therefore brought down earnings and remittances flows. To assess the impact of closures on labour incomes, we first estimate the effect of a reduction in work permits and then add the impact of closures. Since the outbreak of the latest Intifada in September 2000, Israel has significantly tightened its policy of issuing work permits to Palestinians. As a result, the Palestinian workforce in Israel has roughly halved since then. From 2000Q3 to 2000Q4, the Palestinian workforce in Israel fell from 146,000 to 43,000, equivalent to a decline from 22 per cent to 9 per cent in terms of total Palestinian employment (both in Israel and WB&G). A limited recovery was witnessed in 2001 when the number of Palestinians working in Israel rose to 15 per cent of total WB&G employment during the first two quarters of 2001. This increase, however, did not last and since 2002Q4 the number of Palestinians working in Israel has stabilized at around 10 per cent; approximately 65,000.

The loss of access to Israeli labour markets has significantly reduced the income of Palestinian workers: in 2005 WB&G income reached only 36 per cent of its pre-Intifada level. For a counterfactual estimate of workers' earnings in the absence of closures, we apply the following reasoning: had the relative share of Palestinians employed in Israel (of total WB&G employment) remained at its 1999–2000 level, then in 2005 Palestinian employment in Israel would have amounted to 165,000 and earnings would have totaled US$922 million. This stands in stark contrast to observed figures of 63,000 workers and earnings of US$351 million (Figure 6.3). The difference between actual and counterfactual earnings provides an estimate for remittances lost due to a reduction in work permits of US$571 million for 2005 alone.

External closures have added to the negative impact of a reduction in work permits. This impact can be gauged by the strong contraction in workers' earnings since 2000. As wages have remained fairly constant during this period, it seems reasonable to attribute the fall in earnings to a decline in working days due to external closures; had Palestinians worked in 2005 the same number of days and for the same average wage as in 2000, their earnings would have been US$179 million higher in 2005 that they actually were.[5]

---

[5] This is based on the following reasoning: Total annual workers' remittances per number of employed fell from US$84,000 in 2000 to US$43,000 in 2002; this rebounded to US$54,000 and US$56,000 in 2004 and 2005 respectively. Since wages of Palestinians employed in Israel did not fall, the drop in remittances per employee can be attributed to the loss of days worked in Israel due to closures. The estimate is based on remittances per employee in 2000.

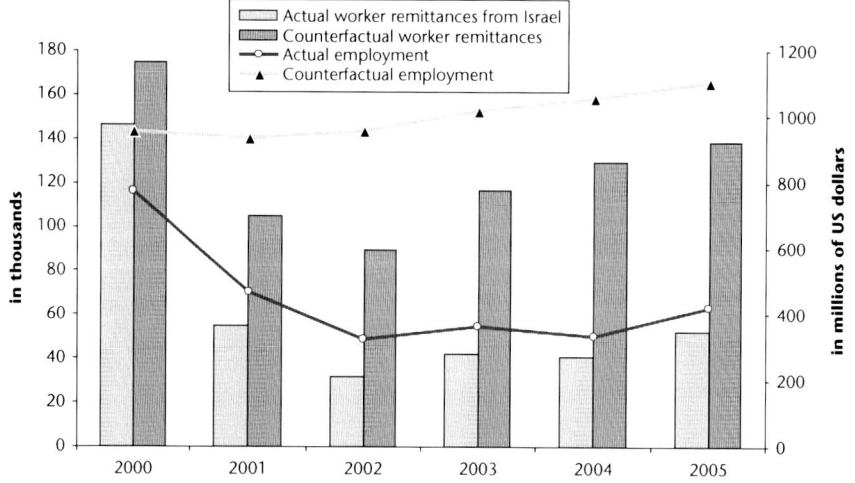

Figure 6.3. Employment and workers' remittances from Israel in 2000–5

Source: Authors' calculations based on remittances reported by Israel Central Bureau of Statistics (ICBS) and employment reported by Palestinian Central Bureau of Statistics (PCBS).

Table 6.2. Estimated losses in workers' remittances from Israel because of cuts in employment and closures in 2001–5 (in millions of US$)

	2001	2002	2003	2004	2005	Total in 2001–5
Losses because of the fall in employment	342	385	500	588	571	2,386
Losses because of closures	222	200	178	149	179	928
Total losses	564	585	678	737	750	3,314

Source: Remittances from ICBS and employment as reported by PCBS.

Table 6.2 brings together the combined impact of a relative decline in Palestinian employment in Israel and a fall in remittances per employee due to the closure-related reduction in number of days worked. For 2001–5, the employment-related loss is estimated at US$2.4 billion and the closure related loss at US$928 million: equivalent to total losses of US$3.3 billion (Table 6.2). In 2005, employment- and closure-related losses are estimated at US$750 million—the equivalent of 58 per cent of total foreign aid (US$1.3 billion) provided to the Palestinian Authority in that year.[6]

These estimates are likely to represent a lower bound estimate of the income lost to external closures. The overall income effect of the reduction in Palestinian employment in Israel is expected to be much higher as indirect effects

---

[6] See *West Bank and Gaza Update*, a quarterly publication of the West Bank and Gaza office of the World Bank.

of reduced expenditures on total production would also need to be factored in, but cannot readily be quantified.

The adverse impact of the Israeli security regime on economic welfare in WB&G is further exacerbated by the fact that wages in Israel are generally higher and dependency ratios in WB&G are very high. For example, average wages earned by Palestinians in Israel are about two-thirds higher than in WB&G. Dependency ratios of 5.5 for the West Bank and 8.2 for Gaza imply that 600,000 to 800,000 individuals, i.e., 18 to 24 per cent of the total population in WB&G, were affected by 100,000 closure-related job losses.

6.5 The Impact On Current Movement Of Goods and Services

This section analyses the impact of closures on the current movement of goods and services. Section 6.5.1 investigates the impact on trading costs that may be directly attributable to the fragmentation of economic space both within the WB&G and with Israel. Section 6.5.2 studies the impact of closures on external trade. An assessment of the impact of closures on future economic activity is attempted in section 6.5.

6.5.1 *The impact of closures on trading costs*

Closures raise the costs of doing business in WB&G. The uncertainty of closures implies higher transaction costs for production and trade; these are because of higher transport costs and shipment delays. In addition, the high probability of outright closures makes shipments both within and outside the WB&G extremely risky. Potential losses depend on product specifics and can range from the loss of the entire shipment (e.g., in the case of perishable agricultural products) to the cost of capital tied up in a shipment (see Appendix A). The uncertainty of in-time delivery (both on the demand and the supply side) further completely eliminates WB&G producers from participating in supply chains with short response times—for example, specialized garments or automobile parts.

Back-to-back transit arrangements further add to transportation costs. As trucks are generally not allowed to enter Palestinian urban areas, upon arrival at a checkpoint cargo is unloaded and then reloaded onto another truck at entry point. Back-to-back transport is not only costly in terms of additional handling charges, delivery delays, and lost time, but quality also often suffers due to handling. Khatib (2005) estimates that around 50 trucks per day and per city pass through commercial checkpoints in this back-to-back manner.

The back-to-back system increases the cost of transportation for both finished products and raw materials. It is estimated that the added costs of transport are as follows:[7]

- The transfer of raw materials from one trailer to another costs about US $75–86 because of additional handling and increased trailer costs.

- Waiting in line at the checkpoint, demurrage, delays because of closure, and security checks.

- In the case of bulk materials, associated costs are even more important because of product damage during the loading and unloading process.

- Vegetable exporters from the West Bank state that the back-to-back transit arrangements imposed on them since October 2005 have introduced regular 24 hour delays.[8]

Since the increase in transportation costs has taken effect over five years of extensive closures, higher transport costs have been gradually 'internalized'. Relative to 2001 and 2002, the difference between transport price inflation (a proxy for transaction costs) and overall consumer price inflation declined in 2003 and 2004 and was negative in 2005, suggesting no further aggravation to movement restrictions in that year (Figure 6.4).[9]

The change in transportation costs relative to CPI does not take into account the closures-induced decline in the (total factor) productivity level of the transport sector. The estimated decline has amounted to about 33 per cent since the outbreak of the Intifada. For example, a truck that was able to

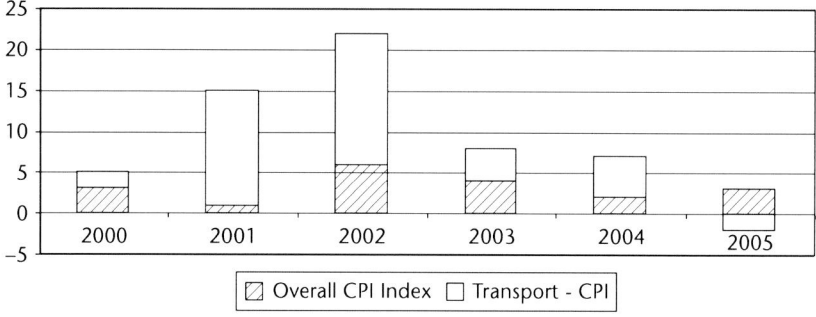

Figure 6.4. Change in CPI index and in transportation costs relative to CPI, 2000–5 (in %)

Source: ICBS and PCBS.

---

[7] Data from Khatib (2005) complemented by interviews.
[8] World Bank (2006a, 2006b, and 2006c).
[9] World Bank (2006d).

make three rotations per day before the Intifada now makes only two rotations.[10] This has significantly raised unit transportation costs.

Interviews with two major Ramallah-based transport companies provide further evidence of substantial increases in transportation costs along major trading routes in the West Bank since the outbreak of the Intifada. Table 6.3 presents cost estimates of increased travel distance during the Intifada years. To provide proxy costs for extra travel distance (abstracting from other transportation costs, i.e., increases in fuel prices, labour costs), we apply the same fuel and labour costs as in 2005 to both pre- and post-Intifada years. Fuel cost estimates are based on 4.4 NIS per litre and a fuel consumption of 5 km per litre per truck. Labour costs include additional time spent by one driver, assuming a monthly salary of 2200 NIS and a workweek of 48 hours (192 hours a month).

The back-to-back system, longer waiting times, and higher uncertainties often prompt companies to send more than just one driver. These additional labour costs are however not factored into our above estimates, as they are related with higher uncertainty that is distinct from costs associated with extra travel distance. The estimates presented here also do not account for the resulting drop in total factor productivity of the transport sector.

A series of interviews with transport companies further indicates that by restricting access to major agricultural trading centres such as Nablus, Jenin, and Jerusalem, closures have raised transportation costs more than 100 per cent along major trading routes, compared to the pre-Intifada period. This suggests that our data-driven estimates are very conservative.

Although both Palestinian and Israeli firms operate in the same trading zone (the Israeli customs envelope), closures are not the only differentiating factor between them. For security reasons, shipments originating in WB&G face different border procedures and Israeli firms do not confront 'internal economic' borders. As a consequence, WB&G businesses experience significantly larger transaction costs, although their impact on the cost of imported goods varies depending on their unit values. Low value, bulky products are more affected (see Appendix B).

An Israeli firm operating in the same sector as its WB&G counterpart is better situated to compete both externally and internally. An Israeli firm has one important advantage over a WB&G firm: even if it has higher costs, it can compete in WB&G markets, whereas a WB&G firm with a similar cost structure would be unable to compete in Israel because of higher trading costs owing to discriminatory procedures at the crossing points and back-to-back

---

[10] World Bank (2006d).

Table 6.3. Increase in transport costs along major trade routes because of longer distances in December 2005

From Ramallah	Pre-September 2000				December 2005 Alternative Route 1					December 2005 Alternative Route 2				
	Time	Distance (km)	Cost (NIS)		Time	Distance (km)	Cost (NIS)	% change in cost over pre-Sept. 2000		Time	Distance (km)	Cost (NIS)	% change in cost over pre-Sept. 2000	
To:														
Bethlehem	35	25	29.1		90	80	86.0	195		210	105	130.4	348	
Nablus	60	50	54.4		90	60	68.6	26		180	90	111.8	105	
Jenin	90	90	94.6		210	140	160.5	70		420	200	252.2	167	

Source: Interviews conducted by Nithya Nagarajan.

operations. The disadvantage of a WB&G firm in terms of its capacity to compete in Israel rises again when production requires imported inputs.

6.5.2 *The impact of closures on external trade*

While back-to-back transit arrangements increase transport costs inside West Bank and Gaza, transport costs for external trade are further inflated by special security requirements for Palestinian firms at the external border. Both exporters and importers from WB&G are confined to the use of Israeli transport companies when goods are destined for WB&G or leaving WB&G through Israel. Furthermore, shipments have to be reloaded at the crossing points with Israel and are subjected to screening procedures.[11] In this section we attempt to estimate the impact of closures on external trade.

Estimating the impact of closures on trade is a complicated endeavour. For one, it is almost impossible to fully isolate these impacts from other effects, such as supply side disruptions due to civil unrest,[12] breakdowns in output, and a shift in preferences of foreigners away from WB&G exports, due to uncertainties about contract fulfilments.[13] For imports, it seems reasonable to assume that, with the exception of perishable goods, all contracted imports were honoured, although possibly at a premium. For exports, the picture is even more complicated since WB&G firms have to compete with firms not affected by the closures regime and therefore faces higher transaction costs.

We focus on closure-related losses of exports and apply a similar strategy as for labour income losses: we assume that in the absence of the latest Intifada, exports would have grown at historical rates. The difference between these extrapolated exports and observed exports provide a first proxy of the impact of closures, although this measure does not attempt to separate closures from disruptions. Figure 6.5 shows actual exports and extrapolated exports, based on an observed 3.5 per cent annual average growth rate from 1997 to 2000. To illustrate, the difference between cumulative extrapolated and actual values of exports from 2001 to 2005 amounted to US$693 million.

To arrive at a more precise measure of closures-induced export losses, we consider the impact on exports either already shipped, or about to be shipped, but never delivered due to closures. This analysis builds on earlier work at the

---

[11] Khatib (2005) further alludes to less favourable treatment of Palestinian firms at the border.

[12] The contraction in exports was not only due to closures but also to difficulties in sustaining production activity during the civil unrest. Furthermore, many industrial sites were either damaged or destroyed. Thus, the supply side was also negatively affected not only by closures but an overall unstable business environment.

[13] Foreign importers of WB&G products can choose from a wide range of suppliers. There is no data available on the number and value of contracts cancelled by foreign importers due to the unpredictability of deliveries. One can only speculate as to the value of contracts not awarded because of uncertainty concerning deliveries.

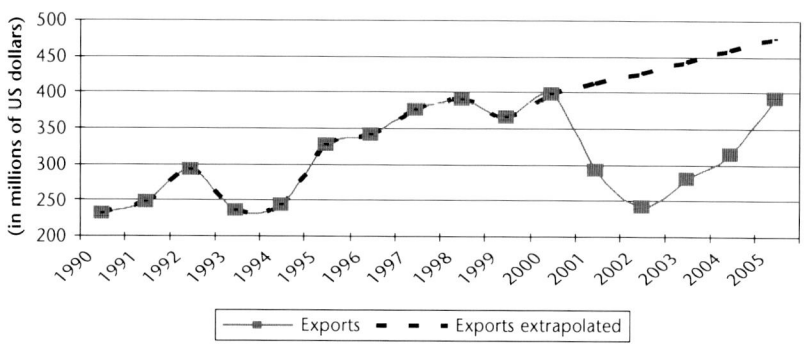

Figure 6.5. Total and extrapolated exports in current prices, 1990–2005 (in millions of current US$)

Source: Based on data provided by PCBS.

World Bank by Diwan and Shaban (1999). Using 1999 as a benchmark,[14] we compare exports in 1999 and in 2003 by month and take these differences as a proxy for closure-related losses. We find that exports in 2003 were on average 30 per cent lower than in 1999. Furthermore, we assume that portions of exports were lost, either because of delayed shipment, or because foreign importers cancelled because of continual delays. When terminals were open more frequently, as happened in 2003 and in 2004, some export activities resumed. Nevertheless, we estimate that at least 30 per cent of export capacity disappeared between 1999 and 2003.

While very conservative, these estimates show a significant loss in exports. Without closures, exports would have been 5 per cent higher in 2000, 23 per cent higher in 2001, and 15 per cent higher in 2003 (Table 6.4).

Uncertainties associated with closures impact merchandise trade in the short and medium terms through three channels: first, closures erode competitiveness since WB&G exporters must include higher transportation costs and extra transaction costs in their end price, and these prices may become uncompetitive in external markets.[15] Second, closures may compel producers of agricultural products to shift from higher value-added perishable exports to lower value-added products produced for domestic markets. Third, prolonged closures erode further existing export capacity by leading to bankruptcies of WB&G companies.

---

[14] The year 1999 is used as a benchmark as it immediately precedes the Intifada and is also the year with the lowest number of closure days.

[15] According to textiles and garments producers, the cost of using Israeli ship forwarders adds 10–25 per cent to the cost of raw materials (see World Bank 2006a).

Table 6.4. Exports lost because of closures in relation to actual and hypothetical exports during 1999–2003 (in millions of US$ and %)

	1999	2000	2001	2002	2003
Lost exports (in millions of US$)	3	20	67	23	41
Lost and actual exports in % of actual exports	100.8	105.0	123.1	109.7	114.5
Export loss in % of actual exports	0.8	4.8	18.7	8.9	12.7
Export loss in % of difference between extrapolated and actual exports	0	0	55.4	12.6	25.2

Source: Based on data from UNSCO database on closures, and PCBS for exports.

6.6 Hypothetical Impact On Future Economic Activity

The main difficulty with quantifying the economic costs of the closures regime is that its major impact is on activities that are unlikely to occur as long as these policies are in place. We do not know what would have happened without the closures regime but we can be certain what will not happen while it is in place. This section presents the likely impact of the closures regime on investment activity; it is expected that the closures regime suppresses new investments and erodes the competitiveness of existing firms simply because closures make the following extremely difficult:

- The shift from a currently dominant type of inter-industry trade to intra-industry or intra-product trade, associated with a more sophisticated division of labour based on narrow industrial specialization within global value chains.[16]

- Attracting foreign and domestic investment to more sophisticated manufacturing, which requires imported inputs.

- Expansion of existing firms through economies of scale.

- Effectively coping with competition from imports.

Throughout this chapter we alluded to the fact that our estimates are likely to be highly conservative; they do not capture all aspects of closures on both current as well as future economic activity. The true costs of closures are likely to be much higher. Besides economic multiplier effects, there are also large social costs, which are even more difficult to quantify, for example, patients not receiving timely medical treatment, children missing out on education, or families being forced to live apart; all these aspects contribute to greater fragility.

---

[16] Global value chains usually require short, predictable delivery schedules unattainable under the closures regime.

6.7 Concluding Remarks

Israeli security measures, increased in response to the Intifada, have imposed a major cost on the WB&G and increased its fragility, heavily undercutting its current and future developmental capacity. The closures regime affects the WB&G through three distinct channels: workers' remittances, current movement of goods and services, and future capacity to export. In this chapter we have attempted to quantify the impact of closures mainly within the first two channels.

The direct current cost relates to the reduction in the number of work permits issued by the Israeli authorities to Palestinians for work in Israel, the reduced number of days worked in Israel, the uncertainty of closures, and other measures affecting Palestinian imports (back-to-back arrangements, extra security measures). Cumulative losses between 2001 and 2005 run to billions of dollars: income forgone by Palestinian workers in Israel is estimated at more than US$3 billion, greater than any other financial loss due to the closures regime. Cumulative loss in export earnings over this period is estimated at approximately US$693 million. Other current losses are more difficult to capture, although it can be safely assumed that the costs of imports increased considerably as a result of Israeli security measures.

The current security regime eats away at the capacity for growth. We find a strong adverse impact of closure on growth in WB&G since their widespread introduction. But today's closures have also a legacy for future growth: closures do not only undercut the competitiveness of existing businesses but also dramatically curtail the range of feasible future investment opportunities in WB&G. In the absence of security measures, unfettered access to markets of such a highly developed economy as Israel would be a powerful magnet for domestic and foreign investments alike. Unfortunately, losses associated with forgone future capacity to export are impossible to assess—except that these are likely to be substantial, as the tight and unpredictable closures regime rules out the participation of WB&G firms in the modern division of labour based on in-time production and inventory management. It also removes incentives to invest in these sectors, as well as in those critically dependent on economies of scale.

Although much remains to be done to improve the quality of governance and business climate in WB&G, reforms and foreign aid will have limited impact on economic development unless they simultaneously remove security measures affecting movements of goods and people between Israel and WB&G, and within the West Bank.

Suspension of closures in 1998–2000 coincided with an almost three-year-long economic recovery in WB&G, with real GDP growing 5 per cent in 1998 and 6 per cent in 1999 before coming to a grinding halt in the last quarter of

2000 after the outbreak of violence. In a similar vein, for the first time in more than a decade, exports of goods showed some signs of growth in the second half of the 1990s, expanding in current prices at an average (least square) rate of 3.5 per cent per year from 1996 to 2000.

While economic theory leaves little doubt that North–South integration is beneficial for a less developed economy, Israeli–Palestinian integration strongly indicates that such benefits will only materialize with an accommodating political economy. As long as closures remain an instrument of Israeli security policy, there will be further disintegration of WB&G and divergence between the two economies.

APPENDIX A

Case study: a furniture producer in WB&G

Our case study highlights the adverse impact of uncertainty in delivery and shipment on transport cost and the profitability of furniture exports. The particular case of the furniture industry has wider implications for at least three reasons: first, the furniture industry has developed significantly in Gaza, accounting for a relatively large sector of Gaza's economy today. In 2005, it included more than 600 firms employing more than 5,500 people. Second, the sector is highly dependent on imports and, to a lesser extent, on exports. Imported inputs account for almost 98 per cent of raw materials, whereas exports make up an estimated 15.5 per cent of production, most of which is destined to Israeli markets. But overall, fewer than 50 furniture manufacturers are engaged in export activities, and very few have successfully exported to markets outside Israel. Third, it shows the lack of prospects for future development. Furniture production is increasingly organized around large multinational retailers (for example, Ikea) establishing value chains across continents and countries. Prolonged closures forestall participation in global value chains and increase the costs of doing business in this sector.

Table 6.A1 presents data assessing the impact of closure of the Karni crossing point on a producer of furniture in Gaza, which relies on imported inputs from Slovenia and exports to the EU. When the Karni crossing is open, total transport costs of imports from Slovenia to Gaza are 17 per cent of import value; total transport costs of exports amount to 9 per cent of the value of exports. On balance, total transport costs (12,905 NIS) amount to 40 per cent of the difference between the value of exports and the value of imported inputs (32,500 NIS), which approximates the value-added created in Gaza.

The profitability picture changes rather significantly when the Karni crossing is closed. Traders estimate that in the case of closures lasting more than a week, land transport cost increases up to four times of the 'normal' cost, as importers and exporters have to pay extra charges for shipments stuck at the terminal. The computations presented in Table 6.A1, assuming a four-time increase in transport charges because of a one-week closure, demonstrate the degree to which prolonged closures cut into the

Table 6.A1. The impact of uncertainty on transport costs: an example from the wood industry in Gaza

	IMPORTS OPEN		IMPORTS CLOSED	
	Costs (in NIS)	In % of load value	Costs (in NIS)	In % of load value
Furniture parts				
Total transport costs	6,355	16.9	10,855	28.9
of which:				
Maritime transport	2,600	6.9	2,600	6.9
Port charges	1,875	5.0	1,875	5.0
Insurance	140	0.4	140	0.4
Ashdod-Gaza	1,500	4.0	6,000	16.0
Costs at Karni	240	0.6	240	0.6
Truckload value	37,500	100.0	37,500	100.0
Furniture				
Total transport costs	6,550	9.4	14,050	20.1
of which:				
Maritime transport	3,600	5.1	3,600	5.1
Port charges	0	0.0		0.0
Insurance	210	0.3	210	0.3
Gaza-Ashdod	2,500	3.6	10,000	14.3
Costs at Karni	240	0.3	240	0.3
Truckload value	70,000	100.0	70,000	100.0

Source: DAI (Development Alternatives, Inc.) Gaza.

value-added remaining in Gaza. These extra costs amount to 77 per cent of the value added in the Gaza Strip. This drastically reduces profit margins, especially since higher land transportation costs are not the only costs incurred by a producer of furniture because of a closure. Part of the uncertainty is absorbed by raising inventories of imported inputs, but this comes at a price.

APPENDIX B

Differential treatment within the 'customs envelope': ports of entry and exit

Although Article III (13) of the Paris Protocol states that 'the import and export of Palestinians through the points of exit and entry in Israel will be given equal trade and economic treatment', reality is different, as the security regime puts Israeli firms in an advantageous position vis-à-vis their WB&G counterparts.

For imports, different treatment starts at Israel's external border. Although shipments destined for Israel and WB&G are subject to the same procedures by virtue of a customs envelope, they tend to be treated differently already at the port of entry into Israel. Higher costs do not depend on the mode of transportation—that is, by sea or air: clearance of shipments usually takes longer due to security. Israeli imports face a 'risk' of security checks amounting to 15–20 per cent, whereas WB&G importers face a 'certainty' of security checks: all shipments destined for WB&G are subject to security procedures. The cargo dwell time is one or two days for Israeli importers and at least one week for a WB&G importer. According to a study by the Federation of the Palestinian Chambers of Commerce, Palestinian companies exporting through the port of Haifa (as well as at Ashdod Port) faced higher costs (18 per cent) and longer delays (20 per cent) than comparable Israeli companies, whereas importers incurred higher costs (11 per cent) and experienced much longer delays (52 per cent) than Israeli companies in 2001. Nothing indicates that the situation has changed for the better since the survey was conducted.

At Ben Gurion airport, WB&G importers and exporters also face rather costly discrimination: in contrast to their Israeli counterparts, they must use dedicated cargo planes, as they are banned from using passenger planes (where some space is reserved for cargo). This is significantly more expensive, as wide-bodied passenger planes have large (often not fully used) cargo space available at attractive freight rates.

On top of the opportunity cost of capital tied up in a shipment, other expenses add up to extra costs. Containers and partial shipments weighing up to 10 tons landed in Israel may be stored free of charge at the port or placed in public bonded warehouses or other places approved by customs for a period up to four days only. Subsequently, they are subject to a port storage fee with additional charges applied after 30 days. Containers weighing more than 10 tons are charged after six days. Other places approved by customs often include the premises of an importing firm, but only if the firm is in Israel.

Another form of asymmetrical treatment regarding WB&G importers is that they are not allowed to run wholesale operations in either Israeli or WB&G markets. In contrast to Israeli importers, WB&G importers are required by Israeli authorities to sign a pledge that they will not sell their imported goods in Israel.

In sum, the security arrangements discriminate against WB&G shipments in points of entry and exit in Israel, wiping away benefits that would be usually associated with deeper integration with a much more developed economy. They not only curb the capacity of WB&G firms to compete in international markets but also subject them to competition from Israeli firms on an unequal footing. These conditions discourage entry of new firms and investments in WB&G.

In addition, they also provide incentive to imports through Israeli intermediaries, although the scope of these indirect imports resulting in customs revenue losses to the WB&G is difficult to estimate. To avoid paying extra costs because of border security measures, many firms directly purchase goods imported into Israel by Israeli firms. Palestinian importers of telecommunications and other high technology products resort to Israeli intermediaries. The cost of use of Israeli middlemen is some indication of extra costs incurred by importers because of security measures. Garment producers buying through these channels estimate that these costs amount to 10 to 25 per cent of the value of imported materials. Since freight forwarding is a highly competitive sector in Israel, this is probably a fairly accurate estimate of these costs.[17]

---

[17] For detailed discussion on selected industries, see the second volume of World Bank (2006a).

References

Arnon, A. and J. Weinblatt (2001). 'Sovereignty and Economic Development: The Case of Israel and Palestine'. *The Economic Journal*, 111 (June): 291–308.

Cobham, D. (2001). 'Economic Aspects of the Israeli–Palestinian Conflict: Introduction'. *The Economic Journal*, 111 (June): 249–53.

Dessus, S. (2004). 'A Palestinian Growth History, 1968–2000'. *Journal of Economic Integration*, 19 (3): 447–69.

Diwan, I. and R. A. Shaban (1999). *Development under Adversity: The Palestinian Economy in Transition*. Washington, DC: World Bank.

Fisher, S., P. Alonson-Gamo, and U. E. von Allmen (2001). 'Economic Developments in the West Bank and Gaza since Oslo'. *The Economic Journal*, 111 (June) 254–75.

Khatib, S. (2005). *Trade and Transport Facilitation Audit*. Ramallah: Paltrade.

OCHA oPt (2005). West Bank and Closure and Access, April 2005, available at <http://www.ochaopt.org>.

Pesaran, M. H. and Y. Shin (1999). 'An Autoregressive Distributed Lag Modeling Approach to Cointegration Analysis', in S. Strom (ed.), *Econometrics and Economic Theory in 20th Century: The Ragnar Frisch Centennial Symposium*. Cambridge: Cambridge University Press.

Pesaran, M. H., Y. Shin, and R. J. Smith (2001). 'Bounds Testing Approaches to the Analysis of Level Relationships'. *Journal of Applied Econometrics*, 16: 289–326.

World Bank (1993). *Developing the Occupied Territories: An Investment in Peace*. Washington, DC: World Bank.

World Bank (2006a). *West Bank and Gaza Country Economic Memorandum: Enhancing the Prospects for Economic Recovery and Growth*. Washington, DC: World Bank.

World Bank (2006b). 'An Update on Palestinian Movement, Access and Trade in the West Bank and Gaza'. World Bank Technical Team Report. Washington, DC: World Bank.

World Bank (2006c). 'An Interim Assessment of Passages and Trade Facilitation', available at <http://go.worldbank.org/RRG3KGWK90>.

World Bank (2006d). 'West Bank and Gaza Country Economic Monitoring Note', April. Washington, DC: World Bank.

World Bank (2006e). 'West Bank and Gaza Country Economic Monitoring Note', Fall. Washington, DC: World Bank.

7

Gender and Ethnicity in Fragile States: The Case of Post-Conflict Kosovo

Sumon Kumar Bhaumik, Ira N. Gang, and Myeong-Su Yun

7.1 Introduction

It is stylized in development literature that female-headed households are more vulnerable to adverse economic conditions such as poverty (Barros et al. 1997; Buvinic and Gupta 1997). Indeed, even in mature industrialized economies such as the USA, the poverty rate among female-headed families without a husband present was 28.3 per cent in 2005 while the corresponding proportion for married couples was 5.5 per cent and 13.4 per cent for male-headed families with no wife present (DeNavas-Walt et al. 2006: table 4).

This is often the case because women find it more difficult to find formal sector employment with the attendant benefits (Buvinic 1990). This problem is further aggravated when the female head has to take on domestic roles that make it difficult for her to accept employment that is less flexible but offers higher pay. A related scenario is a high dependency ratio in female-headed households. In some cases, female-headed households are small—the limiting case of which is a widow living on her own—and thereby unable to enjoy economies of scale (Drèze and Srinivasan 1997).

Intuition suggests that the challenges encountered by female-headed households are even greater in fragile states. To recapitulate, as argued by Naudé, Santos-Paulino, and McGillivray in this book, a fragile state has the following characteristics: they are usually characterized by conflicts and low development status. Large sections of their populations are vulnerable to adverse shocks that can easily push them below the poverty threshold. Finally, governments in these countries typically do not pursue policies that address this vulnerability of the population. As such, fragility of a state is a condition whereby an exogenous shock such as a conflict can propel large sections of the population into poverty, often without the prospect of recovery as low endowments of human capital and assets—correlates of a low development status—coexist with inadequate government support.

In a context such as this, the labour market related vulnerabilities of female-headed households are exacerbated (Loughna and Vicente 1997; Deininger and Castagnini 2004). With violent conflicts, not only do they lose the men in the households, who are the main earners, but they are also displaced from locations within which they have historically had support from family and social networks (Meertens and Stoller 2001). Crimes like rape are rampant and the associated psychological trauma and health problems might impede economic recovery after the conflict (Hamilton 2000). Post-conflict reconstruction programmes often have a gender bias that fails to address the specific vulnerabilities of females (and, by extension, female-headed households) (Zuckerman and Greenberg 2004). More generally, as vulnerable sections of the population they receive little or no support from government apparatus in non-developmental states.

The literature documents the nature and extent of vulnerability of widows and female-headed households in countries characterized by conflicts (for details, see Brück and Schindler 2008). For example, in post-conflict Rwanda, widows faced different forms of discrimination that, among other things, made it difficult for them to access land (Newbury and Baldwin 2000). In post-war rural northern Mozambique, income and (food) consumption of female-headed households are, on average, 33 per cent and 43 per cent (53 per cent) less, respectively, vis-à-vis their male-headed counterparts (Bruck 2001). Evidence from Rwanda suggests that female-headed households are also less likely to move out of poverty (Justino and Verwimp 2008).

As evident from the above discussion, much of the literature about women in general and female-headed households in particular, in the context of post-conflict countries, focuses on Africa and, less often, on Latin America. The observation that female-headed households are disadvantaged in these contexts, however, may not be generalized to all fragile states marked by conflicts. This is especially true if women in a fragile state are historically equally educated, by and large, as their male counterparts (or spouses) and are equal participants in the labour market. Possibly even less so if the post-conflict reconstruction process is overseen or monitored by agencies such as the United Nations and the European Union, which strongly favour gender equality. Such contexts have emerged over the past two decades, especially among the former Soviet and Yugoslav republics. There is no evidence to suggest, for example, that female-headed households were at a disadvantage in post-conflict Bosnia and Herzegovina (Smajic and Ermacora 2007). And yet very little has been written about female-headed households in these contexts. We address this lacuna in the literature by examining the differences in per capita consumption levels between male- and female-headed households in Serbian and Albanian households in the strife-torn Balkan region of Kosovo.

We use regression models to identify covariates of per capita household expenditure in Kosovo,[1] and use the regression estimates to address two empirical questions: (i) whether, *ceteris paribus*, an average female-headed household in Kosovo is worse off than an average male-headed household, and (ii) whether the extent of relative deprivation by gender applies equally to both ethnic groups, that is, whether the extent of relative deprivation of Serb female-headed households is greater (less) than that of Albanian female-headed households. The exact empirical methodology is discussed later in this chapter.

Our results suggest that female-headed households generally do not suffer more than male-headed households, but there is substantial variation among ethnic groups. In fact, Albanian female-headed households are marginally better-off than Albanian male-headed households. The living standard of Serb households is lower than that of Albanians households, and Serb female-headed households suffer substantially lower living standards than male-headed households. Indeed, Serb female-headed households have the lowest standard of living among the four groups defined by ethnicity and gender of head of household.

The rest of the chapter is structured as follows. In the next section we provide a brief background of the context of our analysis, namely, Kosovo. Then we describe our empirical methodology followed by reporting of the data and estimation results. The final section concludes.

7.2 Kosovo

Kosovo is a small landlocked territory on the Balkan Peninsula. The political strife in Kosovo involving the Serbs and Albanians can be traced back to 1948 (Artisien 1984). While the shared political ideology between Yugoslavia and Albania pre-empted an Albanian response to Yugoslavia's re-annexation of Kosovo in 1945, after Yugoslavia's expulsion from the Cominform in 1948, the Albanian government raised the issue of Kosovo's 'unsettled' status, presumably with Soviet backing. The Kosovo issue was put on the backburner after Rankovic's departure in 1968, and, over time, the Yugoslav government granted the autonomous province of Kosovo two major concessions: the borders of the autonomous province could not be changed without the

---

[1] Throughout this chapter, per capita household expenditure is used synonymously with per adult equivalent expenditure.

consent of the residents of the province, and, by 1974, the province had the same rights as the republics of the Yugoslav Federation.

The hostilities resumed after the death of Tito, and both the Serbs and Albanians hardened their positions, even as the province witnessed significant Serb (and Montenegrin) out-migration to other parts of Yugoslavia. The hostilities escalated in 1989 as the Milosevic government began removing Kosovo's autonomy. In 1990, Kosovo Albanians declared independence from Serbia, and Albania recognized Kosovo's independent status in 1991. The resultant armed conflict lasted until 1999, with NATO intervening militarily to persuade Milosevic to withdraw Serb forces from Kosovo. Since 1999, Kosovo has been a protectorate under the guidelines of UN Security Council Resolution number 1244.

Even prior to the changes in Central and Eastern Europe (CEE), people in Kosovo were poor by the standards of the region. In 1988, the year before Kosovo's autonomous status was revoked, the per capita output in Kosovo was only 28 per cent of the average per capita output in Yugoslavia. The economic crisis in Kosovo was aggravated during the 1991–9 period. The civil war reduced the number of able-bodied people of working age, damaged the housing stock and utilities such as power and telecommunication, and disrupted the flow of commerce. A reconstruction boom financed by international donors significantly aided the recovery of the economy soon after the end of the war. By the second half of 2000, agricultural output was estimated to have reached 75 per cent of its pre-conflict level, the investment–GDP ratio had climbed to almost 40 per cent, and per capita GDP stood at US$759. This recovery was marked by two major distortions, namely, total domestic consumption in 2000 was 146 per cent of GDP and imports stood at approximately 80 per cent of GDP.

The UN Mission in Kosovo (UNMIK) is responsible for Kosovo's administration and has established institutions to support the process of economic re-invigoration. The UNMIK helped to create a central fiscal authority (CSA); this authority implements tax policy and formulates an independent budget for Kosovo that is non-overlapping with the budgets of (former state of) Serbia and Montenegro. Together the UNMIK and CSA established a new tax system and a tax administration to replace both the old system inherited from Yugoslavia and the parallel tax systems that had emerged during the conflict. The import regime was simplified and deregulated; no quantitative restrictions remain and the tariff rate is a flat 10 per cent for all goods and services. A department of reconstruction was created to coordinate donor assistance with public investments. Finally, the jobs of overseeing the payments system and domestic banks were entrusted to the newly created Banking and Payments Authority of Kosovo (BPAK).

The economic recovery continued through 2001 with Kosovo's 2001 per capita GDP growing at a rate of 18.4 per cent. However, the earlier imbalances persisted. For example, total consumption in 2001 was 121 per cent of GDP, which clearly is not sustainable in the long run. Moreover, despite the high consumption-to-GDP ratio, most Serbs and Albanians lived in poverty. Bhaumik et al. (2006a) estimate headcount poverty among Serb and Albanian households to be 57.4 per cent and 45.5 per cent, respectively.

7.3 Empirical Strategy

We use regression models to identify covariates of per capita expenditure of households, a measure of living standard, in our sample. The focus of our analysis is the gender and ethnicity of the household head. Other characteristics contributing to the level of a household's per capita expenditure are well-documented in the literature (see Bhaumik et al. 2006b). For example, per capita expenditure may decrease with youth and old age dependency ratios, i.e., the proportion of household members in the age groups 0–15 years and over 65 years. The presence of young children and elderly people, whose employability and earning abilities are low, reduces the overall labour power of the household and, in some cases, working-age household members are not able to participate fully in the labour market because they are required to care for family members, as Pezzin and Schone (1998) discuss. Even among working-age adults, the ability to participate effectively in the labour market may depend on age and gender, as Scott et al. (1995) and Stanley and Jarrell (1998) suggest. Hence, we take into account the age distribution of the households—the proportion of household members in each age category—as well as the proportion of males among working-age adults.

Per capita expenditure is also influenced by the earnings potential of the working-age household members which, in turn, depends on their educational attainment. The literature suggests that both employability and the returns on education vary significantly for individuals with different levels of education, e.g., Grubb (1993) and Arum and Shavit (1995). To capture this effect, we include the proportion of working-age household members with different levels and types of education, namely, no formal education, primary education, general secondary education, vocational training, and tertiary or university education.

The wealth of a household may also be an important determinant of its income and expenditure. We measure the tangible wealth of households in Kosovo by the extent of their land ownership and the value of their livestock. As land and livestock contribute directly towards expenditure, these are particularly relevant in a geographic region where markets were either disturbed or non-existent due to the prolonged military conflict. Furthermore, we take into account social capital in the form of extended families and networks of friends who also contribute towards the economic well-being of a household. The literature on *inter vivos* transfers argues that such social capital plays a crucial role in expenditure smoothing both in developing and developed economies, as Bhaumik and Nugent (2000) discuss. Therefore, the proportion of households that receive private transfers from friends and extended family is an important factor to consider. In the same vein, public transfers may add to the well-being of households but these two types of transfers should be treated differently because, as Maitra and Ray (2003) suggest, their marginal impacts on the expenditure of a household are different. Hence, we also take account of the proportion of households that receive public support because of some disability among their adult members. However, the disability card may be more of a reflection of the failing health of one or more adult household members, i.e., the health related capabilities of the household, rather than public transfers per se.

In addition to these stylized potential covariates, some other factors may also influence per capita household expenditure in the specific context of Kosovo. For example, the location of a household and whether or not it was uprooted from its place of origin may contribute significantly to its economic well-being or economic deprivation. Geographic displacement brought about by war leads not only to job loss and subsequently long-term unemployment, but can also disrupt established social networks. Because of the war, migration may not have been voluntary and migrants might have lost wealth. In addition, emigration out of the country may not have affected all income classes evenly. Therefore, we include the proportion of households living in urban areas as well as the proportion of households that reported having had to migrate after the disintegration of Yugoslavia.

Our empirical strategy involves the estimation of three sets of regression models. First, we estimate the following model separately for the Serb and the Albanian households in our sample:

$$PCHE = \alpha_0 + \alpha_1 FEMHEADED + \Phi'X + u, \tag{7.1}$$

where *PCHE* is (log) per capita household expenditure, *FEMHEADED* is a dummy variable that takes the value unity for female-headed households, X is a vector of the control variables discussed above, and u is the familiar *iid* error term. Next, we estimate a similar specification for female-headed households:

$$PCHE = \beta_0 + \beta_1 SERB + > \Omega'X + v, \tag{7.2}$$

where *SERB* is a dummy variable that takes the value unity for Serb-headed households, and v is the *iid* error term. Finally, we estimate the following model for the pooled sample of all households:

$$PCHE = \delta_0 + \delta_2 SERB + \delta_1 FEMHEADED + \delta_3 (SERB \times FEMHEADED) + \Psi'X + \epsilon \tag{7.3}$$

where ϵ is the *iid* error term. Equation (7.3) not only controls for all non-ethnic and non-gender characteristics that affect per capita household consumption, it also enables distinction between the impact of ethnicity and female-head-edness of households.

If, indeed, female-headed households in Kosovo are worse off than male-headed households, then the coefficients of the *FEMHEADED* variable in Equation (7.1) should be negative for both the Serb and Albanian samples. A comparison of the estimates of α_1 for the Serb and Albanian samples would also provide an indication about whether the relative deprivation of female-headed households is more (less) among Serbs than among Albanians. Equation (7.2) directly sheds light on this latter issue. If the extent of deprivation, as manifested in lower per capita household expenditure, is higher for Serb female-headed households, then the coefficient of the *SERB* dummy variable would be negative, and vice versa.

Finally, it is easily seen that the models outlined by Equations (7.1) and (7.2) are nested in Equation (7.3), and the estimates of δ_1, δ_2, and δ_3 shed light on the same two issues, thereby facilitating a robustness check for our results. Specifically, δ_0 is the estimate for the baseline category, namely, Albanian male-headed households, δ_1 is the general difference in per capita household expenditure between Serbs and Albanians, δ_2 is the general difference in the same between female- and male-headed households, and δ_3 is the special effect of being a Serbian female-headed household.[2] For Albanian households, the difference in the per capita expenditures of an average female-headed household and an average male-headed household is δ_2 [$= (\delta_0 + \delta_2) - \delta_0$]. Similarly, for Serb households, the difference in the per capita expenditures of an average female-headed household and an average male-headed household is $\delta_2 + \delta_3$ [$= (\delta_0 + \delta_1 + \delta_2 + \delta_3) - (\delta_0 + \delta_1)$]. Hence, the coefficient of the interaction term, δ_3, represents the extra burden of being female-headed among Serb households.

7.4 Data And Empirical Results

To better assess the economic well-being of the population in Kosovo, including the width, depth, and correlates of poverty, the World Bank organized a

---

[2] As is true in any discussion using regression analysis, the coefficients represent partial effects, meaning the changes in per capita household expenditure when the value of dummy variable changes from zero to one, e.g., changing from Albanian households to Serb households, while keeping values of other household characteristics constant.

living standards measurement survey (LSMS). The survey, carried out between September and December of 2000, collected data from 2880 households and is statistically representative of both the Albanians and Serbs in Kosovo. After accounting for missing values, the survey provides information on 2101 Albanian households and 416 Serbian households.[3]

We report key descriptive statistics associated with the variables of interest in Table 7.1. In keeping with our empirical strategy, we report comparative figures for male- and female-headed Serb and Albanian households, as well as for all male- and female-headed households in the sample.

The descriptive statistics indicate the following:

— In general, female-headed households have per capita consumption levels 3.6 per cent below male-headed households (122.11 vs. 126.64).

— Albanian female-headed households have per capita consumption levels 2.3 per cent above Albanian male-headed households (131.07 vs. 128.09).

— Serbian female-headed households have per capita consumption levels 23.9 per cent below Serbian male-headed households (87.36 vs. 114.77).

— The incidence (headcount ratio) of poverty is greater for female-headed households regardless of ethnicity.

— There are relatively more female-headed households among Serbs.

— Age structure, educational attainment, assets, and transfers differ by ethnicity and gender, indicating it is important to account for these factors in discussing the true extent of gender and ethnicity gaps.

The regression estimates are reported in Table 7.2. The rationale for the use of these models and the associated specifications were discussed earlier. The F-statistics for the specifications are significant at the 1 per cent level, indicating that the regression models yield meaningful results. Further, the adjusted R-squared values, which range from 0.18 to 0.29 and are comparable with other cross-section estimates of per capita expenditure functions for similar-sized samples, indicate that the regression specifications explain inter-household variations in per capita expenditures quite well.

The regression estimates indicate that the presence of young and elderly people in the households reduces the per capita expenditure of households. For example, in the combined sample of all 2517 households, an increase in the proportion of children in the age groups of 0–15 years and even 16–25, as also people older than 65 years, reduces (log) per capita expenditures by 0.61,

---

[3] The survey over-samples Serbian households. In a sample containing only these two ethnic groups in Kosovo, Serbs should account for 7.4 per cent and Albanians 92.6 per cent of the observations. In our data, 83 per cent of the households are Albanians and the rest are Serbs.

Table 7.1. Mean household characteristics

	Albanians		Serbs		Serbs & Albanians	
	Female-headed	Male-headed	Female-headed	Male-headed	Female-headed	Male-headed
Per capita household expenditure and poverty incidence						
Per capita expenditure (DM)	131.07	128.05	87.36	114.77	122.11	126.64
Headcount poverty ratio	0.50	0.45	0.77	0.54	0.56	0.46
Ethnicity of household head						
Dummy = 1 if head is a Serb					0.20	0.11
Demographic characteristics of households						
Proportion of household members in 0–15 age group	0.30	0.35	0.11	0.19	0.26	0.31
Proportion of household members in 16–25 age group	0.27	0.21	0.15	0.16	0.25	0.20
Proportion of household members in 26–35 age group	0.13	0.14	0.09	0.13	0.13	0.14
Proportion of household members in 36–45 age group	0.09	0.11	0.10	0.13	0.09	0.11
Proportion of household members in 46–55 age group	0.10	0.10	0.10	0.15	0.10	0.11
Proportion of household members in 56–65 age group	0.06	0.07	0.24	0.15	0.09	0.08
Proportion of household members older than 55	0.05	0.04	0.21	0.09	0.08	0.05
Proportion of male household members	0.29	0.49	0.19	0.53	0.27	0.49
Education of working-age household members						
Proportion of working-age adults with no formal education	0.12	0.09	0.08	0.02	0.11	0.08
Proportion of working-age adults with primary education	0.47	0.45	0.42	0.30	0.46	0.43
Proportion of working-age adults with secondary education	0.27	0.30	0.39	0.53	0.30	0.32
Proportion of working-age adults with vocational education	0.09	0.03	0.07	0.07	0.08	0.08
Proportion of working-age adults with university education	0.06	0.09	0.05	0.08	0.06	0.09
Household assets						
Acres of land owned by household	0.06	0.07	0.03	0.13	0.06	0.08
Value of domestic animals owned by household	0.44	0.57	0.22	0.50	0.40	0.56
Public and private transfers						
Dummy = 1 if at least one household member has disability card	0.05	0.10	0.10	0.10	0.06	0.10
Dummy = 1 if at least one household member receives private transfers	0.62	0.42	0.10	0.04	0.51	0.38
Location and migration						
Dummy = 1 if head of the household migrated from native place of residence	0.68	0.76	0.06	0.09	0.56	0.69
Dummy = 1 if household is resident in an urban area	0.31	0.27	0.56	0.40	0.37	0.29
Sample Size	139	1,962	54	362	193	2,324

Source: See text.

Table 7.2. Female-headed households, ethnicity, and per capita consumption

	Equation (7.1)		Equation (7.2)	Equation (7.3)
	Albanians	Serbs	Female-headed	All
Constant	4.35 ***	3.92 ***	4.34 ***	4.40 ***
	(0.11)	(0.23)	(0.24)	(0.10)
Gender and ethnicity of household heads				
Dummy = 1 if head is a Serb				-0.29 ***
				(0.03)
Dummy = 1 if head is a female	0.07 ***	-0.08		0.07
	(0.05)	(0.09)		(0.05)
Female-headed × Serb head				-0.19 *
				(0.10)
Demographic characteristics of households				
Proportion of household members in 0–15 age group	-0.60 ***	-0.43 **	-0.47 *	-0.61 ***
	(0.10)	(0.21)	(0.25)	(0.09)
Proportion of household members in 16–25 age group	-0.28 ***	-0.24	0.46 **	-0.26 ***
	(0.08)	(0.17)	(0.20)	(0.08)
Proportion of household members in 36–45 age group	0.04	0.10	0.35	0.03
	(0.09)	(0.16)	(0.24)	(0.08)
Proportion of household members in 46–55 age group	0.14	-0.16	-0.10	0.02
	(0.10)	(0.17)	(0.29)	(0.09)
Proportion of household members in 56–65 age group	0.05	-0.25	0.02	-0.10
	(0.12)	(0.18)	(0.27)	(0.10)
Proportion of household members older than 65	-0.21	-0.31 *	-0.21	-0.29 ***
	(0.14)	(0.17)	(0.27)	(0.10)
Proportion of male household members	0.14	0.20	-0.36 *	0.16 **
	(0.09)	(0.16)	(0.19)	(0.08)
Education of working-age household members				
Proportion of working-age adults with primary education	0.24 ***	0.31 *	0.27	0.22 ***
	(0.08)	(0.18)	(0.18)	(0.07)
Proportion of working-age adults with secondary education	0.69 ***	0.87 ***	0.71 ***	0.68 ***
	(0.08)	(0.19)	(0.21)	(0.08)
Proportion of working-age adults with vocational education	0.63 ***	0.92 ***	0.50 **	0.65 ***
	(0.08)	(0.19)	(0.19)	(0.08)

	(0.11)	(0.22)	(0.20)	(0.10)
Proportion of working-age adults with university education	0.93 ***	1.44 ***	0.91 ***	0.95 ***
	(0.09)	(0.21)	(0.27)	(0.09)
Household assets				
Acres of land owned by household	0.32 **	0.01	1.46 ***	0.06
	(0.15)	(0.01)	(0.57)	(0.04)
Value of domestic animals owned by household	0.07 ***	0.05	– 0.01	0.08 ***
	(0.02)	(0.03)	(0.07)	(0.02)
Public and private transfers				
Dummy = 1 if at least one household member has disability card	– 0.01	– 0.12 *	0.15 *	– 0.02
	(0.04)	(0.07)	(0.09)	(0.04)
Dummy = 1 if at least one household member receives private transfers	0.06 **	0.31 ***	0.11	0.07 ***
	(0.02)	(0.10)	(0.08)	(0.02)
Location and migration				
Dummy = 1 if head of the household migrated from native place of residence	0.001	– 0.12 *	– 0.22 **	– 0.01
	(0.03)	(0.10)	(0.10)	(0.03)
Dummy = 1 if household is resident in an urban area	0.02	0.03	0.17	0.02
	(0.03)	(0.05)	(0.11)	(0.03)
F-statistic	26.23 ***	10.61 ***	5.04 ***	30.53 ***
Adjust R-square	0.18	0.29	0.27	0.19
Sample size	2,101	416	193	2,517

Note: The values within parentheses are robust standard errors. ***, **, and * indicate significance at 1%, 5%, and 10% levels, respectively.

Source: See text.

0.26, and 0.29 log-points, respectively. Per capita expenditure increases with the human capital of working-age household members; the increase is higher for households whose working-age members have secondary or tertiary education, as opposed to primary or vocational education. It increases with household assets as captured by the value of domestic animals, and is higher for households that receive private transfers. These results are reasonable on their own, and are consistent with the results reported by Bhaumik et al. (2006b).

The estimates for the smaller sample of 193 female-headed households indicate that the presence of young children in the 0–15 year age group and elderly people over 66 years reduces per capita expenditure of these households. However, presence of young people in the 16–25 year age group increases their per capita expenditure, possibly indicating that in female-headed households children and younger adults close to adulthood contribute to the household income by participating in the labour force relatively early. A plausible explanation for this is that the well-understood vulnerability of female-headed households results in greater effort by other household members, including the older children, to increase household income. Education of working-age adults once again adds to the per capita expenditure of these households.

However, in contrast to the estimates of the overall sample of 2517 households, per capita expenditure of female-headed households is positively affected by land ownership and *public* transfers, the proxy for which is the ownership of a disability card by at least one household member. This is consistent with the literature discussed earlier in this chapter which concluded that access to land and government aid for female-headed households should be a key element in post-conflict reconstruction policies (Newbury and Baldwin 2000; Justino and Verwimp 2008). In further contrast to the estimates of the overall sample, per capita expenditure of female-headed households is negatively affected by migration, typically as a consequence of the unrest in the region. This too is consistent with the existing literature (Meertens and Stoller 2001).

The regression results also clearly show the differential impacts of ethnicity and gender in Kosovo on per capita household expenditure while holding other household characteristics unchanged. The reported estimates of Equation (7.1) indicate that, other things remaining the same, female-headed Albanian households are actually *better-off* than their male-headed counterparts ($\alpha_{1,\text{Albanian}} = 0.07 > 0$ at the 1 per cent level), while, though not statistically significant probably due to small sample size, female-headed households among Serbs are worse off than male-headed households ($\alpha_{1,\text{Serb}} = -0.08$). The significant and negative coefficient of Serb dummy variable in Equation (7.2) ($\beta_1 = -0.59 < 0$ at the 1 per cent level) confirms that among the female-headed households ethnicity still matters. The compounded effect of ethnicity and gender is further verified by the estimates reported in the last column of the table.[4]

To recapitulate, from the last column of the table, the benchmark for this regression model is the male-headed Albanian household. The estimates indicate that Serb households, irrespective of the gender of the household, have a lower per capita household expenditure, on average, than the benchmark male-headed Albanian households ($\delta_1 = -0.29 < 0$ at the 1 per cent level). Further, while the estimate of the interaction term between Serb-headed and female-headed households, $\delta_3 = -0.19 < 0$, significant at 10 per cent level, indicates that the degree of deprivation of female-headed households relative to male-headed households among Serb households is further exacerbated when compared to the degree of deprivation by the gender of head among Albanian households.

7.5 Concluding Remarks

The results reported in the previous sections are striking on two counts.[5] First, they demonstrate that ethnic differences explain inter-household differences in per capita consumption than female-headedness. Second, and more importantly for this chapter, they better demonstrate that there is a significant inter-ethnic difference in the impact of female-headedness of a household. We can only speculate on the reasons why female-headedness reduces consumption among Serb households but not among Albanian households. If, for example, Serb women were represented disproportionately more in formal sector employment in pre-conflict Kosovo, they were more likely to experience challenges to employability in post-conflict Kosovo, where most jobs were likely to be in the informal sector. In order to shed more light on this difference, one would require in-depth case studies that outline the differences in the nature of challenges encountered by women and female-headed households of the two different ethnic groups, and perhaps also on the (often culturally determined) intra-household dynamics of female-headed households of Serb and Albanian communities. In other words, we need to study welfare in fragile states, where conflicts among ethnicities or tribes or political ideologies are at the forefront, not only from ethnicity/tribe/ideology perspectives, but also

---

[4] Regression results are consistent with the descriptive statistics reported in Table 7.1 that indicate that the distribution of per capita household expenditure is defined by the following hierarchical pattern: Albanian female-headed households > Albanian male-headed households > Serb male-headed households > Serb female-headed households.

[5] Here, we refer to the estimates of Equation (7.3) that is 'complete' in the sense that this equation nests Equations (7.1) and (7.2).

from gender perspectives. Specifically, we need to understand better how contexts interact with factors such as ethnicity and associated cultures to have different impacts on the vulnerability of women and female-headed households. This understanding is essential for formulation of targeted policies that better account for gender in post-conflict and fragile states.

References

Artisien, P. F. R. (1984). 'A Note on Kosovo and the Future of Yugoslav–Albanian Relations: A Balkan Perspective'. *Soviet Studies*, 36 (2): 267–76.

Arum, R. and Y. Shavit (1995). 'Secondary Vocational Education and the Transition from School to Work'. *Sociology of Education*, 68 (3): 187–204.

Barros, R., L. Fox, and R. Menonca (1997). 'Female-Headed Households, Poverty, and the Welfare of Children in Urban Brazil'. *Economic Development and Cultural Change*, 45 (2): 231–57.

Bhaumik, S. K. and J. B. Nugent (2000). 'Wealth Accumulation, Fertility, and Transfers to Elderly Households in Peru'. In A. Mason and G. Tapinios (eds), *Sharing the Wealth*. New York: Oxford University Press.

Bhaumik, S. K., I. N. Gang, and M.-S. Yun (2006a). 'A Note on Poverty in Kosovo'. *Journal of International Development*, 18 (8): 1177–87.

Bhaumik, S. K., I. N. Gang, and M.-S. Yun (2006b). 'Ethnic Conflict and Economic Disparity: Serbians and Albanians in Kosovo'. *Journal of Comparative Economics*, 34 (4): 754–73.

Brück, T. (2001). 'Determinants of Rural Poverty in Post-War Mozambique: Evidence from a Household Survey and Implications for Government and Donor Policy', Queen Elizabeth House Working Paper No. 67, University of Oxford.

Brück, T. and K. Schindler (2008). 'The Impact of Conflict and Fragility of Households: A Conceptual Framework with Reference to Widows', WIDER Research Paper No. 2008/83, Helsinki: UNU-WIDER.

Buvinic, M. (1990). 'The Vulnerability of Women-Headed Households: Policy Questions and Options for Latin America and the Caribbean'. Mimeo, ICRW, Washington, DC, and Population Council, New York.

Buvinic, M. and G. R. Gupta (1997). 'Female-headed Households and Female-maintained Families: Are They Worth Targeting to Reduce Poverty in Developing Countries?' *Economic Development and Cultural Change*, 45 (2): 259–80.

Deininger, K. and R. Castagnini (2004). 'Incidence and Impact of Land Conflict in Uganda', WB Policy Research Working Paper No. 3248. Washington, DC: World Bank.

DeNavas-Walt, C., B. D. Proctor, and C. H. Lee (2006). 'Income, Poverty, and Health Insurance Coverage in the United States: 2005', US Census Bureau, Current Population Reports, P60–231. Washington, DC: US Government Printing Office.

Drèze, J. and P. V. Srinivasan (1997). 'Widowhood and Poverty in Rural India: Some Inferences from Household Survey Data'. *Journal of Development Economics*, 53: 217–34.

Grubb, W. N. (1993). 'The Varied Economic Returns to Post-Secondary Education: New Evidence from the Class of 1972'. *Journal of Human Resources*, 28: 365–82.

Hamilton, H. B. (2000). 'Rwanda's Women: The Key to Reconstruction'. *Journal of Humanitarian Assistance*, <http://www.jha.ac/greatlakes/b001.htm>.

Justino, P. and P. Verwimp (2008). 'Poverty Dynamics, Violent Conflict and Convergence in Rwanda', MICROCON Research Working Paper No. 4. Brighton: University of Sussex.

Loughna, S. and G. Vicente (1997). 'Population Issues and the Situation of Women in Post-Conflict Guatemala'. Mimeo. Geneva: ILO.

Maitra, P. and R. Ray (2003). 'The Effect of Transfers on Household Expenditure Patterns and Poverty in South Africa'. *Journal of Development Economics*, 71 (1): 23–49.

Meertens, D. and R. Stoller (2001). 'Destruction, Rebuilding Life: Gender and Internally Displaced in Colombia'. *Latin American Perspectives*, 28 (1): 132–48.

Newbury, C. and H. Baldwin (2000). 'Aftermath: Women in Postgenocide Rwanda', Working Paper No. 303. Washington, DC: Center for Development Information and Evaluation, USAID.

Pezzin, L. E. and B. S. Schone (1998). 'Intergenerational Household Formation, Female Labour Supply and Informal Care Giving'. *Journal of Human Resources*, 34 (3): 475–503.

Scott, F. A., M. C. Berger, and J. E. Garen (1995). 'Do Health Insurance and Pension Costs Reduce the Job Opportunities of Older Workers?' *Industrial and Labour Relations Review*, 48 (4): 775–91.

Smajic, S. and S. Ermacora (2007). 'Poverty amongst Female-Headed Households in Bosnia and Herzegovina: An Empirical Analysis', *South East European Journal of Economics and Business*, 3: 69–88.

Stanley, T. D. and S. B. Jarrell (1998). 'Gender Wage Discrimination Bias? A Meta-Regression Analysis'. *Journal of Human Resources*, 33 (4): 947–73.

Zuckerman, E. and M. Greenberg (2004). 'The Gender Dimensions of Post-Conflict Reconstruction: An Analytical Framework for Policymakers'. *Gender and Development*, 12 (3): 70–82.

Part III
Responses

8

Enforcing Peace Agreements in Fragile States through Commitment Technologies

S. Mansoob Murshed and Philip Verwimp[1]

8.1 Introduction

The introductory chapter in this volume discusses in detail various definitions of 'state fragility'. Fragility can result from factors external to the country such as the dangers of foreign invasion, external economic shocks, and global climate change. These features may be regarded as exogenous sources of fragility. There are also internal, more endogenous, origins of fragility that relate to the failure of economic policies to reduce mass poverty, as well as the failure to develop an acceptable and legitimate polity. Related to both these factors, and a prominent source of fragility in general, is the risk of recurring violent internal conflict in a country that has recently experienced civil war (see Chapter 1). This is the issue that is addressed in this chapter.

Usually when conflicts break out in the developing world attempts are made to mediate between the warring parties by outside powers. These often result in peace agreements. Why is it so difficult to sustain peace agreements following civil wars in developing countries? Well-known examples of broken peace agreements are the Addis Ababa Agreement (Sudan 1972); the Arusha Agreement (Rwanda 1993); and the Angola Peace Agreements (1991 and 1994). Not only do peace treaties need to be brokered by outside powers (Nordic countries or United Nations agencies, for example), but their continued engagement as financiers and enforcers of the peace is required if the negotiated settlement that is mediated is to last. In other words, most peace agreements between warring factions in contemporary developing country civil wars are not

[1] Mansoob Murshed is grateful to Scott Gates and other participants of the PRIO (WG 7) workshop in Oslo, 14–15 May 2004, for their comments and suggestions.

self-enforcing. Walter (2002) points out the empirical regularity with which peace deals break down, and civil wars resume. She also points out the fact that it is much more likely that belligerents will agree to a deal if they are able to share power following the agreement, and when a third party guarantees the peace arrangement. Similarly, Fortna (2004) extends the analysis as to why some peace treaties endure while others flounder. Hastily cobbled together power sharing deals, in particular, do not always ensure that the peace will last because of various temptations to renege on current undertakings in the future, see Rothchild (2005). And, in many instances this future period may not be too far away, as is often the case when valuable resource rents are at stake, or if long-standing collective grievances exist, calling into question the credibility of the peace agreement in the first place.

Arguably, therefore, the greatest impediment to sustaining peace agreements is the imperfect or insincere nature of the *commitment* to peace. The theme of commitment in the context of modern conflict can be traced back to the work of Schelling (1960). More generally, a costly commitment problem arises when an agreement or contract may be reneged upon, usually because the undertaking cannot be enforced by a third party or court of law; see Hart (1995) on commercial applications of contracts that require renegotiation. If breaches of contract cannot be remedied, the credibility of the agreement is questionable. One side will not be able to successfully 'bribe' another group into always adhering to peace, because the recipient's commitment to the deal is suspect. Therefore, there is no potential political 'Coase' theorem because there is no enforcement of the bargain. In political science, for example, an absolute monarch who is not subject to constitutional constraints can never credibly commit to a future course of action, as he or she can easily go back on earlier undertakings. Ultimately, a peace treaty is only a piece of paper. It will be self-enforcing as long as it is in the interests of the parties concerned to adhere to its stipulations. If not, it will collapse, unless there is some form of (outside) enforcement.

Peace agreements are unsustainable when they are not in the interests of at least one side entering into the agreement. Stated in another way, the benefits from peace are not incentive compatible. Also, we often see that repeated attempts at peace-making are often necessary before lasting peace is established. Even when a side in civil war is not ready for peace, it might engage in 'cheap talk' about peace in order to curry favour with donors and international agencies. It has to be borne in mind that many peace conferences, temporary cease-fires, and even peace agreements are reached after mediation by well-meaning outside parties such as the governments of Finland, Norway, or Switzerland. Furthermore, civil wars are sometimes temporarily halted by outside military peace enforcement as in Liberia (ECOMOG) and Somalia (USA)—in other instances peace may be more lasting as with the British intervention in Sierra

Leone. Barring outright military victory by one side, most civil wars cannot be ended without outside intervention, including the use of aid, trade restrictions, and peace keeping efforts to sustain the agreement following the cessation of hostilities.

An illustration of the various mechanisms we model in our chapter may be found in the Rwandan case (Verwimp 2004). In 1993, after two and a half years of civil war, the Rwandan President, Major-General J. Habyarimana signed a peace agreement with his opponents, the Rwandan Patriotic Front (RPF), in the Tanzanian town of Arusha. He signed under immense pressure from donors, domestic opposition, and the military threat of the rebel force. Western donors were heavily engaged in the entire peace process, including military support and promises of financial aid. With the economy in subsistence mode, coffee prices down, and crop failure hurting the population, the regime was struggling to survive. But one may ask: were the president and rebel army (RPF) genuinely *committed* to peace? The answer must be 'no'. In a speech before his supporters, the president called the agreement 'just a scrap of paper'. A group of officers and leading administrators from the president's inner circle were organizing small-scale massacres of Tutsi far from the frontline in which a total of 2000 people were killed (FIDH 1993) and the presidential clan set up a hate radio station (Radio des Mille Colinnes) that vehemently attacked the peace agreement and the Rwandan Patriotic Front (RPF). The fact of the matter was that the ruling elite around Habyarimana was used to ruling the country on their own, and had no long-term interest in sharing power with the RPF. Even sharing power with the domestic Hutu opposition was only accomplished after intense pressure from within and outside the country. The campaign of hate ultimately ended in genocide that cost the lives of at least 500,000 Tutsi people. The Rwandan Patriotic Front on their part repeatedly engaged in surprise attacks (January 1991, February 1993) which cast doubts on their commitment to peace as well. With a weak mandate to enforce the peace, the small and under-equipped UN contingent tragically failed to prevent violence as soon as the peace agreement collapsed.

Relating the Rwandan case to the model that we develop in this chapter, we can summarize it as follows: (i) the presence of deep-seated historical grievances; (ii) a civil war leading to a peace agreement; (iii) the inability to share power; (iv) the use of surprise attacks; (v) weak and inadequate enforcement of the agreement; (vi) worsening of the civil war and ultimately genocide, which shows that inadequate enforcement of a treaty may make matters worse; and (vii) the reconstruction phase with greater international support in terms of aid and implicit threats of violence.

The theoretical modelling literature on civil war persistence as a failure of commitment to peaceful behaviour is characterized by its paucity. Of the few models that do exist, Addison and Murshed (2002) argue that discounting future costs of reneging on treaty obligations causes peace agreements to crumble. They also point out that uncertainty about honest/dishonest types of agents engenders extra costs. Azam (1995) models the imperfect credibility of transfers made by a ruling group to potential armed rebels. Azam (2005) also models imperfect commitment to peace treaties and outside intervention to enforce the peace based on incomplete information about the true nature of the protagonists. Fearon (2001) characterizes ongoing civil war as a consequence of the phenomenon that might make the remote possibility of outright military victory a more attractive option to compromise and peace. Wood (2003) analyses the self-enforcing robustness of settlements to civil war, pointing out that one important reason for the breakdown of peace deals is the indivisibility of what is contested, be it the post-war economic surplus or intrinsic symbols, such as Har'm-al-Sharif or Temple Mount in Jerusalem, or ideological aims such as the abolition of the monarchy in Nepal.

This chapter builds an analytical signalling model of a peace agreement based on Addison and Murshed (2002). In the next section, we establish the imperfect credibility of a peace agreement when greed based on the desire to acquire natural resource rents, or equally, deep-seated grievances make it incentive incompatible for one side to commit to peace. In our example it is the rebel side, but that role can be assigned to the government or any spoiler group without loss of generality. So why are incentive-compatible or self-enforcing peace treaties not arrived at? One reason is that in some cases the parties have intractable differences, and can never agree to a sharing rule in a post-war situation, without outright military victory for one side, or an outside power altering the incentive structure. Second, one party or faction within a party may have such a bad reputation that they cannot credibly commit to an agreement even if they wish to. There may be no institutions upon which to anchor genuine commitments to peace; most conflict-ridden countries experience war because of weak state capacity in the context of a degenerated political system. Third, information may be imperfect. The presence of lootable resource rents—such as those associated with alluvial gemstones, illicit narcotics, or fuels—may make it difficult to see through avaricious tendencies to grab more for oneself or the group through the resumption of fighting. Finally, a high rate of discount for future costs. One side or faction may wish to break the agreement in order to satisfy its current impatience to consume, discounting the future consequences of reneging on a commitment to peace. This chapter attempts to address all these considerations.

The role of externally imposed commitment technologies (mechanism design) to make peace more likely to last are considered next. In particular, it is shown that sanctions (such as a peace keeping force) imposed by outside powers can only work if they too turn out to be credible. This result is the analytical counterpart of the all too often observed phenomenon of failed and imperfect peace keeping. For example, peace keeping is considerably more robust in the Balkans than in many parts of Africa. Larger and better equipped forces patrol smaller territories in the former region. Former conflict-afflicted regions in the Balkans, such as Bosnia-Herzegovina, receive more external assistance per capita than their counterparts in Africa. The efficacy of the sanctions imposed by peace keepers is also a function of their mandate. UN peace keepers may be less empowered to intervene compared to NATO forces or the militaries of unilaterally imposed peace keepers. Ultimately, sanctions that enforce the peace cost money. To this end, we also discuss the 'production' of where the sanction is financed by an outside power but executed by another, closer, party. For instance, peace keeping in the Darfur in the Sudan is being carried out by African Union members, but financed by Western donors such as the European Union. When these arrangements in distant lands yield little utility to outside sponsors, or are very expensive, the sanction and bite of the peace keeping operation can become largely ineffective.

8.2 The Imperfect Credibility Of Peace Agreements

The basic set-up of the model involves two sides, referred to as government and rebels. One side is either tired of fighting or it has an interest in peace. This group is the government in our example. The other side, the rebels, may have something to gain from the resumption of fighting. Note that the roles played by the government and rebels in the games that follow can be reversed without altering the results. Both sides have entered into a peace deal. The government side derives no benefit from breaking this agreement. Consider the utility function of the rebel group (U^R):

$$U^R = -(1/2)c_1 w^2 + E\theta c_2(w - w^e) + Iw \tag{8.1}$$

$$c_1 > 0, w, w^e, \theta, c_2 \geq 0.$$

$$\theta = B + \epsilon, B \geq 0, \ldots \epsilon = \epsilon_{t-1} + \eta, \eta(0, \sigma^2)$$

In Equation (8.1) and what follows, the utility functions correspond to expected utilities. The expectation operator (E) is introduced for the value of a random variable within the function, and a superscript e is used for an expectation of a variable on which information is (or may be) incomplete. The first term on the right-hand side of Equation (8.1) is the pure cost of conflict in quadratic (squared) form, where w represents warfare or belligerent behaviour[2] and c_1 is the parameter measuring the direct cost of warfare. The negative sign before it is to indicate the cost or disutility from fighting. The quadratic form of the cost illustrates that the costs of war rise more than proportionately as the level of w rises. The parameter $(1/2)$ is introduced for analytical tractability.

The second term on the right-hand side of (8.1) indicates the gains to the rebels from reneging on a peace agreement, or the benefit from a 'surprise' war, where the level of actual conflict (w) exceeds the level of conflict expected by the opposition, the government in our example (w^e). In other words, the spoils of war (capturable rents) can only be wrested via the ruse of peaceful intentions. The parameter c_2 captures the magnitude of this desire, the higher c_2 is, the greater the gain from feigning to make peace first and looting later. It may also be viewed as a subjective measure of *greed*. In addition to this, the greater the abundance of lootable resources, or rents to be extracted, the higher is the gain from surprise war. This is measured by the expected value (E) of the parameter θ which captures the rent (B) from disputed natural resources such as oil, diamonds, drugs, and so on. The rent or booty is subject to random shocks (ε) with a first-order auto-regressive process resulting in shocks persisting for some time. The purely random component (η) has zero mean and constant variance. Random shocks could arise from terms of trade fluctuations or sudden increases in outside contributions to the war chest.

The third term in Equation (8.1) represents an intrinsic motivation (I) on the part of the rebels to fight the government based on deep-seated historical grievances (such as between Hutu and Tutsi), ideological differences (land reform, monarchy), or intractable indivisible stakes such as the control of a city/shrine (see Wood 2003), or secessionist tendencies. Note that both greed and grievance are incorporated into the utility function for the rebels. Equation (8.1) is the utility function of the rebel leaders and their followers whose participation and incentive compatibility constraints have to be satisfied to induce them to follow their commanders. Note also that the cost of fighting and gains from war are additive separable.

The pecuniary component of the rebel utility function (the second term in Equation (8.1)) may be characterized by the following process of income generation (y^R):

$$y^R = y^N + E\theta(w - w^e) \tag{8.2}$$

---

[2] The variable w may be measured in terms of chosen military expenditure and other costs of war broadly defined. We omit aspects of 'conflict technology' considered by authors such as Hirshleifer (1995), dealing with the trade-offs between peaceful and military production and the probability of winning influenced by decisiveness, as they are of marginal interest to issues addressed in this chapter.

Here the income of rebels is equal to some fixed rate (y^N), plus an additional component arising from surprise warfare. The income associated with the fixed rate is the certain income received by the rebels as a result of the peace treaty, and is therefore omitted from (8.1). It may incorporate the pecuniary value of power sharing with the government. In contrast, the gains from the second term in (8.2) are based upon driving a wedge between actual and expected levels of belligerence on the part of the rebel group's opponents. This implies gains from surprise warfare (reneging on a peace agreement), when there is something to gain based on expected θ which measures the rent from capturable natural resources. More importantly, these rents remain contestable even after the peace settlement and can only be captured through belligerent action. The rebel group wants more than what is considered fair and acceptable in the peace settlement; it gets it through surprise war because of weak institutions of restraint.

The rebels maximize their utility in (1) subject to w, which leads to optimal w^*:

$$w^* = (E\theta c_2 + I)/c_1 \qquad (8.3)$$

Proposition 1: From (8.3), the equilibrium choice of warfare is greater the higher the element of pure avarice, c_2, the higher the expected availability of lootable resources and other sources of finance, θ, the greater the grievance or intrinsic motivation to fight (I), and the smaller the direct cost of fighting, c_1. Both greed and grievance have been incorporated into the rebel decisionmaking calculus.

As far as the government (G) is concerned, a simple version of their utility function is:

$$U^G(w^e/w) = -(w - w^e)^2 \qquad (8.4)$$

The meaning of (8.4) is that government's utility is declining in surprise warfare, when w diverges from w^e. In case actual fighting levels are in excess of the government side's expectation, it is clearly caught less than fully prepared for war. In the event that actual fighting is less than expected, the disutility arises because the government has to engage in unforeseen military expenditure that diverts income from other types of public expenditure or increases its borrowing/aid requirement. Maximizing (8.4) with respect to w^e yields:

$$w = w^e \qquad (8.5)$$

The government reacts at the same time as the rebels. Substituting (8.3) into (8.1) for the rebel group, and (8.5) into (8.4) for the government, gives us:

$$U^R = [-(E\theta c_2 + I)^2 + 2I(E\theta c_2 + I)]/2c_1$$
$$U^G = 0$$
(8.6)

This is the outcome when the rebels have an incentive to renege on an announcement of complete peace, but it does not have a first mover advantage. The only positive term in the rebel utility function emanates from grievance. Both announcements by the rebels and expectations formation by the government take place simultaneously. If the rebels pursue a policy of no warfare, with $w = 0$, the payoffs in (8.6) become:

$$U_P^R = 0$$
$$U_P^G = 0$$
(8.7)

This is the Pareto optimal outcome and superior to the result in (8.6). In the optimal state there is no war, and $y^R = y^N$.

Now, consider a situation where the rebels enjoy a first mover advantage and send signals of peaceful intentions, and then engage in surprise warfare. If their signal is believed, the actual and expected levels of warfare would diverge, $w = (E\theta c_2 + I)/c_1$ and $w^e = 0$ in Equation (8.1). This involves cheating on a pre-announced commitment and the rebel payoff becomes:

$$U^R = ((E\theta c_2 + I)^2/2c_1)$$
(8.8)

Note that the rebels' utility is greater in this case than under (8.6) if we discount the intrinsic gain from warfare. As in Barro and Gordon (1983) the reputation of the rebels is all or nothing (0,1), hinging on past behaviour. Consider the following rule. The government believes the announcement if the rebels acted honestly in the previous period and kept its commitments, otherwise it is not believed. This implies that there is a future cost of cheating. The cost (C) is equal to the loss of reputation and the inability to create future surprises, and is given by:

$$C = -((E\theta c_2 + I)^2/2c_1)$$
(8.9)

Hence, the penalty for cheating (loss of reputation) is exactly equal to the gain from cheating in (8.8). But the punishment *always* comes at some future period. If rebel leaders discount this *future* loss, the cost of cheating in (8.9) is always less than the gain from reneging on a fixed commitment in (8.8). Typically in conflict situations, which primarily occur in low-income developing countries, the future is heavily discounted. The upshot is that the socially optimal policy of zero warfare ($w = 0$) is *time inconsistent* or incentive incompatible, and thus will not be a possible outcome. The optimal policy of no conflict is infeasible, as it is inconsistent with the incentives and expectations of the concerned parties, as was the case, for example, following the

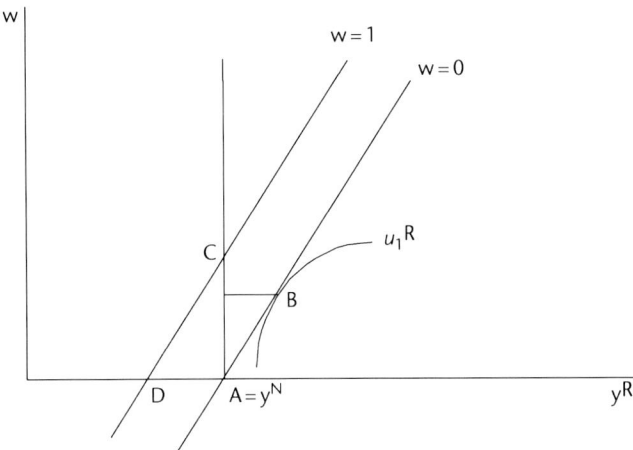

Figure 8.1. Credibility and reputation

Arusha Agreement for Rwanda in 1994 and the Angola peace agreements of 1991 and 1994.

Furthermore, there will be a range of possible conflict intensities that are feasible equilibrium outcomes. Multiple equilibria are possible. The results are depicted in Figure 8.1 in y^R and w space. The upward sloping linear aggregate supply curve has a slope exactly equal to $E\theta$ from Equation (8.2), and is steeper the greater the spoils of war. The rebels' preferences are shown by the concave indifference curves with a slope $= (E\theta c_2 + I)/c_1$, obtained from (8.1). The greedier the group (the greater is θc_2), the steeper the indifference curve is. Similarly, the more intrinsically motivated they are to fight the government, the deeper the grievance and the steeper the indifference curve. The rebels could announce zero conflict at point A. It could then cheat on its commitment and try to move to point B. The aggregate supply curve schedule would shift leftwards because of the process of expectations formation. The vertical distance between B and C gives the range of multiple equilibria depending on the time horizon of the game and the discount rate used to obtain the present value of future reputation losses. The point B defines the lowest feasible rate of conflict. It is the *best self-enforcing outcome*, without outside intervention, and given the objectives of the rebels and the expectations of the government. To reiterate, a no war situation (point A) is simply not incentive compatible for the rebels, or credible to the government. An increase in the expected spoils of war, $E\theta$, shifts the aggregate supply function leftwards and makes the indifference curves steeper pointing to an expansion in the zone of feasible equilibrium warfare. Also, the incentive for conflict cannot be eliminated without removing intrinsic grievances.

8.3 Commitment Technologies For The Rebel Group

Since peace between warring groups is not self-enforcing, let us consider an externally devised mechanism design to reduce conflict. Much of this implies manipulating the attitudes of the rebel leadership via sanctions, arms controls, trade restrictions, and foreign aid. Consider a reformulated version of the rebel utility function where we embed external conflict prevention policy parameters, and an additional cost component associated with an international agreement:

$$U^R = -(1/2)c_1(M)w^2 + E\theta c_2(T)(w - w^e) - c_3(S)[(w - w^e) + Iw] \qquad (8.10)$$

where: $c_1 > 0, c_2 \geq 0, c_3 \geq 0; c_{11}, c_{31} > 0; c_{21} < 0$

Also: $c_1(M) \geq c_1 \forall M, c_2(T) \geq c_2 \forall (T), c_3(S) \geq 0 \forall S^e \geq 0, c_3(S) < 0 \forall S^e < 0$

In Equation (8.10) the *behavioural* parameters of the rebel group, c_1, c_2, and c_3 are now functions of actions undertaken by external actors. The final term in (8.10) represents an institutional innovation, a deep intervention or mechanism design in the sense of Dixit (1996). The objective function of the external actor is not yet explicitly modelled, except that their own domestic security interests will motivate their actions.

Trade sanctions (T) on items such as 'conflict' diamonds, money laundering, and the activities of foreign entrepreneurs (in supplying arms and finance) may be utilized by a foreign power to reduce greedy attitudes, c_2. International controls on arms transfers (M) and/or sympathetic assistance from non-residents could be utilized to raise the direct cost of war, c_1. In either case, the indifference curve in Figure 8.1 will flatten out, and lower equilibrium ranges of fighting will emerge. These interventions are, however, shallow (Dixit 1996) as they do not alter the rules of the game.

Another way of reducing conflict is through an international agreement or understanding. This must also work on *intrinsic grievances*, provide a peace dividend, and also hold out a forceful sanction in the event of deviations from agreements. Participation in these agreements implies a strategic pre-commitment to peace by delegation to a treaty or outside adjudicator. Although this method does not always eliminate conflict, it does raise the costs of war and reneging on peace deals. The last term in (8.10) represents such a *commitment technology* or *delegation* via mechanism design, and c_3 measures the costs of reneging on peace agreements as a function of sanctions (S) imposed by other signatories or parties to the agreement. Sanctions consist of the carrot of conditional aid, and the stick which militarily enforces adherence to the peace treaty. The sanction works if and only if its expected value (S^e) is positive; it must not be perceived as 'cheap talk' (a signal without commitment). When the sanction works, $S^e > 0$, and it could be the force or delegated sanction imposed on warring parties by some outside power, such as an effective UN or another multinational peace keeping force. To take an example each of effective versus ineffective peace keeping, the peace enforcement works better in Kosovo with nearly 100,000 troops compared to the Congo, where a group of a mere 16,000 troops polices a state the size of Western Europe.

Maximizing (8.10) with respect to w yields the level of w with commitment ($w_c{}^*$):

$$w_c^* = [E\theta c_2 - c_3(1 + I)]/c_1 \tag{8.11}$$

Proposition 2: The presence of external commitment technologies in the form of sanctions, conditional aid, and controls in international trade lowers the optimal level of belligerency amongst rebels, if and only if $S^e > 0$.

The proposition can be verified by noting that w_c^* in (8.11) is less than w^* in (8.3) if $c_3 > 0$ when $S^e > 0$. If so, these commitment technologies lead to lower levels of warfare when compared to (8.3). Even though the commitment technologies and sanctions are independent of actual w in (8.10), for simplicity, our result will hold through if T, M, and S are increasing in w. First, there is a *direct* effect of the external sanction or outside commitment technology innovation when it works, c_3. Then we have the *indirect* effects emanating from the manipulation of the behavioural parameters of the rebels (shallow interventions). Chiefly, this involves restrictions on the export/import of the rebels' international revenue/financial sources, which lower c_2. Also, controls on arms transfers and financial flows from sympathetic outsiders raise c_1. Note, however, that the sanctions and policies are a result of external intervention, and involve costs to outside parties, which is something we turn to in the next section.

Corollary 1: If sanctions are expected to be ineffective, because the level of force and developmental aid is inadequate making them cheap talk, $S^e < 0$, and $c_3 < 0$ in (8.10) and (8.11). A half-hearted sanction package will be a complete failure, and the levels of conflict that ensue are greater than without the cheap talk sanction, as illustrated by the tragic failure of the UN peace keepers to prevent the Rwandan genocide of 1994.

8.4 The Finance And Production Of Sanctions

Typically the policies considered in the previous section, especially sanctions, S, will involve costs to outside powers and agencies, as it is they who initiate them. The external powers could be the USA, the EU, or an international organization like the UN. By sanctions, we mean the enforcement of a peace deal via peace keeping forces.[3] Normally, it also includes some conditional development assistance or aid. Either way, the production of sanctions and the aid that accompanies it cost money. This section considers the benefit of sanctions to outside sponsors. It also looks at it in a situation where the finance and production of the sanction, S, is not carried out by the same party. The separation of finance and enforcement of peace deals is not uncommon. Often the financiers of peace treaties, especially the aid component, are donors such as Norway and Finland without a direct security interest in the conflict zone. An organization like the African Union, through the armed forces of its member states, may actually enforce a peace deal, whereas the funding and logistical support for the operation may be provided by Western donors like the EU, as is practised in Darfur at the time of writing of this chapter. Even UN peace keeping mandates are carried out by the military forces of member states who are paid for their pains in this regard. The idea here is that the sponsor or financier of peace keeping derives some utility from peace in other parts of the world due to security considerations (terrorism, refugee influxes), humanitarian considerations, or because promoting peace enhances the sponsor's international prestige. But how much is the external sponsor of the peace willing to pay, and how far are they willing to go in this respect?

In many ways, the sponsor or financier of the sanction can be regarded as the principal, and the implementer of the sanction the agent, in a principal–agent framework of the type considered by say, Laffont (2005). In general, the marginal utility of sanctions cum aid production is equated to its marginal cost. Also, the lower the marginal utility of sanctions to the sponsor, the more expensive the aid cum military sanctions package is in terms of 'price', the greater the shadow cost of the distortionary tax that has to be levied to finance it and the greater the effort levels by the agent or implementor of the sanction that are needed to produce sanctions, the lower the optimal level of sanction chosen.[4]

This outcome relates to the cheap talk result in proposition 2 and corollary 1 above. If the optimal level of sanctions and aid produced is low, then the peace keeping force's sanction is cheap talk or ineffective, as $S^e < 0$. This is likely to happen if the conflict is in a distant land, which lowers both the marginal utility of the sanctions–aid package and raises the cost of doing so because of the endemic poverty in the country in question, as well as logistical

---

[3] It is beyond the scope of this chapter to dwell upon various nuances of peace keeping including disarmament, demobilization, and reintegration.

[4] Detailed derivations are available from the authors.

difficulties. Also, the financing of such projects through taxation might be hard to sell to the ordinary median voter in the sponsoring country. Finally, the effort level required on the part of the sponsor's agent might just be too great to make it worthwhile, and the probability of the agent's success in this regard may be too uncertain. Perhaps, the result above helps to explain the security dilemma in African civil wars. There is just not enough will in the West to finance security in far away war torn places, in contrast to problems at their back door, say in the former Yugoslavia, which are considerably more menacing. Arguably, an incipient civil war was prevented in FYR of Macedonia. In former conflict zones in the Balkans, aid per capita is very high, and those regions are policed by high quality, well-motivated, and adequately mandated Western and NATO forces. Yet, at the same time, lip-service is paid to the need to end civil wars in Africa, and weak and ineffectual forces are despatched there from inside and outside the continent, usually under the aegis of virtually impotent Security Council-sanctioned UN mandates. Hence, the saliency of the expression, 'cheap talk', meaning that in the absence of a willingness to pay by external sponsors, many of the peace deals brokered in far flung places of the world like Africa are doomed to failure.

8.5 Concluding Remarks

We have analysed the non-self-enforcing nature of peace treaties caused by imperfect commitment. Where war provides economic gains to one side or there are deep-seated grievances, peace is not incentive compatible, and peace agreements will necessarily degenerate. Socially optimal policies of no conflict may become time inconsistent. A range of equilibrium conflict levels may appear, implying the existence of multiple equilibria. The levels of conflict are an increasing function of grievances and pure greed over lootable resources, but decreasing in the direct costs of war. Externally devised commitment technologies (mechanism design) could be key to ending conflict where the peace treaty is otherwise not self-enforcing. Sanctions, aid, and trade restrictions, if effective, might eliminate conflict. These include controls on the sale of 'blood' diamonds and restrictions on arms transfers to combatants. Foreign aid can play a pivotal role in reducing poverty and lowering the pecuniary and intrinsic incentive to fight via growth and income redistribution (pro-poor growth). It might also be used to make credible promises of redistributive reconstruction that close the gap in living standards between rebels and government supporters, thereby reducing the intrinsic incentive to fight. There is also a role for the use of *force majeure*, military intervention mandated by regional alliances along with the UN. In order for this threat to work, military force must be credible, as is sadly not the case in many contemporary civil wars. In summary, conflict prevention by outside parties involves manipulating the utility function of combatants and their leaders so as to make fighting a less attractive proposition, and imposing settlements when they are otherwise not self-enforcing. But, external military sanctions, in particular, must not be perceived by potential combatants as cheap talk. This can make matters worse, and warfare might resume at a higher level of intensity. We also examine the production of sanctions where, in accordance with contemporary practice, the finance and execution of the sanction are made independent of one another. If the cost of effective sanctions is too high, or it yields little security benefit to the sponsor, as is likely to be the case for conflicts in distant lands, there is under-production of the sanction, making it more likely that it really is ineffective cheap talk. Perhaps, that is why we do not see a speedy end to many civil wars in Africa. In the ultimate analysis, credible commitments to peace must be found in effective domestic solutions that involve constitutional restraints and delegation of power. As discussed in Rothchild (2005), mechanisms leading to the *separation of powers*, and where decisions on different issues are taken by diversely constituted bodies, may prove more durable in sustaining the peace when compared to cruder quick-fix power sharing arrangements between warring parties.

References

Addison, T. and S. M. Murshed (2002). 'Credibility and Reputation in Peace-Making'. *Journal of Peace Research*, 39 (4): 487–501.

Azam, J.-P. (1995). 'How to Pay for Peace? A Theoretical Framework with Reference to African Countries'. *Public Choice*, 83 (1/2): 173–84.

Azam, J.-P. (2005). 'Can the Peace be Imported'. Paper presented at a workshop on 'Hastening the Day: When Can Peace-Enforcers Leave?', 17 June. Montréal: McGill University.

Barro, R. and D. Gordon (1983). 'Rules, Discretion and Reputation in a Model of Monetary Policy'. *Journal of Monetary Economics*, 12 (1): 101–21.

Dixit, A. K. (1996). *The Making of Economic Policy: A Transaction-Cost Politics Perspective.* London: MIT Press.

Fearon, J. D. (2001). 'Why Do Some Civil Wars Last So Much Longer than Others?' Available at: <www.hypatia.ss.uci.edu/gpacs/newpages/agenda.htm>.

FIDH (Fédération Internationale des Droits de l'Homme) (1993). *Rapport sur la Commission d'enquête sur les violations des droits de l'Homme au Rwanda depuis le 1er Octobre 1990.* Paris-New York: Africa Watch.

Fortna, V. P. (2004). *Peace Time: Cease-Fire Agreements and the Durability of Peace.* Princeton: Princeton University Press.

Hart, O. (1995). *Firms, Contracts and Financial Structure.* Oxford: Oxford University Press.

Hirshleifer, J. (1995). 'Anarchy and its Breakdown'. *Journal of Political Economy*, 103 (1): 26–52.

Laffont, J.-J. (2005). *Regulation and Development*. Cambridge: Cambridge University Press.

Rothchild, D. (2005). 'Reassuring Weaker Parties after Civil Wars: The Benefits and Costs of Executive Power-Sharing Systems in Africa'. *Ethnopolitics*, 4 (3): 247–67.

Schelling, T. C. (1960). *The Strategy of Conflict*. Cambridge, MA: Harvard University Press.

Verwimp, P. (2004). 'Games in Multiple Arenas and Institutional Design on the Eve of the Rwandan Genocide'. *Peace Economics, Peace Science and Public Policy*. Available at: <www.bepress.com/peps>.

Walter, B. F. (2002). *Committing to Peace: The Successful Settlement of Civil Wars*. Princeton: Princeton University Press.

Wood, E. J. (2003). *Modeling Robust Settlements to Civil War: Indivisible Stakes and Distributional Compromises*. Oslo: International Peace Research Organization.

9

Aid Allocation and Fragile States[*]

Mark McGillivray

9.1 Introduction

Does aid work by increasing growth and reducing poverty? The answer to this question, based on recent research on the macroeconomic impact of aid, evidence from micro studies and field experience, is, in general, a clear 'yes'. Growth would clearly be lower than would otherwise have been the case in the absence of aid.[1] One can reasonably infer that by implication poverty would be higher without aid. Yet, it is also clear that the contribution of aid to growth differs across countries: An additional dollar of aid to one country does not have the same impact as an additional dollar to every other country. Burnside and Dollar (1997, 2000) found that aid works better in countries with better policy regimes or, more generally, that its effectiveness in promoting growth was contingent on the quality of these regimes. This very well-known finding has been questioned by some subsequent research.[2] There is,

[*] This chapter was written with Sophie Pongracz, from DFID's Poverty Reduction in Difficult Environments Team. It was commissioned by DFID for the Learning and Advisory Process on Difficult Partnerships of the OECD-DAC. The author is especially grateful to Sophie Pongracz, but also to Tony Addison (UNU-WIDER), Michael Anderson (DFID), Sarah Cliffe (World Bank), James Gilling (AusAID), Paul Isenman (OECD), Max Willis (AusAID), Adrian Wood (DFID), and Peter Versegi (AusAID), for very useful comments, suggestions, background discussions, or information. The usual disclaimer applies. A previous version of this chapter was circulated as a background chapter at the joint UK-DFID, OECD-DAC, EU, UNDP, and World Bank Senior Level Forum on Development Effectiveness in Fragile States held in January 2005 at Lancaster House, London

[1] A brief survey of the literature on aid and growth is provided in the Appendix.

[2] Studies that do not find empirical evidence of the link between policy and aid effectiveness include Hansen and Tarp (2000, 2001); Dalgaard and Hansen (2001); Guillaumont and Chauvet (2001); Hudson and Mosley (2001); Lu and Ram (2001); Ram (2003, 2004); and Dalgaard et al. (2004). The acceptance that policies generally matter is based on theoretical reasoning, micro studies, and field experience. To this extent, much of the debate has been over whether one can validly observe a link between aid effectiveness and policy in the context of the type of econometric exercise conducted by Burnside and Dollar (1997, 2000) and not per se over the

however, an acceptance among researchers that better policies, however defined, should in all probability result in more effective aid.[3] Other studies find evidence of a number of alternative contingencies.[4] These findings have clear implications for aid allocation, for if one wishes to maximize its global poverty reducing effectiveness, one primarily allocates it to countries in which it has the greatest impact. The Collier and Dollar (2001, 2002) aid selectivity model, discussed in detail later in this chapter, is built partly on this principle. By taking into account recipient country policy and institutional performance in aid allocation, so too is the IDA's long-standing country allocation system (World Bank 2003).

The selectivity approach, or more broadly giving preference to countries that can use external resources more effectively in allocating aid, is one that donors are embracing to such an extent that it has become a dominant paradigm in international aid policy and practice. Donors are in general linking aid allocation to assessments of the quality of recipient country policies and institutions, in the belief that aid works better in countries that do better in terms of these assessments. Some donors are concentrating aid on relatively small samples of countries that inter alia are rated higher on the basis of these assessments. But this paradigm does have drawbacks, some of which are receiving increased scrutiny within the international development community. One is the allocation of aid to countries that score poorly in policy and institutional assessments, especially those that are poor and in great need of assistance. These countries are penalized with less aid in a pure selectivity regime.[5] A specific concern has arisen for 'fragile states'. These states

relevance of policy for this effectiveness. See Robinson and Tarp (2000); Beynon (2001, 2002); Gunning (2001); Morrissey (2002); Collier (2002); McGillivray (2003a); and Collier and Dollar (2004) for further details.

[3] See Robinson and Tarp (2000); Collier (2000); Beynon (2001, 2002); Gunning (2001); Morrissey (2002); McGillivray (2003a); and Collier and Dollar (2004). This acceptance is based on theoretical reasoning, micro studies and field experience. To this extent, much of the debate has been over whether one can validly observe a link between aid effectiveness and policy in the context of the type of econometric exercise conducted by Burnside and Dollar (1997, 2000) and not per se over the relevance of policy for this effectiveness.

[4] These studies are cited in section 9.2.

[5] It should be acknowledged, though, that the Collier-Dollar selectivity model gives more aid to many poor countries than is the case in practice. The model also gives a higher weighting to aid to populous poor countries than to those that score highly in policy and institutional assessments. Regarding the growth relationships underpinning the model, one can further speculate that the link between aid effectiveness (defined in terms of its impact on growth) and policy might not be as systematic or consistent across countries at the bottom end of the policy scale as otherwise might be the case. Aid might still be reasonably effective in some of them, and the case for reducing or giving less aid than would otherwise be the case to all of these countries is weakened. This speculation is consistent with some residual disagreement in the donor community regarding how much aid to give countries with bad or weak governments, and possibly warrants further research on the link between aid effectiveness and policy in countries that do poorly in terms of indices like the CPIA. It is also consistent with a view expressed in Beynon (1999), that one should not apply the Collier-Dollar model in a mechanistic or inflexible way.

have difficult development environments in that, according to conventional wisdom on aid effectiveness, they are 'unable or unwilling to harness domestic and international resources effectively for poverty reduction' (Torres and Anderson 2004: 1).[6] Nations engaged in or recently having emerged from conflict tend to feature heavily among states classified as fragile. Countries that descend into a state of fragility remain in it for decades, and the human and financial costs of this are staggering. Estimated financial costs, for any one country, are well in excess of the current world aid budget (Chauvet and Collier 2004).

This chapter reviews the different research strands and views in the international development community on (i) how aid *should* be allocated among developing countries, and (ii) how aid *is* being allocated among these countries. Special consideration is given to allocations to fragile states, as defined above. The first of these issues is examined in section 9.2. It looks at the different allocation models proposed in recent years, including the Collier-Dollar 'selectivity model' and cases for and against aid to fragile states. Special attention is given to absorptive capacity constraints and recent research looking at whether aid can promote policy and institutional reform in fragile states. Section 9.3 addresses the second of the above issues. It reports evidence that donors are increasingly taking into account developmental criteria in aid allocation, in particular the notion of aid selectivity. The question of whether fragile states receive aid allocations appropriate to their population and poverty levels and policy and institutional environments is examined. Evidence is shown that most fragile states are under-aided in this sense. Also considered is aid volatility. It is observed that aid to these countries, especially the under-aided countries, is highly volatile. Section 9.4 looks at possible directions for future research and policy.

9.2 How *Should* Aid Be Allocated?

Early approaches to the issue of how aid should be allocated among developing countries tended to be based on notions of equity, efficiency, or a

---

[6] At present there appears to be no universally accepted 'fragile states' definition. As Torres and Anderson (2004: 1) note, these states 'take many forms, and have been defined in various ways'. Selecting a group of countries that fall into the category of a fragile state can be problematic, therefore. Jones et al. (2004) refer to 'difficult partnership countries' (DPCs), as do Levin and Dollar (2005). According to the former study a country was assigned to that group if it was a member of the World Bank low-income country under stress (LICUS) group, while according to the latter a DPC was defined as one belonging to the World Bank low-income country group and was in the bottom two World Bank Country Performance and Institutional Assessment (CPIA) quintiles. There is, however, very substantial overlap between these two groups.

combination of both criteria.[7] These approaches were not linked in a systematic way to findings from the aid effectiveness literature.[8] This is understandable given the inability of the aid effectiveness literature to provide consistent, reasonably unambiguous results for country-level effectiveness. Collier and Dollar (1999, 2001, 2002) changed this state of affairs with their aid selectivity model of inter-country aid allocation. This model provides a 'poverty-efficient' inter-country aid allocation that provides a benchmark guide to donors pursuing poverty reduction as the prime operational criterion.[9] A poverty-efficient allocation is one that minimizes the total number of people living in the world below the chosen, international income poverty line. According to the prescriptive Collier-Dollar model, aid allocated to each country is an increasing function of its poverty level and CPIA score and a decreasing function of its national per capita income. Countries with inferior policy regimes receive less aid in this model, therefore, as these regimes are thought to reduce the impact of aid on growth and thus poverty reduction. The poverty-minimizing optimal allocation is one in which an extra dollar of aid in any given country decreases the number of people living below the income poverty line by an identical amount as in any other country.

The Collier-Dollar selectivity builds on the empirical work of Burnside and Dollar (1997, 2000), in particular the notion that the effectiveness of aid in promoting growth is contingent on the policy regimes of recipient countries. A number of other aid-growth studies provide empirical findings that lend support for additional contingencies. These include the extent of democracy (Svensson 1999), structural vulnerability (Guillaumont and Chauvet 2001), the presence of trade shocks (Collier and Dehn 2001), climatic conditions (Hansen and Tarp 2001), the extent of political stability (Chauvet and Guillaumont 2002), the existence of a post-conflict scenario (Collier

[7] The equity-based approaches favoured the allocation of aid according to relative need, typically proxied by per capita income levels. See, for example, Bhagwati (1972); Mosley (1987); McGillivray (1989); McGillivray and White (1994); and Rao (1994, 1997).

[8] The IDA's country allocation system, mentioned above, had for many years been in part based on recipient country policy and institutional performance, but this was not linked to findings from the research community, but instead on field experience. Kanbur (2004) charts the link between this system and the contemporary aid effectiveness literature, showing how it is consistent with the findings of Burnside and Dollar (1997, 2000) and other studies that show a link between aid effectiveness and CPIA (or similar) scores.

[9] Collier and Dollar (2002) acknowledge that donors will also have valid, non-developmental criteria for the allocation of aid, and that actual allocation of aid will deviate from the benchmark guide for this reason. The use of the Collier-Dollar model allocations is articulated further in Collier and Dollar (2004). They argue that the poverty-efficient allocation is a benchmark guide if a donor lacks other information about the likely impact of aid on poverty reduction in the recipient country and the ability to change or prevail over recipient government preferences (hence avoiding fungibility). This is consistent with the above-stated view of Beynon (1999), that the model should not be applied mechanistically. Collier and Dollar (2004) argue that since that ability is uncommon, the main reasons for departing from the benchmark are that the donor has the above-mentioned information or if poverty reduction is not the objective.

and Hoeffler 2002, 2004), the presence of a totalitarian government (Islam 2003), the degree to which aid is fungible across sectors (Pettersson 2004), and the quality of institutions (Dalgaard et al. 2004).[10]

McGillivray (2003a) advocates an extension of the Collier-Dollar model on the basis of some of the preceding findings, involving augmenting it with additional contingencies.[11] McGillivray speculates that this might see more aid being prescribed for countries with not-so-good CPIA ratings. Whether this might see more aid to fragile states is a matter of speculation. The Collier and Hoeffler (2002) finding that, ceteris paribus, aid works better in post-conflict scenarios might on the surface provide a basis for such an outcome. A closer inspection reveals, however, that their finding relates not to countries that have just emerged from a conflict, and which might be classified as fragile, but to those four-to-seven years into a post-conflict episode and is contingent on the CPIA-assessed quality of the recipient policy and institutional regime. Thus, according to Collier and Hoeffler, aid will not be especially poverty-efficient in post-conflict countries with inferior CPIA scores.

A defining feature of the Collier-Dollar selectivity model is that it minimizes aggregate global poverty. It does not seek to minimize poverty in each individual country. Reallocating aid from one country to another is globally poverty-efficient if the increase in poverty in the former is less in absolute terms than the decrease in poverty in the latter. An alternative approach is to seek to equalize poverty differences or poverty reduction across countries. This lies at the heart of the allocation model implicit in the strategy for achieving the Millennium Development Goals (MDGs), outlined in the *UN Millennium Project Report*. This strategy involves allocating aid in such a way as to minimize the shortfall between actual levels of MDG variables and their target values, in each country. These targets can in a sense be defined as poverty lines, but defined in spaces or dimensions in not only income but others as well, corresponding to the various MDG variables. The greater the shortfall, and presumably its size, the greater the amount of aid a country can expect to receive. The implicit poverty-efficient outcome is one that equalizes the above mentioned shortfalls across all countries irrespective of the amounts of aid required to do this in each country.[12] This will result in different amounts of

---

[10] Kosack (2003) finds that the impact of aid on the quality of life across countries (measured by the Human Development Index) is contingent on the level of democracy practised. Unfortunately there are comparatively very few studies linking aid to such variables.

[11] These contingencies have not been subject to the extent of scrutiny to which the aid-policy-growth link reported in Burnside and Dollar (1997, 2000) has. It would be appropriate that they be further scrutinized prior to being incorporated into a selectivity model.

[12] Wood (2004) provides a critique of the *UN Millennium Project Report*, arguing that this outcome violates the basic principle of equity, which is to treat like cases alike. The example is given of a situation in which it takes US$1000 to lift one person out of poverty in one country, while in another country this amount of aid will lift three people out of poverty. Assuming these four people are equally poor, it means that the person in the first country effectively gets three times as

aid being used across countries to lift one person above the poverty line if we assume that the effectiveness of aid differs across countries, as is the case. The MDG strategy is largely blind to this point, implicitly assuming that the marginal effectiveness of aid is equal across all countries, at all levels of aid.[13] It also does not take into account possible disincentive effects of increased aid. As Wood (2004) notes, aid can make weak states even weaker by reducing the incentives for self-help and diverting effort into rent-seeking.

Cogneau and Naudet (2004) provide an equal opportunity (EOp) model of aid allocation.[14] This model is in part a response to the above mentioned criticism of the Collier-Dollar model, but unlike the *UN Millennium Project Report* it takes into account differential aid effectiveness at the country level. Cogneau and Naudet's analysis is based on the recognition that a country's CPIA score (which they call an 'effort' indicator) is influenced by structural disadvantages over which the country has little or no control. Not to take this into account in the allocation of aid is thought to be inconsistent with notions of fairness. The Cogneau-Naudet model's optimal allocation is one that equalizes differences in poverty risk by a chosen point in time between countries facing different disadvantages but making the same degree of effort Thus, countries with lower projected poverty declines get more aid for any given effort. This equal poverty risk principle leads to an allocation of aid that minimizes projected poverty-level differences between countries by that point in time. The point of time in Cogneau and Naudet's application is 2015.

A key variable in the Cognea-Naudet EOp model is an effort variable adjusted for disadvantage. It is a country's CPIA quintile that is predicted by its growth prospects of its region and its initial poverty level. The Cogneau and Naudet prescribed allocation gives more aid to poor countries than that of the Collier-Dollar model. Fragile states typically are prescribed more aid by the former as compared to the latter.[15] But for a number of states the reverse is true, with the former model giving zero aid to them. These outcomes notwithstanding, the Cogneau-Naudet model offers some prospects for providing larger

much aid as the people in the second country. It is in this sense that the outcome is inequitable. Wood makes the general point that the *UN Millennium Project Report* needs to show a greater awareness of the existing literature on aid effectiveness.

[13] The report does acknowledge that aid should not be given to countries in which it would be ineffective or counterproductive, although these countries are extreme cases ('thugocracies') where the pathology is visible and the leaders are often irrational.

[14] Llavador and Roemer (2001) provide a similar analysis. However, it suffers from serious methodological flaws and prescribes a questionable inter-country allocation of aid. See McGillivray (2003b, 2004c) and Cogneau and Naudet (2004) for further details. McGillivray (2003b, 2004c) also provides a general survey and critique of the approaches discussed in this section.

[15] For example, Laos, Papua New Guinea, and the Solomon Islands would receive US$6.5 million, 3.2 million, and 4.8 million, respectively, from the Collier-Dollar model but under the Cogneau-Naudet model they receive zero aid.

shares of aid to fragile states than might otherwise prevail, in an objective and scientific manner. The key question, though, is whether the notion of fairness, implicit to the Cogneau-Naudet approach, results in fewer people being lifted out of poverty.

The Collier-Dollar and Cogneau-Naudet models share an important common feature: a saturation level of aid. They result from the recognition of diminishing returns to aid, and equate to a level of aid at which its incremental impact falls to zero. Diminishing returns to aid effectiveness have been examined closely by most recent aid-growth studies. This tests for non-linearity in the aid-growth relationship, with aid being positively related to growth up to a certain level of aid and negatively related thereafter. That there are diminishing returns is a seemingly highly robust finding, with almost all studies reporting such a relationship, with negative returns setting in when the aid inflow reaches anywhere between 15 and 45 per cent of GDP. This has been interpreted as indicating limited aid absorptive capacities, with recipient governments being limited in the amounts of aid they can use effectively (Clemens and Radelet 2003).[16] This issue is especially relevant to fragile states as they will inevitably have very limited absorptive capacities, as conventionally defined. Increased aid to these countries, in line with proposals to achieve the MDGs, could actually reverse poverty reduction. This is obviously a compelling case against additional aid to fragile states.

Chauvet and Collier (2004) look at whether aid can assist in the improvement of policies and institutions in situations in which they are particularly weak, viewing their analysis as an extension of the Collier-Dollar selectivity model discussed above.[17] Two questions were considered, both in the context of the low-income country under stress (LICUS) group. The first was whether aid is significantly effective in promoting policy and institutional turnarounds sufficient to take a country out of LICUS status on a sustained basis.[18] Chauvet and Collier found that two forms of aid—support that achieves an expansion of secondary education and aid in general other than technical assistance—have significantly favourable effects on the changes of a

---

[16] Gupta and Heller (2002) provide a useful discussion of this issue, along with the related problem of Dutch Disease. Killick (2004) cautions against increased aid to Africa on, inter alia, absorptive capacity and Dutch Disease grounds. Note, though, that Gomanee et al. (2003), using a general technique specifically designed to detect threshold effects, struggle to find evidence of such returns, and therefore question the inferences drawn by previous studies. They do however find evidence of a non-linear impact of aid on growth.

[17] Note that the Chauvet and Collier (2004) analysis reported throughout this chapter is preliminary and for discussion only. It is not yet sufficiently conclusive to be used as a basis for policy.

[18] This outcome was deemed to have occurred if a country meets each of the following criteria: has a pre-turnaround CPIA score of no greater than 2.5; achieves an increase in its CPIA of 1.4 points above its pre-turnaround nadir; and can maintain a CPIA score of greater than 3.0 for at least five consecutive years after passing the 2.5 point threshold.

sustained turnaround. Technical assistance was found to have a negative impact on the chances of such a turnaround. The level of aid required to achieve a turnaround, for any typical LICUS, was estimated to be an additional one per cent of its GDP per year for five years. In present value terms, this cost is US$240.8 million. The estimated payoff, defined in terms of the reduced costs to the LICUS and neighbouring countries (due to spillovers) in terms of GDP foregone, is US$3.1 billion.

The second question addressed by Chauvet and Collier was whether aid affects policy during the early stages of a pre-existing reform. Collier and Chauvet addressed this question by looking at countries in the LICUS group that embarked on 'incipient turnarounds', defined as a 0.5 point CPIA improvement, asking whether they matured into sustained turnarounds. It was found that both technical assistance and other aid have significant effects on the time which an incipient turnaround takes to become a sustained one. But these effects were quite different in nature. Small amounts of other aid slow down the process of sustained turnaround, but large amounts accelerate it. The threshold at which the effect becomes positive, at which aid begins to acceler-ate the process, was found to be around 12 per cent of GDP. Technical assis-tance had the opposite effect, being associated with a slowing down of the time an incipient turnaround becomes a sustained one at around 4 per cent of GDP.

Chauvet and Collier (2004) also examine the LICUS duration and costs. They estimate that once a country meets the criteria for LICUS status it typically remains so for 69 years. They also estimate that the cost of a country descending into this status, to the country itself and its neighbours, is in present value terms approximately US$100 billion. This is a lower bound cost, and based on a typical LICUS. Most of this cost, which is well in excess of the current annual world aid budget, is met by neighbouring countries. Thirty countries are currently in the LICUS group. There is also the concern that fragile states can descend into conflict. Chalmers (2004) estimates that on average for every GB£1 spent on conflict prevention GB£24 of savings are generated. Added to this of course is the loss of life associated with conflict. These findings do not alone provide a case for allocating aid to fragile states. But they would appear to provide a compelling case for finding ways of making aid work in fragile states, given the potential costs of non-intervention, and if so providing more aid to them.

9.3 How *Is* Aid Allocated?

A number of empirical studies have tested for selectivity in aid allocations. Dollar and Levin (2004) provide a comprehensive analysis of this issue, cover-ing aid allocations of 41 donor agencies for the period 1984 to 2002. Based on

panel data, they find that selectivity is present in aid allocation, being practised by most donors, bilateral and multilateral, but that it is a new phenomenon that has emerged since the mid 1990s. Dollar and Levin (2004) also
examined the poverty focus of aid, finding that it had increased as well.[19]
They found that the donor agencies that are most selectivity-focused also
tended to be the most poverty-focused. McGillivray (2004b) looks at evidence
from 1968 to 1999 time series data, controlling for a range of developmental
and donor self-interests. Evidence of selectivity was found in seven of the ten
recipient countries under consideration. For a number of these countries it
became increasingly important from the early 1990s.[20]

The econometric evidence of increased selectivity in aid allocations is consistent with the widespread view that since the end of the Cold War, and
especially since the late 1990s and early 2000s, donors have given much
greater emphasis to developmental criteria.[21] This view is further supported
by survey research. A 2002 survey of ten donors, conducted by DFID indicated
that increased emphasis is being given to selectivity, defined broadly as en-
compassing not only the quality of policy regimes but also a range of other
developmental concerns, such as governance, programme implementation,
and absorptive capacity (McGillivray 2003a). Jones et al. (2004) provide a
comprehensive survey of donor allocative behaviour, finding that aid allocations and policies have become more poverty-driven as international consensus regarding support for the MDGs has grown.[22] They also found that donors
had become more selective as they became more aware of evidence suggesting
that policies were important for aid effectiveness. Jones et al. looked closely at

[19] The IDA, the IMF's Enhanced Structural Adjustment Facility, Denmark, the United Kingdom,
Norway, Ireland, and the Netherlands were ranked most highly in terms of selectivity- and poverty-
focus. France and the United States were among the least selectivity-focused donors.

[20] Dollar and Levin's results appear to be robust with respect to the choice of policy index.
Among the indices used was the CPIA. McGillivray's analysis employed an index combining the
inflation rate, economic openness, and the central government budget deficit. For Kenya,
McGillivray observed a negative relationship between policy quality and aid from the early
1990s, contrary to the selectivity approach. Birdsall et al. (2002) struggle to find evidence of
selectivity in official net resource transfers to sub-Saharan Africa, although there is a case for
suspecting that this result is an outcome of the empirical methods employed by this study.

[21] More recent studies, examining data extending to the mid- to late 1990s, do though find that
donor non-developmental interests remain important determinants of aid allocation. See, for
example, Alesina and Dollar (2000); Alesina and Weder (2002); Berthelemy and Tichit (2002);
Neumayer (2002, 2003a, 2003b, 2003c, 2003d); Feeny and McGillivray (2004). These studies do,
however, report a statistically significant, negative relationship between aid and recipient country
income per capita, indicating that donors give preference to poorer countries in allocating aid. This
is quite a robust result. Some studies test for population biases in aid allocation, finding biases
against larger countries in per capita aid allocation. See, for example, Arvin (1998); Arvin and
Drewes (2001). Note that this result is not as robust across studies as that concerning income per
capita. Concerns for this bias have been long-standing, and have been observed over many
decades. See, in particular, Isenman (1976).

[22] Dollar and Levin (2004) also found that the poverty focus of aid has increased. It was also
found that the donor agencies that were most selectivity-focused tended to be the most poverty-
focused as well.

the allocation processes of nine donors, finding five built formal performance criteria (such as CPIA scores) into allocation decisions.[23] The World Bank has shown increased concern for poorly performing countries, as evidenced by its LICUS initiative and the IDA's framework for aid delivery to conflict-affected countries (World Bank 2002; IDA 2004).[24]

Jones et al. (2004) examined whether greater selectivity had led to a bias against failed states and those defined in terms of LICUS group membership. It was concluded that the potential for such a bias between 2000 and 2002 was offset due to not only the provision of humanitarian aid, but by the 'increasing attention to those failed or failing states that are regarded as significant for regional and global security and geo-political reasons' (Jones et al. 2004). Evidence presented in partial support of this contention was that the LICUS group had received increased shares of total aid from the nine donor agencies under consideration between 2000 and 2002. This is broadly consistent with the finding of Nunnenkamp et al. (2004) that shares of both total bilateral and total multilateral aid to the bottom two CPIA quintile groups remained approximately constant between 1993–8 and 1999–2002.[25] Jones et al. note, however, that some difficult partnership countries could be considered as 'aid orphans'. That is, they received very low amounts of aid, in part because the costs of their state failure was not of sufficient consequence to the international community or to particular donors to justify larger aid amounts. This is in part reflected by a lack of diplomatic engagement, and is made worse by a lack of media attention in many fragile states.[26]

Levin and Dollar (2005) conduct a closer, empirical examination of aid during 1992 to 2002 to difficult partnership countries (DPCs). Levin and Dollar look at aid to these countries in the context of their population, poverty, and policy and institutional performance levels. It was concluded that the difficult partnership countries received 58 per cent less bilateral aid and 34 per cent less multilateral aid than predicted by these variables. Overall, these countries received 43 per cent less aid than predicted by their population and poverty levels and policy and institutional environment. This is a particularly incisive finding, and more meaningful than the shares of aid reported above. The extent of under-aiding, in the context considered by Levin and

---

[23] The donors were Australia, Canada, the European Commission, France, Germany, Japan, the Netherlands, Norway, Sweden, the United Kingdom, and the United States.

[24] The IDA in its IDA13 mid-term review announced that countries eligible for special post-conflict allocations would receive support for four years instead of three, as was previously the case. IDA (2004) acknowledges that further, special consideration may be needed to cover 'failed states' that do not qualify for exceptional post-conflict assistance.

[25] Note though that Nunnenkamp et al. (2004) find that the shares aid to the poorest quintile of low-income countries had fallen from 1981–6 to 1999–2002.

[26] ODI (2004) discusses the importance of the media in aid responses to various circumstances, poor country performance among them.

Dollar, varies tremendously among the DPC group. Some countries received substantially less aid than predicted and others received far more. Post-conflict DPCs were found to receive more aid than predicted, and this gap has increased after September 11th. Among those countries receiving less aid than predicted were those that are aided by a relatively small number of donors. The under-aided countries (the 'orphans') included Burundi, the Democratic Republic of Congo, Nigeria, and Sudan. The most over-aided countries (the 'darlings') included Cambodia, Laos, Papua New Guinea, and Sierra Leone.

Aid flows have been shown to be more volatile than other sources of developing country government revenue (Gemmell and McGillivray 1998). High aid volatility makes budgetary policy more difficult and can increase exchange rate variability, thus potentially offsetting any positive impacts of aid (Edwards and van Wijnbergen 1989; Bulíř and Hamann 2003). Levin and Dollar (2005) also examined the volatility of aid per capita to the DPC group. Specific for fragile states would be that results take longer to materialize in these environments, therefore volatility is particularly damaging. It was found that aid to the DPC group was almost twice that of other low income countries. This result was not altered after controlling for the specific circumstances faced by DPCs, namely rapid changes in policies and institutional strength and the onset or cessation of conflict. There is, however, volatility heterogeneity among the DPC group, and this is of serious concern. The aid volatility faced by the darlings, as defined above, is very close to that experienced by other low income countries. Strikingly, the volatility of aid to orphans is more than twice that of the darlings. It is therefore the volatility of aid to the orphans that pushes the average volatility of the DPC group to such a comparatively high level.

9.4 Factoring-In Fragility: Where To From Here?

This chapter has focused primarily on the research literature on aid allocation and related work on aid effectiveness, taking a special interest in what the literature says about fragile states. It is reasonably clear from the chapter's literature survey that while research on policies and institutions is clearly relevant to these states, the fragile state-specific literature is still an emerging one. Chauvet and Collier (2004), Jones et al. (2004), and Levin and Dollar (2005) provide important and comprehensive information, but more fragile state-specific research is clearly needed to sufficiently address the question raised above. This initially, and fairly obviously, requires agreement over the criteria for classifying countries as fragile states. As mentioned earlier in this chapter, a consensus on an appropriate definition of this term has not yet been achieved. One also needs to acknowledge that fragility is primarily a matter of degree, not of kind. One should not, however, become bogged down by this issue as that militates against further research and policy development and implementation. A reasonably expedient, but seemingly valid approach is that adopted by the DAC, which assigns the fragile state classification to a country if it is in the bottom two quintiles of the country policy and institutional assessment (CPIA) or has not been rated by the World Bank.

The key questions that then need to be addressed are whether aid, in all of its current or historical forms, is either ineffective or not sufficiently effective in fragile states, as defined, and if so, how can it be made to work more effectively in them. Chauvet and Collier (2004) provide an insightful response to this question, by looking at the impact of aid on policy and institutional reform. One might infer from their results that by being positively associated with such reform, aid to fragile states can be justified on effectiveness criteria. But their analysis is a partial one, to the extent that it does not look at this relationship in the context of a selectivity model, nor relatedly does it look at implications for growth and poverty reduction. It is also a preliminary one, requiring further investigation.

Answering the preceding questions should provide subsequent information on whether these countries are under- or over-aided and, in particular, on their absorptive capacities. It might also tell us, for example, whether the augmentation of the Collier-Dollar selectivity or Cogneau-Naudet EOp models, discussed in this chapter, would see changes in aid allocations prescribed for fragile states. Augmenting the selectivity model, for instance, would see more aid to fragile states if they are characterized by stable political regimes, trade shocks, structural vulnerability, and the other characteristics mentioned above. Such an augmentation rests on results from research on links between aid and growth. But it needs to be recognized that growth is not the only potential benefit of aid. Prevention of instability and conflict, improvements in human rights, avoiding deterioration of human development indicators, and preventing spillovers on neighbouring countries are other benefits. We need to learn more about the impact of aid on these factors, especially as they apply to fragile states.

Donors can factor-in the results of this research as they become available. But they need to move more quickly than this given the magnitude of issues faced with respect to fragile states, the costs of conflict prevention and a return to violent conflict among them. Three issues emerge.

The first concerns the issue of under- and over-aided fragile states (the orphans and darlings, respectively) that needs to be addressed. This could involve consideration of:

donors agreeing on an annual discussion of their 'partner country' lists to establish where some countries are in danger of losing all or almost all bilateral partners;

compensatory multilateral mechanisms, with some multilateral agencies playing a residual role balancing out the decisions of others;

more explicit tasking and training of diplomatic missions in development dialogue; and

use of mechanisms such as the proposed UN peace-building commission to maintain a focus on orphans.

Second, aid volatility to fragile states must be checked, especially in the case of the under-aided fragile states, the aid orphans. This is both a matter of individual donors being more conscious of year-on-year variation in aid allocations, but also for greater coordination among donors. This coordination could involve:

longer term partnership agreements, possibly facilitated through sector programmes; and compensatory multilateral mechanisms, specifically focused on sector programmes in the 'long term' sectors such as health and education, allowing other types of aid to be more variable.

Third, diminishing aid returns and related absorptive capacity constraints need to be addressed urgently. The literature on aid tends to assume that all aid is provided via governments, or that donors work with governments rather than working around them. Empirical evidence of diminishing returns is based almost entirely on aid flows which have gone to recipient country governments. Diminishing returns will in principle always be an issue in all countries; an economy can only efficiently absorb aid up to a particular level. But clarity is required over the saturation levels of aid that apply in fragile states, and ways of increasing the optimal share of aid in GDP need to be considered. One method of addressing the second of these issues is to allocate aid via non-government channels, such as NGOs, the private sector or 'independent service authorities'. It can be the case that operating through these channels can make aid effective even when policy and institutional settings are deficient, prior to reforms. These channels have been considered in the literature (see Collier 2002; World Bank 2002; Collier and Dollar 2004; ODI 2004). One can and should explore these channels further, as they apply to fragile states.

APPENDIX

Aid and growth: a brief literature survey

For many decades the research literature on the country-level impacts of aid often sent ambiguous messages as to whether aid was effective in promoting growth and reducing poverty. A number of widely cited empirical studies found no evidence that aid contributed to higher growth, while influential writers often provided damning qualitative accounts of aid. The empirical studies include Voivodas (1973), Mosley (1980), Mosley et al. (1987), and Boone (1996). Arguably the best known author critical of aid on qualitative grounds is the late Lord Bauer (see Bauer 1981, 1991). The overall consensus about these impacts was rather pessimistic. This, combined with strong evidence that projects were in general effective in attaining their intended outcomes, led to the well-known 'micro-macro paradox' of aid (Mosley 1986).

The late 1990s saw a fundamental change in the literature on aid and growth. Commencing with the publication of the seminal research of Burnside and Dollar (1997), a new stream of empirical studies has emerged that provides a clear, unambiguous message that aid increases growth. This has proved to be an especially robust research finding drawn by practically all of the increasingly large number of empirical studies of aid and growth post-Burnside and Dollar (1997). This is clear, as a number of recent surveys of the aid-growth and related literatures attest. These include Hansen and Tarp (2000); Beynon (2001, 2002); Hermes and Lensink (2001); (2003a, 2004a); Morrissey (2001). McGillivray (2004a) identifies 35 empirical aid-growth studies that have been conducted since Burnside and Dollar (1997). Each these studies provides original empirical results, obtained from either new or updated data sets, similar data sets but employing different empirical methods or both. Thirty-three of these studies find evidence that aid works. The two studies that fail to find this evidence do not reject the proposition that aid increases growth, but simply that in the context of a Burnside and Dollar analysis of aid one cannot observe a relationship between aid and growth.

Roodman (2004) points to the results of some of these studies being fragile, but does not per se reject the conclusion that aid and growth are positively associated. Full bibliographic details of all 35 studies can be found in McGillivray (2004a). Clemens et al. (2004) cite an additional 11 studies that McGillivray (2004a) does not. Seven of these studies find that aid and growth are positively related. One finds no relationship between these variables and two find that the relationship is negative. Clemens et al. (2004) criticize the methods used by those three studies (very heavily so in the case of the two reporting the negative relationship), to such an extent that their results should be treated with great caution. The well-known macro-micro paradox of aid would appear to be dead and buried, well and truly.

The demise of the macro-micro paradox should imply that aid no longer has its critics. A number of researchers have in fact criticized aid on empirical grounds. Brumm (2003), Easterly (2003), and Ovaska (2003) are among them. They are the three studies cited in Clemens et al. (2004) that provide unfavourable accounts of aid effectiveness. Some go so far as to claim that aid is actually harmful. Data showing increased aid flows and at broadly the same time decreased growth rates are often used to support this claim (see Easterly 2003, for example). The real issue is not whether growth has declined, but whether these declines would have been lower in the absence of aid.

Some critics point to problems in aid delivery, such as fungibility, donor proliferation, lack of harmonization, and tying, citing these as reasons for the failure of aid. These problems are real, and it is valid to criticize aid delivery on the basis of them. But in their proper context, they point to why aid might not have worked better, rather than not having worked at all (McGillivray 2004a). Moreover, as mentioned above, the literature is now very clear in its finding that aid works. While one should always express a degree of skepticism over the findings of most empirical studies, especially econometric analyses of panel data, as Roodman (2004) very skillfully does, the sheer weight of evidence emerging from the literature is such that one can clearly reject the hypothesis that aid, on aggregate, has no beneficial impact on or is harmful for growth. The only context in which one should not reject this hypothesis is if aid inflows are of such a large magnitude that negative returns prevail, to such an extent that they outweigh any positive impact. This would appear to be a case for improving recipient country absorptive capacities and/or reducing aid to manageable levels, not eliminating it entirely.

References

Alesina, A. and D. Dollar (2000). 'Who Gives Foreign Aid to Whom and Why?' *Journal of Economic Growth* 5(1): 33–63.

Alesina, A. and B. Weder (2002). 'Do Corrupt Governments Receive Less Foreign Aid?' *American Economic Review* 92(4): 1126–37.

Arvin, B. M. (1998). 'Biases in the Allocation of Canadian Official Development Assistance', *Applied Economics Letters* 5: 773–5.

Arvin, B. M. and T. Drewes (2001). 'Are There Biases in German Bilateral Aid Allocations?' *Applied Economics Letters* 8: 173–7.

Bauer, P. T. (1981). *Equality, the Third World and Economic Delusion*. London: Weidenfeld.

Bauer, P. T. (1991). *The Development Frontier: Essays in Applied Economics*. Cambridge, MA: Harvard University Press.

Berthelemy, J. C. and A. Tichit (2002). 'Bilateral Donors' Aid Allocation Decisions'. WIDER Discussion Paper DP2002/123. Helsinki: UNU-WIDER.

Beynon, J. (1999). '"Assessing Aid" and the Collier-Dollar Poverty Efficient Allocations: A Critique'. Economic Policy and Research Department Discussion Paper. London: Department for International Development.

Beynon, J. (2001). 'Policy Implications for Aid Allocations of Recent Research on Aid Effectiveness and Selectivity'. Paper presented at the Joint Development Centre/DAC Experts Seminar on Aid Effectiveness, Selectivity and Poor Performers, OECD, Paris, January.

Beynon, J. (2002). 'Policy Implications for Aid Allocations of Recent Research on Aid Effectiveness and Selectivity', in B. Mak Arvin (ed.), *New Perspectives on Foreign Aid and Economic Development*. Westport: Praeger.

Bhagwati, J. (1972). 'Amount and Aid Sharing', in R. Frank, J. Bhagwati, R. Shaw, and H. Malmgren (eds), *Assisting Development Countries*. New York: Praeger.

Birdsall, N., S. Claessens, and I. Diwan (2002). 'Policy Selectivity Forgone: Debt and Donor Behaviour in Africa'. Centre for Global Development Working Paper No. 17. Washington, DC: Centre for Global Development.

Boone, P. (1996). 'Politics and the Effectiveness of Aid', *European Economic Review* 40(2): 289–329.

Brumm, H. J. (2003). 'Aid, Policies and Growth: Bauer was Right', *Cato Journal* 23(2): 167–74.

Bulíř, A. and A. Hamann (2003). 'Aid Volatility: An Empirical Assessment', *IMF Staff Paper* 50(1): 64–89.

Burnside, C. and D. Dollar (1997), 'Aid, Policies, and Growth'. Policy Research Working Paper No. 1777. Washington, DC: World Bank.

Burnside, C. and D. Dollar (2000). 'Aid, Policies and Growth,' *American Economic Review* 90(4): 847–68.

Chalmers, M. (2004). *Spending to Save? An Analysis of the Cost Effectiveness of Conflict Prevention versus Intervention after the Onset of Violent Conflict: Phase 2 Synthesis Report*. Bradford: Centre for International Co-operation and Security, University of Bradford.

Chauvet, L. and P. Collier (2004). *Development Effectiveness in Fragile States: Spillovers and Turnarounds*. Oxford: Centre for the Study of African Economies, Department of Economics, Oxford University.

Chauvet, L. and P. Guillaumont (2002). 'Aid and Growth Revisited: Policy, Economic Vulnerability and Political Instability'. Paper presented at the Annual Bank Conference or Development Economics on Towards Pro-poor Policies, Oslo, June.

Clemens, M. and S. Radelet (2003). 'The Millennium Challenge Account: How Much is Too Much, How Long is Long Enough?' Centre for Global Development Working Paper No. 23. Washington, DC: Centre for Global Development.

Clemens, M., S. Radelet, and R. Bhavnani (2004). 'Counting Chickens When they Hatch: The Short-term Effect of Aid on Growth'. Centre for Global Development Working Paper No. 44. Washington, DC: Centre for Global Development.

Cogneau, D. and J.-D. Naudet (2004). 'Who Deserves Aid? Equality of Opportunity, International Aid and Poverty Reduction'. Mimeo. Paris: DIAL/AFD.

Collier, P. (2002). *Making Aid Smart: Institutional Incentives Facing Donor Organizations and their Implications for Aid Effectiveness*. Forum Series on the Roles of Institutions in Promoting Growth. Washington, DC: USAID and IRIS.

Collier, P. and J. Dehn (2001). 'Aid, Shocks, and Growth'. World Bank Policy Research Working Paper No. 2688. Washington, DC: World Bank.

Collier, P. and D. Dollar (1999). 'Aid Allocation and Poverty Reduction'. World Bank Policy Research Working Paper No. 2041. Washington, DC: World Bank.

Collier, P. and D. Dollar (2001). 'Can the World Cut Poverty in Half? How Policy Reform and Effective Aid Can Meet the International Development Goals'. *World Development* 29(11): 1787–802.

Collier, P. and D. Dollar (2002). 'Aid Allocation and Poverty Reduction', *European Economic Review* 26: 1475–500.

Collier, P. and D. Dollar (2004). 'Development Effectiveness: What Have We Learnt?' *Economic Journal* 114(496): F244–71.

Collier, P. and A. Hoeffler (2002). 'Aid, Policy, and Growth in Post-Conflict Societies'. World Bank Policy Research Working Paper No. 2902. Washington, DC: World Bank.

Collier, P. and A. Hoeffler (2004). 'Aid, Policy and Growth in Post-Conflict Societies', *European Economic Review* 48: 1125–45.

Dalgaard, C. and H. Hansen (2001). 'On Aid, Growth and Good Policies', *Journal of Development Studies* 37(6): 17–35.

Dalgaard, C., H. Hansen, and F. Tarp (2004). 'On the Empirics of Foreign Aid and Growth', *Economic Journal* 114(496): F191–216.

Dollar, D. and V. Levin (2004). 'The Increasing Selectivity of Foreign Aid, 1984–2002'. World Bank Policy Research Working Paper No. 3299. Washington, DC: World Bank.

Easterly, W. (2003). 'Can Foreign Aid Buy Growth', *Journal of Economic Perspectives* 17 (3): 23–48.

Edwards, S. and S. van Wijnbergen (1989). 'Disequilibrium and Structural Adjustment', in H. Chenery and T. N. Srinivasan (eds), *Handbook of Development Economics*. Amsterdam: North-Holland.

Feeny, S. and M. McGillivray (2004). 'Modelling Inter-temporal Aid Allocation: A New Application with an Emphasis on Papua New Guinea', *Oxford Development Studies* 32 (2): 233–50.

Gemmell, N. and M. McGillivray (1998). 'Aid and Tax Instability and the Government Budget Constraint in Developing Countries'. CREDIT Research Paper 98/1. Nottingham: Centre for Research in Economic Development and International Trade, University of Nottingham.

Gomanee, K., S. Girma, and O. Morrissey (2003). 'Searching for Aid Threshold Effects: Aid, Growth and the Welfare of the Poor'. CREDIT Research Paper 02/05. Nottingham: Centre for Research in Economic Development and International Trade, University of Nottingham.

Guillaumont, P. and L. Chauvet (2001). 'Aid and Performance: A Reassessment,' *Journal of Development Studies* 37(6): 66–87.

Gunning, J. W. (2001). 'Rethinking Aid', in B. Pleskovic and N. Stern (eds), *Annual World Bank Conference on Development Economics 2000*. Washington, DC: World Bank.

Gupta, Sanjeev and Peter S. Heller (2002). 'Challenges in Expanding Development Assistance'. IMF Policy Discussion Papers 02/5, International Monetary Fund.

Hansen, H. and F. Tarp (2000). 'Aid Effectiveness Disputed', *Journal of International Development* 12: 375–98.

Hansen, H. and F. Tarp (2001). 'Aid and Growth Regressions', *Journal of Development Economics* 64: 547–70.

Hermes, N. and R. Lensink (2001). 'Changing the Conditions for Development Aid: A New Paradigm?' *Journal of Development Studies* 37(6): 1–16.

Hudson, J. and P. Mosley (2001). 'Aid, Policies and Growth: In Search of the Holy Grail', *Journal of International Development* 13: 1023–38.

IDA (International Development Association) (2004). *Aid Delivery in Conflict-Affected Countries: The Role of the World Bank*. Washington, DC: International Development Association.

Isenman, P. (1976). 'Biases in Aid Allocations Against Poorer and Larger Countries', *World Development* 4(8): 631–41.

Islam, M. (2003). 'Political Regimes and the Effects of Foreign Aid on Growth', *Journal of Developing Areas* 37(1): 35–53.

Jones, S., R. Riddell, and K. Kotonglou (2004). 'Aid Allocation: Managing for Development Results and Difficult Partnerships'. Summary paper prepared for the DAC Learning and Advisory Process on Difficult Partnerships, Oxford Policy Management, Oxford, November.

Kanbur, R. (2004). 'Reforming the Formula: A Modest Proposal for Introducing Developmental Outcomes in IDA Allocation Procedures'. Paper presented at the Second AFD-EUDN Conference, Paris, November.

Killick, T. (2004). 'The Case Against Doubling Aid to Africa'. Notes for House of Commons Presentation, November. Mimeo. House of Commons, London.

Kosack, S. (2003). 'Effective Aid: How Democracy Allows Development Aid to Improve the Quality of Life', *World Development* 31(1): 1–22.

Levin, V. and D. Dollar (2005). 'The Forgotten States: Aid Volumes and Volatility in Difficult Partnership Countries (1992–2002)'. Summary paper prepared for the DAC Learning and Advisory Process on Difficult Partnerships, Oxford Policy Management, Oxford. November. Mimeo.

Llavador, H. G. and J. E. Roemer (2001). 'An Equal-opportunity Approach to the Allocation of International Aid', *Journal of Development Economics* 64(1): 147–71.

Lu, S. and R. Ram (2001). 'Foreign Aid, Government Policies and Economic Growth: Further Evidence from Cross-country Panel Data for 1970 to 1993', *International Economics* 54: 15–29.

McGillivray, M. (1989). 'The Allocation of Aid among Developing Countries: A Multi-donor Analysis Using a Per Capita Aid Index', *World Development* 17(2): 561–8.

McGillivray, M. (2003a). 'Aid Effectiveness and Selectivity: Integrating Multiple Objectives in Aid Allocations', *DAC Journal* 4(3): 23–36.

McGillivray, M. (2003b). 'Descriptive and Prescriptive Analyses of Aid Allocation: Approaches, Issues and Consequences'. WIDER Discussion Paper DP2002/123. Helsinki: UNU-WIDER.

McGillivray, M. (2004a). 'Is Aid Effective?'. Mimeo. Helsinki: UNU-WIDER.

McGillivray, M. (2004b). 'What Determines African Bilateral Aid Receipts?' Mimeo. Helsinki: UNU-WIDER.

McGillivray, M. (2004c). 'Descriptive and Prescriptive Analyses of Aid Allocation: Approaches, Issues and Consequences', *International Review of Economics and Finance* 13: 275–92.

McGillivray, M. and H. White (1994). 'Development Criteria for the Allocation of Aid and Assessment of Donor Performance'. CREDIT Research Paper No. 94/7. Nottingham: University of Nottingham.

Moreno Torres, M. and M. Anderson (2004). 'Fragile States: Defining Difficult Environments for Poverty Reduction'. PRDE Working Paper No. 1, Poverty Reduction in Difficult Environments Team, Policy Division, DIFD, London.

Morrissey, O. (2001). 'Does Aid Increase Growth?' *Progress in Development Studies* 1(1): 37–50.

Morrissey, O. (2002). 'Aid Effectiveness for Growth and Development', *ODI Opinions*, February.

Mosley, P. (1980). 'Aid, Savings and Growth Revisited', *Oxford Bulletin of Economics and Statistics* 42(2): 79–95.

Mosley, P. (1986). 'Aid Effectiveness: The Micro-Macro Paradox', *Institute of Development Studies Bulletin* 17: 214–25.

Mosley, P. (1987). *Overseas Aid: Its Defence and Reform*. Brighton: Wheatsheaf Books.

Mosley, P., J. Hudson, and S. Horrell (1987). 'Aid, the Public Sector and the Market in Less Developed Countries', *Economic Journal* 97(387): 616–41.

Neumayer, E. (2002). 'Is Good Governance Rewarded? A Cross-National Analysis of Debt Forgiveness', *World Development* 30(6): 913–30.

Neumayer, E. (2003a). 'Is Respect for Human Rights Rewarded? An Analysis of Bilateral and Multilateral Aid Allocation Before and After the End of the Cold War', *Human Rights Quarterly* 25(2): 510–27.

Neumayer, E. (2003b). 'The Determinants of Aid Allocation by Regional Multilateral Development Banks and United Nations Agencies', *International Studies Quarterly* 47: 101–27.

Neumayer, E. (2003c). 'What Determines the Allocation of Aid by Arab Countries and Multilateral Agencies?' *Journal of Development Studies* 39(4): 134–7.

Neumayer, E. (2003d). *The Pattern of Aid Giving: The Impact of Good Governance on Development Assistance*. London: Routledge.

Nunnenkamp, P., C. Canavire, and L. Triveño (2004). 'Targeting Aid to the Needy and Deserving: Nothing but Promises?' Kiel Working Paper No. 1229. Kiel: Kiel Institute for World Economics.

ODI (Overseas Development Institute) (2004). *Aid to 'Poorly Performing' Countries: A Critical Review of Debates and Issues*. London: ODI.

Ovaska, T. (2003). 'The Failure of Development Aid', *Cato Journal* 23(2): 175–88.

Pettersson, J. (2004). 'Foreign Aid, Fungibility, Growth and Poverty Reduction'. Mimeo. Department of Economics, Stockholm University, Stockholm.

Ram, R. (2003). 'Roles of Bilateral and Multilateral Aid in Economic Growth of Developing Countries', *Kyklos* 56: 95–110.

Ram, R. (2004). 'Recipient Country's "Policies" and the Effect of Foreign Aid on Economic Growth in Developing Countries: Additional Evidence', *Journal of International Development* 16: 201–11.

Rao, J. M. (1994). 'Judging Givers: Equity and Scale in Aid Allocation', *World Development* 22(10): 1579–84.

Rao, J. M. (1997). 'Ranking Foreign Aid Donors: An Index Combining the Scale and Equity of Aid Giving', *World Development* 25(6): 947–61.

Robinson, S. and F. Tarp (2000). 'Foreign Aid and Development: Summary and Synthesis', in F. Tarp and P. Hjertholm (eds), *Foreign Aid and Development: Lessons Learnt and Directions for the Future*. London and New York: Routledge.

Roodman, D. (2004). 'The Anarchy of Numbers: Aid, Development and Cross-country Empirics'. CGD Working Paper No. 32. Washington, DC: Centre for Global Development.

Svensson, J. (1999). 'Aid, Growth and Democracy', *Economics and Politics* 11(3): 275–97.

Torres, M. M. and M. Anderson (2004). 'Fragile States: Defining Difficult Environments for Poverty Reduction. PRDE Working Papers 1, Poverty Reduction in Difficult Environments Team, Policy Division. London: DIFD.

Voivodas, C. S. (1973). 'Exports, Foreign Capital Inflow and Economic Growth', *Journal of International Economics* 3(4): 337–49.

Wood, A. (2004). 'UN Millennium Project Report: Comments on 23/9/04 Draft'. Mimeo. London: DIFD.

World Bank (2002). *World Bank Group Work in Low-income Countries under Stress: A Task Force Report*. Washington, DC: World Bank.

World Bank (2003). *Allocating IDA Funds Based on Performance: Fourth Annual Report on IDA's Country Assessment and Allocation Process*. Washington, DC: World Bank.

10

Enhancing Effective Utilization of Aid in Fragile States

Sanjeev Gupta[1]

10.1 Introduction

In recent years, there has been much discussion on the macroeconomic consequences of the scaling up of aid in low-income countries (LICs) (Aiyar et al. 2005; Foster and Killick 2006; Gupta et al. 2006; Berg et al. 2007). The debate has centred on whether aid surges experienced since the late 1990s have been absorbed or spent, and on the nature of the macroeconomic and structural policies needed in aid-receiving countries so that they can use aid effectively.[2] The results from these studies show that many countries did not fully absorb or spend the aid. A recent study estimated that aid-receiving countries in sub-Saharan Africa spent between 30 and 80 per cent of aid, depending on the macroeconomic conditions and level of reserves. The proportion of spending was more when inflation was less than 5–7 per cent.[3]

The literature on aid spending and absorption in fragile states is limited. These states comprise countries recovering from conflict and those classified as having weak institutions and policies.[4] A recent paper (Elbadawi et al. 2007)

---

[1] I wish to thank Richard Allen, Shamsudddin Tareq, Menachem Katz, and Marijn Verhoeven for helpful comments on an earlier draft. The views expressed in this chapter are solely those of the author and do not necessarily represent those of the IMF or IMF policy.

[2] Aid absorption is defined as the extent to which a country's non-aid current account deficit widens in response to an increase in aid inflows. This captures the quantity of net imports financed by the increased aid and represents the additional transfer of real resources enabled by the aid. Aid spending is defined as the widening in the government fiscal deficit (net of aid) that accompanies an increase in aid.

[3] See Independent Evaluation Office (2007).

[4] The definition of a fragile state varies. The World Bank defines fragile states as those low income, IDA eligible countries with a country policy and institutional assessment (CPIA) of 3.2 or less (World Bank 2009). There are 29 such countries, plus a few others that do not have a CPIA

shows that while post-conflict countries receive substantial aid flows after the onset of peace, the flows are not well synchronized with country capacity to absorb them. The aid tends to surge immediately after the cessation of hostilities and gradually taper off thereafter. Collier and Hoeffler (2002) argue that this pattern of aid flows is often not optimal, as the capacity of these countries to absorb assistance is rather low in the early post-conflict period. Elbadawi et al. (2007) results indicate that many post-conflict countries did not spend the full amount of aid—akin to the response of other aid-receiving countries.

This chapter further explores the macroeconomic implications of aid flows in countries with weak institutions. In doing so, it lists considerations that are relevant for policy-makers in these countries for promoting effective aid utilization. The chapter is organized as follows: the next section discusses the macroeconomic implications of aid flows for LICs in general and for post-conflict countries specifically. Considerations bearing on the spend/save decision in countries with macroeconomic imbalances and weak institutions are presented thereafter. Then the merits of frontloading and expenditure smoothing approaches for fragile states are discussed, after which the chapter concludes.

10.2 Macroeconomic Implications Of Aid Flows

Aid augments domestic resources, but it can have implications for the real exchange rate, exports, and competitiveness, including in countries with weak institutions. In practice, however, macroeconomic impact of aid depends both on how a country's policies (e.g., monetary, fiscal, and exchange rate) respond to aid inflows and how it spends the additional resources (e.g., traded or non-traded goods). The former can be analysed in terms of the absorb and spend framework discussed below (Aiyar et al. 2005; Berg et al. 2007).

---

rating (e.g., Afghanistan and Somalia). The African Development Bank has used two criteria for its definition: It defines fragile states as those with a CPIA of less than 3 and a Country Vulnerability Index (CVI) of less than 0.351. The latter is a weighted index of various measures of vulnerability, which combine selected aggregates from CPIA, the United Nations Development Programme (UNDP) Human Development Index (HDI) and other sources of vulnerability such as external shocks (oil price increases), high dependence on primary commodities, and exposure to frequent natural disasters. Core fragile states are those whose fragility is captured by both the CPIA and the CVI; they number 12. The African Development Bank is in the process of revising its methodology to include other criteria such as: (i) countries in post-crisis/post-conflict transition; (ii) those at the bottom of the UN Human Development Index (as before); and (iii) those that have had their per capita GDP contract by more than 10 per cent in real terms since 1990 (base year of the Millennium Development Goals—MDGs) to 2005. In Chapter 2, Baliamoune-Lutz and McGillivray question the use of such approaches for identifying fragile states and propose an alternative methodology that relies on the notion that fragility differs along a continuum.

Table 10.1. Basic combinations of absorption and spending in response to aid inflows

Aid is absorbed and spent	*Aid is neither absorbed nor spent*
The government spends the aid.	Government expenditures are not increased.
The central bank sells the foreign exchange.	Taxes are not lowered.
The current account deficit widens.	International reserves are built up.
Aid is absorbed but not spent	*Aid is spent but not absorbed*
Government expenditures are not increased.	The fiscal deficit widens (expenditures are increased).
The central bank sells the foreign exchange.	The central bank does not sell foreign exchange.
Monetary growth is slowed; nominal exchange rates appreciate; inflation is lower.	International reserves are built up.
	Inflation increases.

Source: Gupta et al. (2006).

10.2.1 *Absorb and spend framework*

One could conceive of four basic combinations of absorption and spending in response to aid inflows, although intermediate combinations are also feasible. Each one has different macroeconomic implications (see Table 10.1). The central bank controls absorption through two mechanisms: (i) by deciding how much of the foreign exchange associated with aid it should sell; and (ii) through its interest rate, which impacts aggregate demand. The government has to decide how much of the local currency counterpart it should spend in its budget.

10.2.1.1 *AID IS ABSORBED AND SPENT* (TOP LEFT QUADRANT)
The government spends the aid, and the central bank sells the foreign exchange. The current account widens by the amount of aid received, and the fiscal deficit is fully financed by higher aid. This is the outcome that most donors and international partners are striving for in aid-receiving countries. In this instance, some real exchange rate appreciation may be appropriate to effect reallocation of resources from the traded to the non-traded sector, for example, social services. Studies show that neither LICs nor the post-conflict countries that experienced aid surges in recent years fully absorbed and spent incremental aid.

10.2.1.2 *AID IS NEITHER ABSORBED NOR SPENT* (TOP RIGHT QUADRANT)
In this instance, the countries simply save the entire aid by building up their international reserves. The fiscal deficit does not increase. This strategy was adopted by some countries (e.g., Ethiopia and Ghana) in the short term to increase foreign exchange reserves from a low level—a consideration that is of relevance to countries emerging from a conflict. This may also be an

appropriate response to smooth spending over time if aid flows are viewed as highly volatile (e.g., Ghana).

10.2.1.3 *AID IS ABSORBED BUT NOT SPENT* (BOTTOM LEFT QUADRANT)
Increased aid flows substitute for domestic financing of the government deficit. The sale of foreign exchange draws liquidity out of the economy and lowers inflation. As reported by Elbadawi, Kaltani and Schmidt-Hebbel, (2007) post-conflict countries partially followed this approach to reduce the level of public debt and crowd in the private sector. The receipts from the sale of foreign exchange were used to retire government debt in these countries.

10.2.1.4 *AID IS SPENT BUT NOT ABSORBED* (BOTTOM RIGHT QUADRANT)
In this case, the fiscal deficit widens in response to higher aid flows, but the central bank does not sell the foreign exchange to finance additional imports. This is tantamount to financing government deficit by printing money or borrowing from the domestic private sector, for example, by selling treasury bills. This results in a substantial increase in domestic interest rates, thereby crowding out the private sector. In a way, this reflects inadequate coordination between the ministry of finance and the central bank. Some aid-receiving countries (e.g., Tanzania, Uganda) followed this approach in response to recent aid surges.

10.2.2 *Post-conflict experience*

Elbadawi et al. (2007) report that post-conflict countries saved part of the aid. Because central banks in these countries did not sell all their foreign exchange acquired through aid, there was no significant real appreciation of the exchange rate. The aid literature discusses at length the adverse effects of real exchange rate appreciation on the tradable goods sector—that is, the so-called Dutch disease effect. Rajan and Subramanian (2005) argue that real exchange rate effects on export can be significant, as export-oriented, labour-intensive industries grow more slowly than other industries. These effects are stronger when trade is restricted and when the economy is running at full capacity.

How aid resources are deployed in post-conflict countries or fragile states in general has a bearing on the real exchange rate. If aid is used for productivity-enhancing projects, such as restoring and building critical infrastructure to boost the economy's supply capacity and alleviating constraints to growth, the pressure on the real exchange rate is likely to be mitigated. This is also likely when much of the aid is spent on importables. On the other hand, if aid finances social sector spending, which includes more non-traded goods, the macroeconomic consequences will likely be exacerbated.

Estimation of the equilibrium real exchange rate for such countries on the basis of historical data may not provide useful guidance, particularly when the potential for aid inflows is large. As noted earlier, some real exchange rate adjustment may be necessary and, indeed, appropriate in response to the higher level of aid to facilitate resource reallocation in favour of the non-traded sector. Elbadawi et al. (2007) find that the median post-conflict country suffered from moderate real exchange rate overvaluation after the start of peace, but this could not be traced to aid flows. This does not imply that the policy-makers in these countries can afford to overlook appreciation in the real exchange rate; rather, they should remain alert to this possibility and ensure that appropriate policy actions are taken to offset its adverse consequences.

The empirical evidence from post-conflict countries suggests that a sound fiscal policy (including appropriate expenditure composition) through its positive effects on growth can mitigate the pressure on the real exchange rate. For example, conflict raises the share of defence spending in total government expenditure, which in turn has a negative effect on growth by diverting resources away from the spending on sectors (education, health, infrastructure) that promote economic growth over the long term (Gupta et al. 2004). Elbadawi et al. (2007) find that in post-conflict countries financial development and deepening as well as trade openness alleviate constraints to growth, thereby diminishing the adverse impact of real exchange rate appreciation.[5] They also find evidence that the maximum growth impact of aid is during the six–nine years after the start of peace. This suggests that saving part of the aid received during the initial years is perhaps appropriate.

It is unclear how good the coordination between the fiscal and monetary authorities has been in post-conflict countries during periods of aid surges. Insufficient coordination could partly explain why aid was not fully absorbed. The central bank may have targeted a reserve buildup, sought to prevent an appreciation of the exchange rate, decided to use receipts from the sale of the foreign exchange to retire government debt, or some combination of the three. As saved-up aid is spent, coordination between the two authorities becomes critical; the central bank must sell foreign exchange as the ministry of finance expands spending in the budget by the amount of saved aid. The objective is to ensure that the central bank takes into account the impact of the ministry of finance's fiscal operations. This coordination between the

---

[5] Addison, Chowdhury, and Murshed (2002) find that conflicts have a negative effect on financial development and overall financial depth.

monetary and fiscal policies is relevant whether the country has fixed or flexible exchange rates.[6]

10.3 Considerations Determining Spend/Save Decisions In Fragile States

In deciding how much and how fast they should spend aid, policy-makers in fragile states have to be aware of the country's overall macroeconomic position, its capacity to absorb aid at the sectoral and subnational levels, and the strength of its institutions. The impact of these flows on debt sustainability and growth is also critical. Of course, these considerations do not apply to humanitarian aid, which should be spent as soon as it is received.

10.3.1 *Overall macroeconomic conditions*

Overall macroeconomic conditions affect the amount of aid that could be spent immediately. This point is illustrated first with data from selected post-conflict countries and then followed up by a comparison of fragile states with that of LICs in general. For instance, large macroeconomic imbalances (e.g., a high rate of inflation and a low level of reserves) at the end of conflict may require a more gradual increase in aid-financed spending. Figures 10.1 through to 10.8 give an indication of the macroeconomic conditions prevailing around the end of the conflict.[7] On average, real GDP falls significantly during the conflict, which is consistent with earlier studies on the economic consequences of conflict (Collier 1999; Collier et al. 2003).[8] The figures further show that the average inflation is high, reflecting a relatively high domestic (including bank) financing of the government deficit. At the same time, revenues are lower owing to the decline in economic activity, and raising them domestically may raise political challenges for the postwar government (Boyce and O'Donnell 2007); however, the reduction in the overall spending is not sufficient to offset the revenue drop. The level of foreign exchange reserves is also lower than before the conflict. In such circumstances, further

[6] See Heller et al. (2006) for details.

[7] These data are compiled for a number of countries that went through a conflict situation using an 'event-study' methodology and where the IMF was involved in rebuilding fiscal institutions after cessation of the conflict. That is, data are transformed from calendar time into 'event time'. However, caution is required in interpreting the results because the effect of other influences is not controlled for and the results are not compared with a control group of countries.

[8] Collier (1999) finds that, relative to the counterfactual of peace, the marginal effect of a conflict causes per capita GDP to decline by 2 per cent per annum during the war.

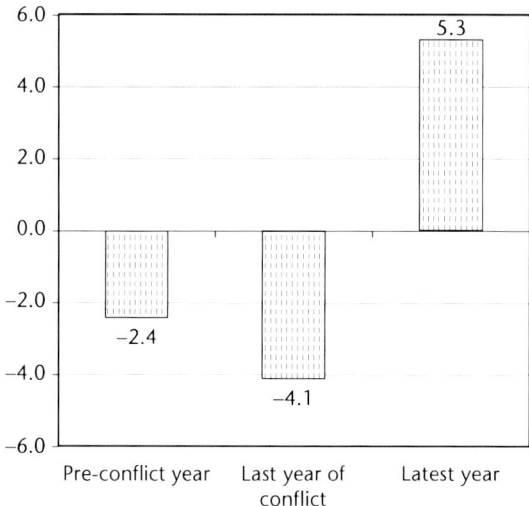

Figure 10.1. Growth in selected post-conflict countries (annual % change)

Note: Based on a sample of 13 countries: Albania, Bosnia and Herzegovina, Cambodia, Dem. Rep. of Congo, Croatia, Lebanon, Liberia, Mozambique, Rwanda, Serbia and Montenegro, Sierra Leone, Tajikistan and Yemen.

'Pre-conflict' refers to the year before the conflict; 'Last year of conflict' refers to the year before the first technical assistance mission by the IMF's Fiscal Affairs Department, either during or immediately following the conflict; 'Latest year' refers to the most recent year for which data are available.

Source: IMF (WEO database, April 2004 and April 2007); World Bank (WDI database).

pressures on domestic demand are likely to aggravate macroeconomic imbalances, although as noted above, how the aid is spent is crucial.[9]

During the conflict, some revenue loss is recouped by seigniorage generated by bank financing of the government deficit. However, the scope for seigniorage revenue is determined by the willingness of the population to hold money balances in local currency vis-à-vis foreign currencies. Post-conflict aid displaces domestic financing of the budget. It restores confidence in the local currency by curbing capital flight, and reduces reliance on seigniorage as a revenue source (Adam et al. 2007; Davies 2007).[10] Aid thus contributes to 'monetary reconstruction'. This effect is reinforced by rising money demand stemming from output growth made possible by aid, although Adam et al. (2007) find that income elasticity of the demand for money is still significantly lower than in normal times. Under such circumstances, unrestrained inflation after the hostilities have ceased would discourage the population

[9] A recent study on sub-Saharan African countries (Independent Evaluation Office 2007) finds that a large proportion of incremental aid (over 80 per cent) was used for retiring domestic debt when inflation exceeded 5 per cent.

[10] According to Adam, Collier, and Davies, a single percentage point increase in GDP in aid reduces seignorage by one-third of a per cent of GDP.

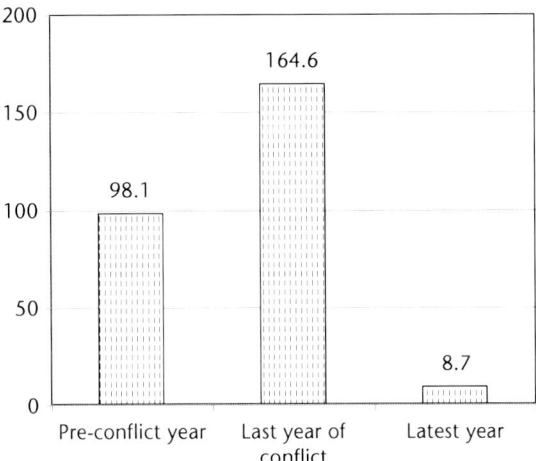

Figure 10.2. Consumer price inflation in selected post-conflict countries (annual %
change)

Note: Based on a sample of 11 countries: Afghanistan, Albania, Cambodia, Dem. Rep. of Congo,
Croatia, Lebanon, Mozambique, Rwanda, Sierra Leone, Tajikistan, and Yemen. 'Pre-conflict' refers
to the year before the conflict; 'Last year of conflict' refers to the year before the first technical
assistance mission by the IMF's Fiscal Affairs Department, either during or immediately following
the conflict; 'Latest year' refers to the most recent year for which data are available.

Source: IMF (WEO database, April 2004 and April 2007); World Bank (WDI database).

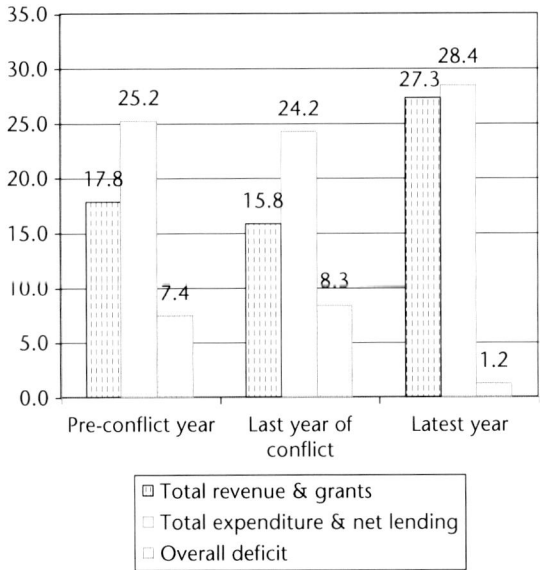

Figure 10.3. Fiscal aggregates in selected post-conflict countries (in % of GDP)

Note: Based on a sample of 10 countries: Albania, Cambodia, Democratic Republic of Congo,
Croatia, Lebanon, Mozambique, Rwanda, Sierra Leone, Tajikistan, and Yemen. 'Pre-conflict' refers
to the year before the conflict; 'Last year of conflict' refers to the year before the first technical
assistance mission by the IMF's Fiscal Affairs Department, either during or immediately following
the conflict; 'Latest year' refers to the most recent year for which data are available.

Source: IMF (WEO database, April 2004 and April 2007); World Bank (WDI database).

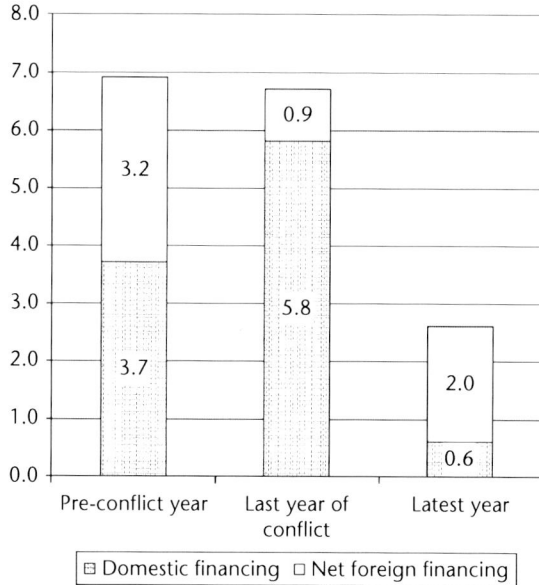

Figure 10.4. Financing of the budget in selected post-conflict countries (in % of GDP)

Note: Based on a sample of 9 countries: Albania, Cambodia, Democratic Republic of Congo, Lebanon, Mozambique, Rwanda, Sierra Leone, Tajikistan, and Yemen. 'Pre-conflict' refers to the year before the conflict; 'Last year of conflict' refers to the year before the first technical assistance mission by the IMF's Fiscal Affairs Department, either during or immediately following the conflict; 'Latest year' refers to the most recent year for which data are available.

Source: IMF (WEO database, April 2004 and April 2007); World Bank (WDI database).

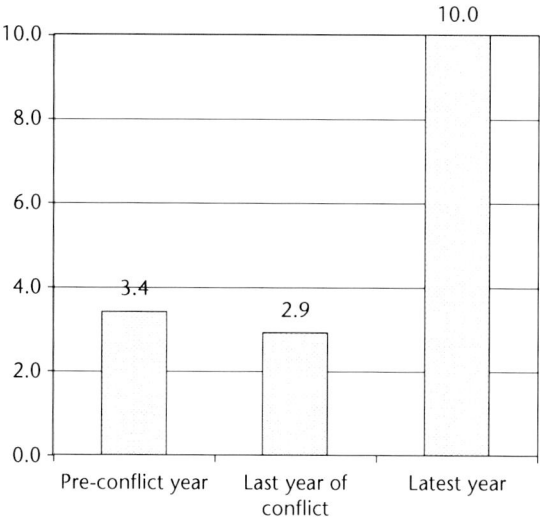

Figure 10.5. Reserves in selected post-conflict countries (in months of imports of goods, average)

Note: Includes Albania, Dem. Rep. of Congo, Croatia, Lebanon, Mozambique, Rwanda, Sierra Leone, Yemen; pre-conflict years adjusted to one year before the conflict.

Source: IMF 2007 (WEO, April).

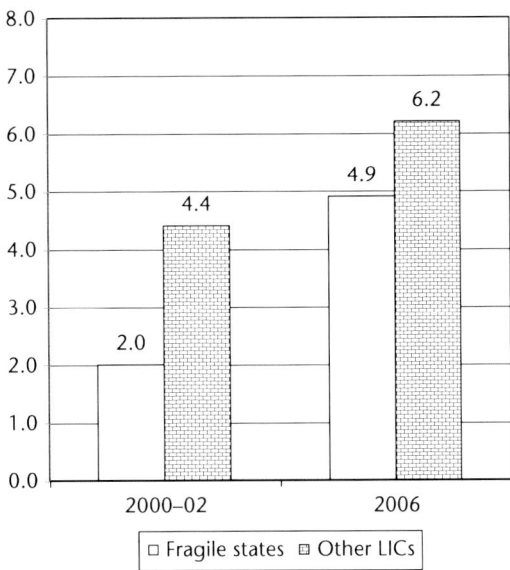

Figure 10.6. Real GDP growth in selected fragile states and other LICs (annual % change, average)

Note: 'Fragile states' include Angola, Burundi, Central African Rep., Chad, Comoros, Republic of Congo, Côte d'Ivoire, Djibouti, Eritrea, Gambia, Guinea, Guinea-Bissau, Haiti, Lao People's Dem. Rep., Mauritania, Myanmar, Nigeria, Papua New Guinea, São Tomé and Príncipe, Solomon Islands, Sudan, Togo, Tongo, Uzbekistan, Vanuatua, and Zimbabwe. 'Other LICs' include Bangladesh, Benin, Bhutan, Burkina Faso, Ethiopia, Ghana, India, Kenya, Kyrgyz Republic, Madagascar, Malawi, Mali, Mongolia, Mozambique, Nepal, Niger, Pakistan, Rwanda, Senegal, Tajikistan, Tanzania, Uganda, Vietnam, Yemen, and Zambia.

Source: IMF 2007 (WEO, April).

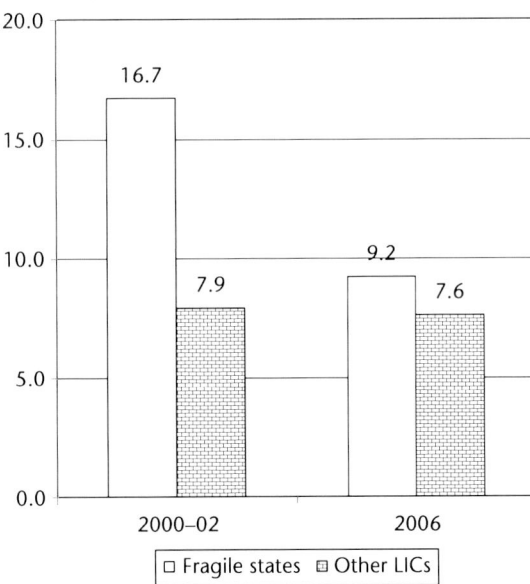

Figure 10.7. Consumer price inflation in selected fragile states and other LICs (annual % change, average)

Note: Includes Albania, Dem. Rep. of Congo, Croatia, Lebanon, Mozambique, Rwanda, Sierra Leone, Yemen; pre-conflict years adjusted to one year before the conflict.

Source: IMF 2007 (WEO, April).

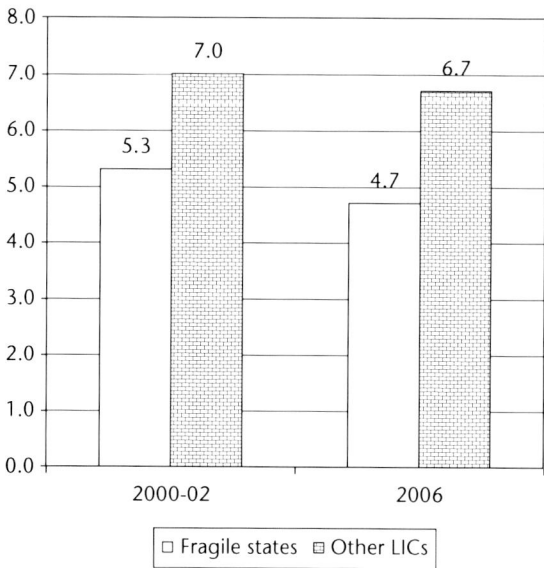

Figure 10.8. Reserves in selected fragile states and other LICs (in months of imports of goods, average)

Note: Includes Albania, Dem. Rep. of Congo, Croatia, Lebanon, Mozambique, Rwanda, Sierra Leone, Yemen; pre-conflict years adjusted to one year before the conflict.

Source: IMF 2007 (WEO, April).

from holding money balances in local currency, and not contribute to 'monetary reconstruction' of the economy. High and sustained inflation would also not help stem and reverse capital flight.[11]

Although macroeconomic indicators of fragile states (as defined by the World Bank) are as poor as those of countries emerging from a conflict, they are nevertheless weaker than those found in LICs in general. Both GDP growth and the level of foreign exchange reserves are lower and inflation higher in fragile states than in other LICs.

10.3.2 *Sectoral absorptive capacity*

Another consideration is the capacity of different sectors to utilize aid-financed spending. According to Collier (1999), conflicts affect the economy in different ways. Besides diverting spending from productive sectors such as education, health, and infrastructure, they destroy physical assets in the economy. That is, the conflict causes a destruction of basic infrastructure

---

[11] Post-conflict inflation increases annual capital flight by up to 0.01 per cent of GDP (Davies 2007). This effect is substantial at high inflation rates.

including schools, health centres, and hospitals. While using aid to rebuild and rehabilitate these assets is an effective use of resources, this effort is likely to be constrained by the lack of trained manpower. A large segment of the skilled population (e.g., teachers and doctors) may have been lost to the conflict or displaced as a result of the conflict. In addition, the conflict may have created a 'lost generation' of a relatively unskilled young population resulting from disruptions to the education systems. In general, fragile states suffer from skill shortages, which limit their ability to expand aid-financed services. These difficulties are more acute at the subnational level where much of the social spending takes place.[12]

10.3.3 *Debt sustainability and growth impact of spending*

Debt sustainability is impacted by (i) the borrowing by the country, including from domestic sources; and (ii) sterilization of aid (even grant) flows. When the central bank decides not to sell the foreign exchange acquired through aid and seeks to sterilize the liquidity impact of aid, domestic interest rates could increase significantly, exerting pressure on public debt dynamics. In the same vein, a sudden drop in aid could cause the exchange rate to depreciate, thereby increasing the cost of servicing external debt.

The aid-financed spending also affects growth, and thus, debt sustainability. Spending on infrastructure would be expected to promote growth in the short to the medium term, which would strengthen the debt dynamics of the country. What is essential is to prioritize capital projects and choose those that have a relatively high rate of return. Similarly, expanding spending on education and health would enhance labour productivity over time and improve health and education outcomes. To be able to achieve desired outcomes, it is necessary that resources are spent efficiently and fiscal institutions are strong.

10.3.4 *Institutional capacity*

According to North (1991) 'institutions provide the broad framework of formal and informal rules and constraints that govern the way organizations, as groups of people, function. Formal rules include constitutions and laws. Informal constraints include customs, codes of conduct and sanctions'. Conflicts can damage these institutions covering the social, economic, legal, and political organization of the society. There are at least five types of market-supporting institutions: property rights, regulatory, macroeconomic

---

[12] The rapid decentralization has increased subnational spending shares quite significantly in recent years; in Nigeria, the share of such spending is over 50 per cent (see IMF 2006).

stabilization, social insurance, and conflict management (Rodrik 2000). These institutions have a strong relationship with growth (Rodrik 2004). The economic institutions influence the ability of the government to effectively conduct macroeconomic management and fiscal operations. Conflicts have been found to significantly weaken the capacity of the central bank and the ministry of finance to formulate and implement sound economic policies. Well-sequenced reforms that take into account country-specific considerations are therefore needed to rebuild or strengthen this capacity.

Are fiscal institutions weaker in post-conflict countries than in LICs in general? In recent years, a number of diagnostic exercises have been carried out to assess the quality of fiscal institutions and public financial management (PFM) systems in LICs. These assessments allow a comparison of relevant fiscal institutions in countries defined as fragile by the World Bank with those in other LICs. Data are available from three diagnostic exercises: the heavily indebted poor countries/assessment and action plans (HIPC/AAP) exercise; IMF's fiscal ROSC assessments; and public expenditure and financial accountability (PEFA) assessments.

Following the granting of debt relief to highly indebted poor countries (HIPCs), their PFM systems were assessed jointly by the World Bank and IMF. Assessment and action plans (AAPs) were prepared by these institutions in consultation with the authorities for 23 countries in 2001 and 26 countries in 2004 to identify weaknesses in PFM systems that could hinder the tracking of poverty-reducing spending and agree on a prioritized set of reforms to strengthen these systems. The assessments were based on 15 indicators classified into three groups: budget formulation, budget execution, and budget reporting. Seven of the indicators related to budget formulation covering issues such as comprehensiveness of the budget, the budget classification system, and medium-term orientation of the budget. Four indicators on budget execution assessed the quality of internal audit and controls. The remaining four indicators relating to budget reporting looked at timeliness of budget reporting and submission of final audited accounts. The 2004 assessment included an additional indicator on procurement practices.

Prior to this development, the IMF introduced a Code of Good Practices on Fiscal Transparency in 1998, which led to a voluntary programme of fiscal transparency assessments called fiscal transparency modules of Reports on the Observance of Standards and Codes (fiscal ROSCs). The fiscal transparency code has four pillars. The first pillar—clarity of roles and responsibilities—emphasizes distinction between government and commercial activities and a clear legal framework governing fiscal administration. The second pillar—open budget process—covers practices related to budget preparation, execution, and monitoring. The third pillar—public availability of information—emphasizes the importance of publishing comprehensive fiscal information.

And the fourth pillar—assurance of integrity—deals with the quality of fiscal data and the need for independent scrutiny of fiscal information. Since 1999, 29 LICs have been assessed against this code of fiscal transparency.[13]

In addition, separately, in 2001 the public expenditure and financial accountability (PEFA) performance measurement framework was developed jointly by the World Bank, the IMF, the EU, and several other bilateral donors. The framework identifies six critical dimensions of an open and orderly PFM system. These are credibility of the budget; its comprehensiveness and transparency; policy-based budgeting; predictability and control in budget execution; accounting, recording, and reporting; and external scrutiny and audit. In addition, the framework also includes an assessment of donor practices. This benchmark comprises three elements: predictability of direct budget support; financial information provided by the donors for budgeting and reporting on project and programme aid; and the proportion of aid that is managed using national procedures.[14] By 2007, PEFA had assessed 12 LICs. The results from the different diagnostic assessments are not surprising: the countries classified as fragile generally fare worse than the rest of the LICs. According to the HIPC/AAP exercise for which data are available for five fragile states, the greatest weaknesses are in budget execution, followed by budget reporting.

In budget formulation and execution, the PFM systems have worsened over time (Figures 10.9, 10.10, and 10.11). The fiscal ROSCs and PEFA assessments have been completed for only two fragile states. The results, which are broadly similar to those for the HIPC/AAP exercise, should therefore be interpreted with caution. Note that for the two ROSCs in fragile states, there are many zero values, suggesting that PFM in these countries lacks vital elements such as internal and external audit systems. Interestingly, PEFA assessments show that donor practices fare better in fragile states than in other LICs.

Given weaknesses in fiscal institutions and the need for funding humanitarian and other operations, there may be a basis for channelling aid to these countries outside the budget in the very short term. However, these flows would need to be fully coordinated with the budget priorities to prevent duplication and waste. Moreover, earmarked aid—provided in part to circumvent institutional weaknesses in these countries—can introduce considerable rigidities in the budget. It restricts governments' choices and prevents them from reallocating spending in response to changing economic circumstances and to sectors consistent with their own priorities. The donors face a dilemma: they would like to spend the aid resources as efficiently as possible in the short term, while striving to build institutions in the medium term.

---

[13] For further information please see IMF 2003 and 2007 (Manual on Fiscal Transparency).
[14] For full information on PEFA indicators, see the PEFA handbook (2005: 50–2).

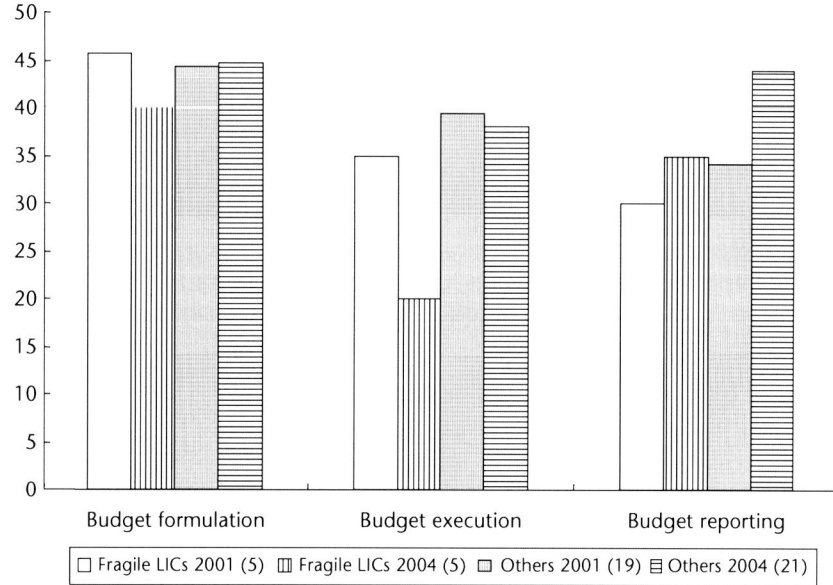

Figure 10.9. HIPC-AAP: Progress in PFM systems by key indicator categories (the number of countries meeting benchmarks in % of total)

Note: The total numbers of assessed countries in parenthesis.

Source: IMF and World Bank estimates.

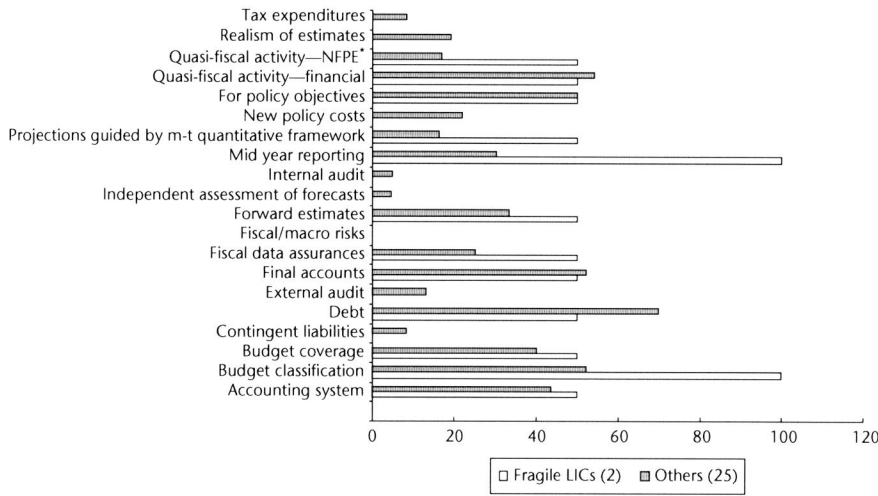

Figure 10.10. Fiscal transparency performance indicators in LICs (the share of countries with strong performance in total)

Note: The number of available ROSC reports in 1995–2005 in parenthesis; * = non-financial public enterprises.

Source: IMF staff estimates based on IMF Fiscal ROSC assessments.

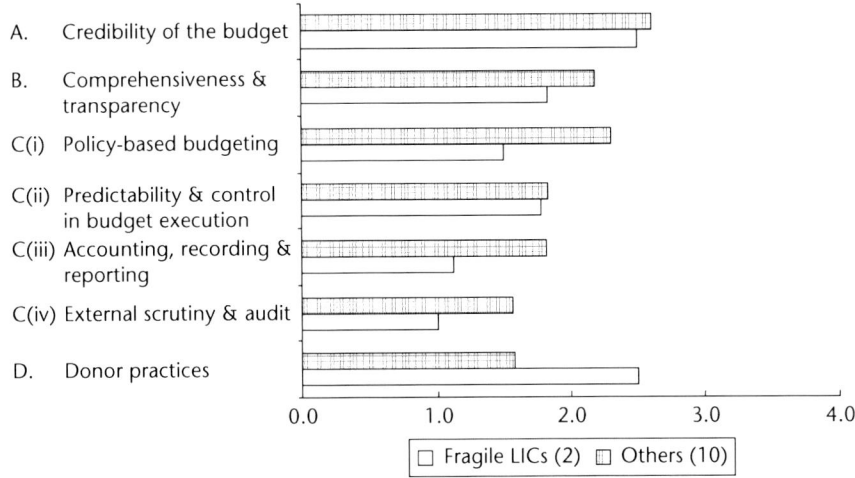

Figure 10.11. Aggregate PEFA ratings by indicator categories (in average aggregate scores: the perfect score = 4)

Source: Based on data provided by PEFA Secretariat.

Thus, the decision to spend aid in post-conflict and fragile states may not be constrained by their weak fiscal institutions because of the option to channel aid through extrabudgetary systems. However, if a country continues to receive external resources outside the budget over a sustained period, there is a risk that little effort will be devoted to building fiscal institutions and aligning external flows with resources mobilized domestically. The overall macroeconomic conditions and the economy's absorptive capacity will nevertheless remain relevant in formulating the budget.

Building fiscal institutions in post-conflict countries is a time-consuming process and involves three basic steps (Gupta et al. 2005). These are: (i) ensuring a functioning legal and regulatory framework;[15] (ii) establishing or strengthening the fiscal authority;[16] and (iii) adopting appropriate revenue and expenditure policies and systems. The sequencing of these steps does not have to follow the preceding order; what is implemented first depends on the country's circumstances.

---

[15] The legal and regulatory framework for fiscal operations is derived from the constitution and tax and budget laws. The former usually specifies the division of taxing powers between different levels of government, and between the executive, the legislature, and the judiciary. Tax laws define the power of the tax administration. The purpose of the budget law is to set out budget classifications; provide guidelines on budget execution; establish a consistent framework for internal and external control and audit; and provide mechanisms for financing budget deficits.

[16] Strengthening the position of the fiscal authority includes strengthening or establishing a budget department (for coordinating the expenditure programme and preparing fiscal projections and budget execution reports), a treasury department (for controlling spending and ensuring that it is accounted for), and customs and domestic revenue administration departments (for implementing tax policy and collecting tax revenues).

10.3.5 *Limits to saving*

Even if the macroeconomic situation is not fully stable and the absorptive capacity of the economy is weak, there are limits to how much aid a country can save. The donors have an interest in seeing that the resources they transfer are in fact used for their intended purposes. At the same time, there are pressures in the aid-receiving country to spend aid to improve economic and social outcomes. Moreover, the scope for saving is circumscribed by the share of project aid in total aid. This aid is already linked to project implementation cycle, and therefore, the aid-receiving country has little discretion on the pace of its utilization. Countries with weak institutions may receive more project aid, in part because donors are reluctant to use the aid-receiving country's own systems to channel external resources.

10.4 Frontloading Or Expenditure Smoothing

As more external resources flow into the country, it must make a key decision on which spending path to adopt. Clearly, this path will be influenced by the country-specific factors and considerations listed above, such as macroeconomic stability and absorptive capacity. One could envisage two options for post-conflict and other fragile states.

Under the frontloaded approach, spending in relation to GDP would increase sharply as resources flow in, and then subside thereafter. This approach would be particularly appropriate for countries emerging from a conflict, where returns to investment in rehabilitating infrastructure are particularly high. Furthermore, there are significant benefits from scaling up spending on providing food and other services to the population affected by the conflict. Resources are also needed to finance demobilization of combatants. However, if frontloading entails domestic borrowing (including from the banking sector), it is likely to exacerbate pressures on domestic prices. Thus, frontloading that is wholly aid-financed would appear to be an appropriate strategy. However, this strategy is not without risks. If frontloaded spending is unproductive and does not contribute to growth, the resulting high spending levels are unlikely to be sustainable over time. This may happen when a country's fiscal institutions are particularly weak, lacking mechanisms to appropriately prioritize spending.

The other option is to keep spending stable as a share of GDP—that is, to smooth it. This may be an appropriate strategy for fragile states (other than those emerging from conflict) in the face of aid volatility and uncertainty regarding the future path of aid. The advantage would be that spending would not rise to unsustainable levels owing to temporary aid surges and it would not have to be compressed when there are aid shortfalls. Thus, there will be no disruptions to spending in critical areas (such as provision of drugs for HIV/ AIDS prevention and treatment). It would also not exert undue pressure on the country's PFM systems. This may be appropriate also when aid increases are temporary. Whether the country adopts a frontloaded or expenditure smoothing approach, casting these plans in a medium-term context would help in fiscal planning. The medium-term frameworks go beyond setting the overall spending limits; they also require that countries allocate their annual spending across different sectors and then allocate sectoral spending across different programmes and projects.

Clearly, fragile states do not have the capacity to formulate these plans in a detailed manner. In fact, their institutions generally have less ability than those of other LICs to develop and/or implement medium-term planning mechanisms. In most LICs, medium-term frameworks do not exist, and where they do exist, they are not well-integrated into the budget. That implies that fragile states should focus essentially on multi-year macroeconomic scenarios prepared by the countries themselves and their partners. These scenarios should be consistent with fiscal sustainability and macroeconomic stability and the overall expenditure allocations in them should reflect the country's own priorities. The annual budget should then be aligned with the chosen medium-term path. In addition, it is important to ensure that there is a strong relationship between the process for preparing the national plan (e.g., PRSP—the poverty reduction strategy papers), and the budget. Furthermore, proper arrangements should be established between the government and donors for coordinating the management of aid, and, over time, for bringing increasing amounts of aid on budget.

10.5 Concluding Remarks

The evidence from LICs that experienced aid surges in recent years suggests that these countries saved part of the aid. In this respect, the behaviour of post-conflict countries has not differed radically from that of LICs in general. This chapter laid out the macroeconomic and institutional considerations that influence how much and how fast aid to post-conflict countries and other fragile states should be spent. The macroeconomic conditions and institutional capacity are typically weaker in fragile states than in other LICs, providing a good argument for using aid gradually, except for aid provided for humanitarian purposes. The real challenge is to create conditions in these countries so that all the aid received can be used effectively. Besides ensuring a stable macroeconomic environment that creates the demand for money balances in local currency and prevents capital flight, development partners would need to assist these countries in strengthening their fiscal institutions. This would also allow them to cast their spending plans in a medium-term context as well as contribute to enhancing the efficiency and effectiveness of resource use. Longer term aid commitments by donors would help in this regard.

There may be some basis for post-conflict countries' frontloading their spending, given the high rates of social return in the aftermath of a conflict. Since the macroeconomic imbalances tend to be severe at this juncture, frontloading should be wholly aid-financed. Other fragile states should seek to smoothen their spending against the background of aid volatility and uncertainty.

References

Adam, C., P. Collier, and V. Davies (2007). 'Post-Conflict Monetary Reconstruction'. Paper presented at the World Bank Conference on Post-Conflict Transitions, Washington, DC, 30 April–1 May.

Addison, T., A. Chowdhury, and S. M. Murshed (2002). 'By How Much Does Conflict Reduce Financial Development?' WIDER Discussion Paper No. 2002/48. Helsinki: UNU-WIDER.

Aiyar, S., A. Berg, and M. Hussain (2005). 'The Macroeconomic Challenge of More Aid'. *Finance and Development* 42 (3): 2831.

Berg, A., S. Aiyar, M. Hussain, S. Roache, T. Mirzoev, and A. Mahone (2007). 'The Macroeconomics of Scaling Up Aid: Lessons from Recent Experience'. IMF Occasional Paper No. 253. Washington, DC: International Monetary Fund.

Boyce, J. K. and M. O'Donnell (2007) (eds). *Peace and the Public Purse: Economic Policies for Postwar Statebuilding*. Boulder, CO: Lynne Rienner Publishers, Inc.

Chen, S., N. Loayza, and M. Reynal-Querol (2006). 'The Aftermath of Civil War'. Paper presented at the World Bank Conference on Post-Conflict Transitions, Washington, DC, 30 April–1 May.

Collier, P. (1999). 'On the Economic Consequences of Civil War'. *Oxford Economic Papers*, 51 (1): 168–83.

Collier, P. and A. Hoeffler (2002). 'Aid, Policy and Growth in Post-Conflict Societies'. WB Policy Research Working Paper No. 2902. Washington, DC: World Bank.

Collier, P., L. Elliott, H. Hegre, A. Hoeffler, M. Reynal-Querol, and N. Sambanis (2003). 'Breaking the Conflict Trap, Civil War and Development Policy'. World Bank Policy Research Report. Washington, DC: World Bank.

Davies, V. (2007). 'Capital Flight and War'. Paper presented at the World Bank Conference on Post-Conflict Transitions, Washington, DC, 30 April–1 May.

Elbadawi, I. and K. Schmidt-Hebbel (2007). 'The Demand for Money around the End of Civil Wars'. Paper presented at the World Bank Conference on Post-Conflict Transitions, Washington, DC, 30 April–1 May.

Elbadawi, I., L. Kaltani, and K. Schmidt-Hebbel (2007). 'Post-Conflict Aid, Real Exchange Rate Adjustment, and Catch-up Growth'. Paper presented at the World Bank Conference on Post-Conflict Transitions, Washington, DC, 30 April–1 May.

Foster, M. and T. Killick (2006). 'What Would Doubling Aid Do For Macroeconomic Management in Africa?' ODI Working Paper No. 06/26. London: Overseas Development Institute.

Gupta, S., B. Clements, R. Bhattacharya, and S. Chakravarti (2004). 'Fiscal Consequences of Armed Conflict and Terrorism in Low- and Middle-Income Countries'. *European Journal of Political Economy*, 20 (2): 403–21.

Gupta, S., B. Tareq, B. Clements, A. Segura-Ubiergo, R. Bhattacharya, and T. Mattina (2005). 'Rebuilding Fiscal Institutions in Post-Conflict Countries'. IMF Occasional Paper No. 247. Washington, DC: International Monetary Fund.

Gupta, S., R. Powell, and Y. Yang (2006). *Macroeconomic Challenges of Scaling Up Aid: A Checklist for Practitioners*. Washington, DC: International Monetary Fund.

Heller, P., M. Katz, X. Debrun, T. Thomas, T. Koranchelian, and I. Adenauer (2006). 'Making Fiscal Space Happen: Managing Fiscal Policy in a World of Scaled-Up Aid'. IMF Working Paper No. 06/270. Washington, DC: International Monetary Fund.

IMF (2003). 'Assessing and Promoting Fiscal Transparency: A Report on Progress'. *International Standards: Strengthening Surveillance, Domestic Institutions, and International Markets*. Supplement 2 of SM/03/86. Washington, DC: IMF.

IMF (2004). World Economic Outlook database, April. Washington, DC: IMF.

IMF (2006). *Regional Economic Outlook, Sub-Saharan Africa*, May. Washington, DC: IMF.

IMF (2007a). World Economic Outlook database, April. Washington, DC: IMF.

IMF (2007b). *Manual on Fiscal Transparency*. Washington, DC: IMF.

Independent Evaluation Office (2007). *An Evaluation of the IMF and Aid to Sub-Saharan Africa*. Washington, DC: International Monetary Fund.

North, D. (1991). 'Institutions'. *Journal of Economic Perspectives*, 5 (1): 97–112.

PEFA (2005). PFM Performance Measurement Framework. June. Available at: <http://www.pefa.org/PEFA%20Website%20–%20CURRENT%204-9-03/www.pefa.org%20WEBSITE/about_test.htm>.

Rajan, R. and A. Subramanian (2005). 'What Undermines Aid's Impact on Growth?'. IMF Working Paper No. 05/126. Washington, DC: International Monetary Fund.

Rodrik, D. (2000). 'Institutions for High-Quality Growth: What They Are and How to Acquire Them'. NBER Working Paper No. 7540. Cambridge, MA: National Bureau of Economic Research.

Rodrik, D. (2004). 'Getting Institutions Right'. Mimeo. Cambridge, MA: Harvard University. Available at: <www//ksghome.harvard.edu/~.drodrik.academic.ksg/ifo-institutions%20article%20_April%202004_.pdf>.

World Bank (2009). 'Definitions of Fragility and Conflict', <http://web.worldbank.org/WBSITE/EXTERNAL/PROJECTS/STRATEGIES/EXTLICUS/0,,contentMDK:22230573~menuPK:4448982~piPK:64171507~theSitePK:511778,00.html>.

Index